Mondrala Press wishes to thank all its friends, fans, patrons, and investors for making this book possible, and especially:

Ms. Randa Dumanian
Mr. and Mrs. Karol and Dagmara Maziukiewicz
de domo Sowul

without whose enthusiasm and open hearts this book could never have happened.

ALEKSANDER'S ANTIQUITIES

TITUS & BERENICE

JEWS, ROMANS, REVOLT, AND LOVE IN THE TIME OF WAR

by Aleksander Krawczuk

translated by Tom Pinch

SECOND EDITION

MONDRALA
PRESS

Originally published in Polish in 1972 as
Tytus i Berenika.

Editing by Mondrala Press
Cover Design by Mondrala Press

ISBN eBook: 978-2-919820-51-1
ISBN paperback: 978-2-919820-52-8
ISBN hardcover: 978-2-919820-53-5

The hand-colored illustrations are by Philippe Cherry (1759-1833), engraved by Pierre Michel Alix (1762-1817), and taken from the 1802 edition of *Recherches sur les Costumes et sur les Théâtres de toutes les nations, tant anciennes que moderns* (*Research on the Costumes and Theaters of all Nations, Ancient as well as Modern*) first published by M. Drouhin, Paris 1790. All refer to *Bérénice*, the 1670 play by Jean-Baptiste Racine.

The book is by theater critic and historian Jean Charles Le Vacher de Charnois (1749-92?) and covers classical tragedies and comedies as well as later interpretations of these dramas by playwrights including Racine. Le Vacher de Charnois intended a series of books encompassing, as the title indicates, theatrical costumes from all nations and from the ancient to the modern; however, the French Revolution interrupted his scheme, and as a monarchist, he was imprisoned in 1792 for his writings in support of the aristocracy. It was long thought that he had died in the massacres at the Abbaye prison in September of that year, but later research indicates that he may have been executed during the Reign of Terror in 1794.

Chorus of Israelite Women

TRANSLATOR'S SPECIAL REQUEST

Translating and publishing this series of books has been a labor of love for me. I grew up reading it, and I have always wanted to be able to share it with my American friends. And so here it is.
It will not make me rich, but if you liked the book, would you please recommend it to a friend?
And if you could give it an Amazon review,
you will be helping others find it!
https://www.amazon.com/dp/2919820494

THANK YOU!

TABLE OF CONTENTS

Palestine at the time of the First Jewish War

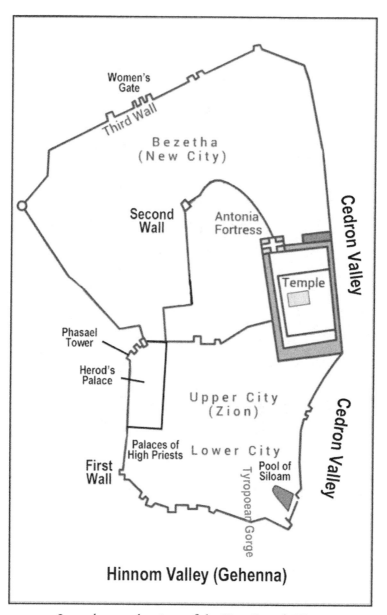

Jerusalem at the time of the First Jewish War

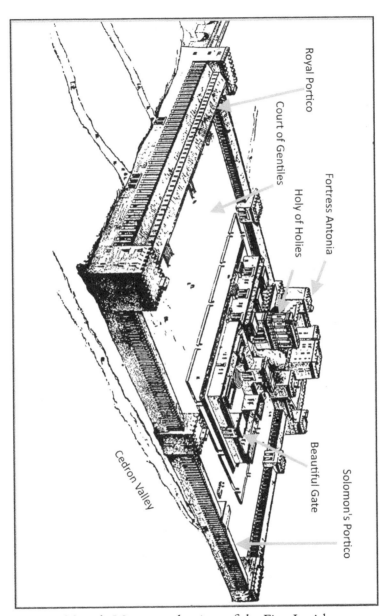

Royal Portico

Court of Gentiles

Fortress Antonia

Holy of Holies

Cedron Valley

Beautiful Gate

Solomon's Portico

Temple Mount at the time of the First Jewish

From the translator
TWO SHORT NOTES IN THE STYLE OF THE AUTHOR

It is probably in keeping with the encyclopedic style of Professor Krawczuk for your translator to append two cultural notes to this delightful book.

1. In the year 1670, at the height of glory of Louis XIV, before rebellions and unlucky wars dimmed somewhat the brilliance of the Sun-King, his cousin and sister-in-law, Henriette d'Angleterre, daughter of the unlucky Charles I of England, and wife of Phillip d'Orleans, staged a bloodless duel: a head-to-head confrontation between two court dramatists, the aging Pierre Corneille (1606-1684) and the up-and-coming Jean Racine (1639-1699), both of whom she commissioned to produce a play on the subject of Berenice, Queen of the Jews. Performed a week apart at the end of November 1670, the two plays caused a furor, a loud war of words and pamphlets between two cultural (and, therefore, as always in France, political) factions—the supporters of either one or the other author. It was a war conclusively won by the new man.

Broken by his defeat, Corneille never wrote another play. For Racine, this victory marked his rise to power. In 1672 he was elevated to a seat in the *Academie* and went on to compose, in short order, his greatest plays: *Bajazet* (1672), *Mithridate* (1673), *Iphigénie* (1674) and *Phèdre* (1677).

The French ruckus sent a veritable cultural tsunami across the shores of European courts, all of which rushed to stage their own versions of the story, whether in dramatic or operatic style. As a result, the sheer volume of "Titus and Berenice" output deposited in the deep layers of European heritage is staggering while Racine's play remains on the playbill in France until this day. As a result, most Europeans have heard of Titus and Berenice: the title rings a bell even if most can no longer say which church is tolling.

2. Pieter Bruegel (also Brueghel or Breughel) the Elder (1525?–1569) was the most significant artist of Dutch and Flemish Renaissance, a painter and printmaker known for his landscapes and peasant scenes (so-called "genre painting"); he pioneered the use of both subjects as the main focus of large paintings. He was a huge commercial success during his lifetime and founded a dynasty of sons and grandsons who continued the business, often copying their founder's designs. Hapsburg Emperor Rudolf II, the famed alchemist and art connoisseur, was a great admirer and collector of his work, which is how the Kunsthistorisches Museum in Vienna has come to feature a special room hung with twelve huge Pieter Breughels, including *The Fall of Icarus, The Tower of Babel, The Hunters in the Snow,* and *The Peasant Wedding.* It is, in my opinion, one of the most profoundly moving museum rooms in the world.

Tom Pinch
Ardennes National Park
Luxembourg

TITUS & BERENICE

GAZING AT ROME FROM THE PALATINE

Things were working out just as Berenice had hoped. Her beloved brother, King Agrippa, and she had been received in Rome with all honors. The Senate granted her the insignia of praetorship, and ample rooms at the imperial palace on the Palatine were placed at her disposal. She could now meet her Titus without any hindrance whenever she wished. It was widely gossiped in the city that the two lived together like man and wife.

They felt all the more at ease because Titus's father, Emperor Vespasian, did not live on the Palatine. He was happiest at the Sallustian Gardens, near the Colline Gate. Once Caesar's private estate, this vast park lay just outside the city walls, on the slopes of the Pintius,[1] in the valley between the Pintius and the Quirinal. Here, villas, gazebos, and temples stood arranged among trees and ponds, meadows, and flowerbeds. It was quiet and spacious, green and idyllic—and yet the city center was nearby.

The gardens were surrounded by a massive wall—a useful thing if one ever had to defend himself. This had been amply proven six years earlier when, in December AD 69, Vitellius's men held off Vespasian's legionaries for a whole day at that wall, pelting them with

---

[1] Modern Pincio.

stones and spears, slings, and arrows. And they would have lasted longer if only Vespasian's cavalry had not broken through from the side of the Colline Gate.

Now, standing on the Palatine and looking down towards the gardens, Queen Berenice had reasons to hope that a formal marriage ceremony might take place soon, and the foremost of these was (it was widely reported) that Titus had promised it. So, she stood there in the role of the bride-to-be of an emperor-in-waiting. She stood proud and dignified, she thought.

Proud and arrogant, thought the Romans.

Titus and Berenice had met after four years of separation. Their love, born in the extraordinary days of a cruel war, proved to be surprisingly durable, alive, and fresh. During their separation, the two had written to each other frequently. Sometimes they also sent trusted courtiers—with greetings and gifts—but also with the secret instructions to espy whether the other side still cared. But the journeys between Italy and Palestine, by land and sea, were long and fraught with danger. And they both knew well that affectionate letters could be skillful deceivers and that emissaries often flattered and conveyed to their masters only what their masters would like to hear—for the simple reason that no one rewards the bearers of bad news.

Their long separation had worried Berenice. Titus's libido and his inclination to erotic excesses were widely known. Malicious "friends" probably "comforted" the queen by noting that Titus had recently preferred boys. Heavy boozing sessions in male company stretched late into the night, invariably ending in wild orgies. This was probably not a great comfort to Berenice. Besides, Titus had other, more orthodox love affairs, too—though, thankfully, all of them fleeting thus far. But perhaps Berenice's most depressing worry concerned the passage of time itself. She was over forty, her beloved—twelve years younger. She saw ever more clearly that she was in a desperate race against time: if she did not win him now, she would lose him forever soon.

However, as soon as they saw each other in Rome, the first glance, the first word told them everything—and her above all—that

4

all those declarations of love, transmitted by letters and messengers, had not lied. And so it happened that their romance rekindled on the Palatine and now burned with the same intensity and beauty as it once had in the distant lands of Syria, Phoenicia, and Palestine. They had moved then through lands captivating with endless contrasts and intensity of color—through lush green valleys and sunburnt fawn-colored wastelands; between intensely blue, vast sea and high mountains covered with ancient, dark forests of cedar. And everywhere, death followed them. There were days when the wind carried the cloying stench of decaying corpses all the way to the queen's bed. And how often Titus's tent stood on a bloody battlefield or near smoking ruins, with heaps of corpses all around!

Those countries were far away, and the terrible years of the evil war behind them. Now peace reigned both in the East and in Italy. The year was, by our reckoning, AD 75: the sixth year of Emperor Vespasian's reign, now firmly established and unchallenged. Titus and Berenice lived in the splendor of imperial majesty, and at their feet lay a huge, rich, populous city, the capital of the world. Living on the Palatine, the queen looked down at Rome every day, walking along the alleys of the Palatine gardens or leaning against the balustrade of the palace balcony. She looked at the great panorama of the metropolis—its temples, basilicas, theaters, circuses, monuments, obelisks, and colonnades. Did she consider it her hour of triumph? She would have had every right to.

We know so much about Berenice—much, much more than this, as you soon shall see. But about her beauty, we know nothing; what her charm consisted in, what her face and eyes were like, her hair, her character, her movements—our sources tell us nothing. No effigy of the queen has survived. You'd think that was only natural since she was Jewish, and the Jewish Law forbids the making of graven images of things in the heavens above, or on earth below, or in the depths of the sea, but that—was not the case. For we know that in her father's palace, there had once stood golden, full-length statues of Berenice and her sisters.

And yet, we so want to know: what clothes did she like to

wear? And how did she style her hair—was she perhaps a brunette? What colors of dresses did she like? Red or blue? Or yellow or green? Only one detail is known about her attire: she had a ring with a magnificent diamond, a gift from her brother. Most Roman women could only dream of something similar. A generation later, the poet Juvenal remembered this diamond, listing it in his sixth satire among the rich gifts that a besotted husband showers upon his capricious wife:

> They bring her great crystal vases; then myrrhine, [2] gigantic; finally, a diamond famous and extremely precious because Berenice once had it on her finger: King Agrippa gave it to her, his shameless sister. And that was over there, where kings keep barefoot on Saturdays, and ancient forbearance allows pigs to live to a ripe old age.

So, only this precious diamond remains to inspire our imagination. Or rather, the sparkle of that diamond—as a ray of sunlight strikes the ring. The queen is standing in the Palatine gardens, under a tall, dark-green cypress in a golden-yellow dress. She put her graceful hand on the stone balustrade and, lost in thought, is gazing at Rome lying at her feet.

But nine years earlier, she had not had that diamond ring on her hand as she ran out of her brother's palace in Jerusalem. She ran out barefoot, weeping, and her dress was not colorful but of simple white linen like the poorest women of her people wore. And thus attired, she, a queen, stood in front of the elevated dais where the Roman procurator sat sprawled on his stool, surrounded by officers in shiny armor and helmets with colored plumes.

That happened in Jerusalem in the spring of AD 66, when Gesius Florus was the procurator of Judea, and the emperor Nero was in the sixth year of his reign.

---

[2] Myrrhinus or Myrrinous was a deme (community, township) in the east of ancient Attica famous for its pottery. The site of Myrrhinus is located near modern Merenda.

THE TEACHINGS OF SIMON THE MAGUS

The followers of Simon the Magus might have said—and they probably did, for though he himself was no longer alive, his followers were still active and remained so for centuries to come in the cities of Palestine and Syria—that such humiliation of even the most majestic of earthly queens was as nothing compared to the humiliations and sufferings that had befallen God's first-born creation.

She was Sophia, or Wisdom, also called Thought, or Idea, or *Logos*, or *Ennoia*. Simon and his disciples liked to use the last term. They taught:

> God—the Supreme Being—conceived the Idea of Creation. She, the first Idea of God, is the Mother of all that exists apart from God, and he is the Father.
>
> Now, as soon as she was conceived and knew His will, she began her descent to earth—for the mere thought of God had already caused all creation to come into being, which was why she could now descend into it. The thought of God had called into existence all the different layers of heavens that exist today, as well as their angels, powers, and thrones; and the angels dwelling on the lowest rung of heaven created the Earth and the mortal men upon it.
>
> But as soon as all this came into being, all these inhabitants of the heavens turned against *Ennoia*. They did so out of pride and envy, for they did not want to admit that they owed their existence to her, and of course, as mere creations of *Ennoia*, they knew nothing about God, the Supreme Being. They knew only *Ennoia*.
>
> Now they seized her and imprisoned her, persecuted and tormented her, and did not allow her to return to the Father. At the same time, the angels fought fiercely among themselves to gain control of her, for they all ardently coveted her beauty.
>
> Fleeing from constant suffering, *Ennoia* fell to ever lower levels. All this took many eons, that is to say, eternity, until she finally reached the bottom of her trajectory: the earth. Here, she had to take the form of a woman. From then on, for many, many centuries, she passed from one woman's body to another—as wine passes from one jug into the next. She was the Helen of Troy, over whom the Trojan War was fought. She was Ariadne

and Cleopatra, and many more besides. For whenever and wherever she appeared, fights broke out among men for control of her—just as there had once been a struggle over her between the inhabitants of the celestial circles. Finally, after many centuries, *Ennoia* met her most terrible fate.

But just then, the Father (who is the Supreme Being) decided to come to the aid of his first creation. And of all creation: for He wanted to save the world, all its heavens and earths, because He could see that the power-hungry angels ruled badly: each of them wanted to be the first, and each exalted himself above the others.

And thus, the Father began to descend through successive heavens himself, as if down the rungs of a ladder. And into whatever circle he entered, he assumed, for concealment, the shape and face proper to its beings. In this way, nowhere recognized, he eventually reached Earth. Here, he became a man—namely Simon, born in Samaria. After a long and adventurous search, he found *Ennoia* in the Phoenician city of Tyre. Her name was Helen again. And to complete the measure of her humiliation and disgrace, she now lived imprisoned in a brothel.

By freeing her, Simon saved both the world and all humanity because her fate is an image and a symbol of the suffering of the human soul, imprisoned in the body, unworthily humiliated, and longing for salvation.[3]

Anyone studying the teachings of Simon the Magus and reflecting on them must have noticed three thoughts in particular—unusual and even shocking, but popular and fertile in the succeeding generations and well worth remembering.

The first was that the earth and all the creatures within it, including man, are not the work not of God but of beings which themselves had been created: secondary, imperfect, proud, quarreling both among themselves and with the Wisdom of God, and above all, willing to inflict suffering. Hence, the conclusion that the world is both inherently evil and badly governed.

---

[3] Main sources for reconstructing the teachings of Simon the Magus are: Justin, *Apologia*, I 26; Irenaeus, *Against Heresies*, I 23; Eusebius, *History of the Church*, II 13.

The second was that God arrived on Earth from outside, from beyond the circle of all heavens, unknown to anyone, and constantly exposed to pain and humiliation.

Finally, the third was that *Ennoia*, the firstborn of God, experienced on earth the worst humiliation that can befall a woman and, at the same time, is always the indirect cause and helpless witness of all suffering, war, and bloodshed.

And since the epoch was fond of unusual symbolism and strange comparisons, we would remain in keeping with its mindset if we said:

As Berenice did in Jerusalem in the spring of AD 66.

THE NAZARITE VOW OF BERENICE

In the spring of AD 66, King Agrippa II left his capital and went on a long journey. His capital, Caesarea Philippi, recently renamed Neronias, lay slightly north of the Sea of Galilee, near the source of the River Jordan, for the lands subjected to the king extended on the border of Syria, to the north and east of this lake. These lands were called in Greek: Gaulanitis, Batanea, Trachonitis, Auranitis. On the western coast of the Sea of Galilee, however, only two districts belonged to his royal domain: Tiberias and Tarichaea.

Agrippa traveled to Alexandria in Egypt. He had come to the conclusion that it was necessary to congratulate in person the new governor of Egypt, Tiberius Julius Alexander, just appointed to this high office by Emperor Nero. Berenice accompanied her brother for a part of the way—her brother from whom she had hardly parted for years, as the wife never leaves her husband—which, of course, was a source of all kinds of talk. This time, however, the siblings—to everyone's surprise—parted in Jerusalem. The king continued south alone while his sister stayed in the holy city. Her reason for remaining in Jerusalem soon became public and met with general approval as evidence of her piety.

Not long ago, Berenice had been bedridden, and while ill, perhaps in the hope of becoming cured, she made a vow known as Nazarite. According to the Jewish Law, a person bound by it had to abstain for thirty days from wine and all intoxicants and even from the fruit of the vine in any form. He was not allowed to trim his hair. And if, during those thirty days, he should accidentally come in contact with a human corpse—even if the deceased were a member of his own family—he had to cleanse himself immediately by performing the appropriate rites, and the thirty days of his vow started all over again. The offerings he had to make at the end of his vow were costly: not everyone could afford to bring three yearling lambs, two male and one female, to the altar of the temple and a basket of unleavened bread and a basket of unleavened cakes—and both of these types of bread had to be made of the finest flour and oil.

The period of Berenice's vow was set to end during her stay in Jerusalem, meaning that she could immediately make the sacrifices prescribed by Law at the Temple. But everything turned out differently and against her best intentions. The queen was unable to complete her vow. She saw blood and corpses in the streets and many who died martyr's death on the cross.

Who was to blame for these misfortunes? Procurator Gesius Florus—that was what Berenice and the Jews said. However, he and his men had a different view of the matter. And, of course, the followers of Simon the Magus saw things yet differently.

Berenice was already in Jerusalem when Florus approached the city, leading a cohort of infantry and several dozen cavalry. The day was the 15th of Iyar,⁴ the beginning of May. The Roman column marched not from Caesarea by the sea, where the governor usually resided, but from Samaria, where he had recently stayed.

---

⁴ Iyar is the eighth month of the civil year (which starts on 1 Tishrei) and the second month of the Jewish religious year (which starts on 1 Nisan). The name is Babylonian in origin. It is a month of 29 days. Iyar usually falls in April–May on the Gregorian calendar.

SAMARIA-SEBASTE

More than eighty years earlier, Herod, king of Judea, had rebuilt the city of Samaria from scratch. He enlarged it many times: from ten hectares to eighty. He surrounded the entire hill on which Samaria stood with a mighty wall "twenty furlongs long," that is, almost four kilometers. He built many grand buildings. He wanted the city to become not just an invincible fortress but also a beautiful monument in honor of Emperor Augustus—and since the Greek equivalent of the Latin *Augustus* is *sebastos*—he gave the city a new name: Sebaste. About six thousand veterans of his army were settled in Samaria-Sebaste. They received plots of land and many privileges. They came from different lands and spoke different languages. There were Greeks, Syrians, Thracians, Gauls, and Germans among them, as well as native Samaritans.

American and British archaeological missions conducted wide-ranging excavations on the hill—first between 1908 and 1910 and then again between 1931 and 1935—and found many artifacts from the first period of splendor of Samaria, that is, from the 9th and 8th centuries BC, but even more from a much later era: from the heyday of the Roman Empire. But there were also many remains of art and architecture dating back to the reign of Herod I and the decades immediately following. Among these were the foundations of defensive walls, towers, and gates; the ruins of a huge temple dedicated to Augustus; the remnants of the main street, almost a kilometer long, flanked by colonnades on both sides; and—finally—the essentials of any Roman city: the forum, the basilica, and the aqueduct.

All these discoveries confirmed what we could have expected based on ancient written sources. But there were also other findings, completely unexpected. And thus, a little north of the Temple of Augustus, there was a large rectangular square, and on its western side lay the foundations of a spacious rectangular temple. The method of processing the boulders dated the building to the period of Herod's reign—the beginning of the first century AD, that is, to the time when

Simon, called the Magus, lived and worked in Samaria. The temple, built strictly on the Greek model and surrounded by supporting colonnades, had an interior consisting of two rooms: a small vestibule—the *pronaos*—which led to the sanctuary, the *naos*. Greek inscriptions told us that the goddess of this tabernacle was called *Kore*. In another district of Samaria, within a large sports stadium, a statuette of this goddess was found—unfortunately, very damaged, as well as an altar dedicated to her and several Greek inscriptions. One of them contained an invocation: "To the One and Only God, the Great *Kore*, Invincible." Another contained a prayer: "May the Goddess *Kore* remember the rhetorician Marcialis and his friends."

In Greek myths and religion, the name *Kore* was most often used to refer to Persephone, the daughter of the goddess Demeter, kidnapped by the god of the underworld, Hades, and thereafter, his queen. However, the word *kore* may also simply mean *a girl,* and so, sometimes other goddesses, when they were depicted in the form of young women, were also called *kore*, especially Athena and Artemis, and sometimes even nymphs. Thus, the name *Kore* alone is not enough to determine what goddess was worshiped in the mysterious temple in Samaria. To figure this out, we needed more clues.

By luck, an interesting bas-relief was eventually discovered in our mystery temple. Although it has no artistic value and is very rough—almost schematic—it does provide an unmistakable clue. It represents, carved on a stone tablet, two tall caps. Under each is a laurel wreath, and above each—an eight-pointed star. For experts on Greek symbolism, the meaning was immediately obvious: such caps, wreaths, and stars were the attributes of the Dioscuri, Castor and Pollux. These twins were the sons of Zeus and Leda and the brothers of Helen. And while some said that they were the sons of Tyndareus and Leda, in which case Helen was only their half-sister, all the myths agreed that the brothers had freed Helen from captivity when Theseus, prince of Athens, had kidnapped her as a young girl and taken her to his city. After having performed many famous deeds—Castor distinguished himself as a tamer of stallions and Pollux as a wrestler—the brothers died young in an armed skirmish with another pair of divine twins, from whom they tried to steal cattle. But only Pollux was admitted to Olympus, and only he was given immortality; his brother Castor had to go to Hades like any ordinary man. However, the former managed to entreat a special favor from Zeus: he was allowed to remain with his brother, but on the condition that they both spend one day on Mount Olympus and the next in the underworld: justice and fairness must prevail in the afterlife.

The Dioscuri were worshiped in many Greek city-states, and in some—and this is the crucial business here—they were worshipped *together with their sister Helen.* She had been regarded divine since times immemorial. In some myths, Helen, over whom the Trojan War had once been fought, was identified as an incarnation, or better yet—manifestation or emanation—of the goddess Persephone.

Who was called *Kore.*

And so, it seems that the worshipers of *Kore* in Samaria may have invoked her by another name also: the name of Helen, the daughter of Zeus: a goddess who had suffered great privations, had been kidnapped and imprisoned, but then finally reclaimed. And so, it seems at least possible that Simon the Magus may have been the priest at the temple of *Kore* and the preacher of a myth blending in a strange way Greek and Near-eastern ideas, just like people of different languages and beliefs mixed in the city itself.[5]

But while we were talking, the procurator Gesius Florus had taken leave of Samaria and was approaching Jerusalem.

JERUSALEM WELCOMES FLORUS

None of the Roman governors of Judea ever earned much sympathy from its inhabitants, mainly because they exercised their rule firmly and ruthlessly. Compared to Florus, however (many said), his predecessors were harmless lambs, men of extraordinary probity and

---

[5] About Samaria see A. Parrot, *Samarie*, Neuchâtel 1955, pp. 79-92.

honor, kind and tender shepherds who had cared for the welfare of their flock. By comparison, the current administrator of the country was a sadist, a psychopath, an insatiable robber, a dishonorable and avaricious creature. He had provoked riots, it was reported, because riots provided an opportunity to "pacify," which meant—to sack and plunder with impunity.

The accusations laid against Florus were almost certainly exaggerated: he was just another ordinary Roman military governor on the make. But the fact remained that on the 15th of the month Iyar, the procurator was approaching Jerusalem full of burning hatred for its people because the city had dared to wound his pride in a particularly painful way. Florus did not hide how this infuriated him. He ordered this to be declared openly to the crowds gathered outside the city walls.

In those days—days of ruthless and absolute Roman rule, it had become customary for the inhabitants of any subject city to greet a high Roman official and his soldiers outside the city walls with a show of groveling submission every time he entered. The crowd lined up in rows and shouted pious greetings, waving flowers and palm fronds. And, as per this custom (which had never been formalized as a written law), also on that day, the 15th of Iyar, crowds of citizens came out in front of the Women's Gate and onto the road coming from the north, from Samaria-Sebaste.

They waited and waited, and finally, they saw, galloping towards them, a unit of Roman cavalry. The Romans rode like the devil, rushing straight for the crowd. They stopped their foaming horses just before they crashed into it. Their commander—his name was Capiton—shouted in a loud voice:

"Disperse immediately, you worthless rabble! The procurator does not want this wretched comedy of feigned cordiality! You have just taunted him brazenly, and now you want to greet him? If his enemies are men, let them joke now in front of him! Let them show their love of 'freedom' not with words but with swords!"

And while the crowd was still hesitating, the riders pushed their horses into it. The people scattered and slowly returned to their homes, frightened and helpless, cursing that fateful, ill-considered joke of their youths.

A few days ago, the procurator, through emissaries, had ordered the priests of the Temple to give him seventeen talents from the treasury for what he called "state purposes." The order was obediently carried out, but the matter caused an unprecedented stir in the city. Great crowds gathered in the courtyards of the sanctuary, shouting slogans hostile to Florus. It was then that some young people took up a collection: they took a large basket and, pleading with tearful voices, begged the assembled crowd for a modest donation "for our poor viceroy."

It was all fun and games, and only too late did everyone realize that the governor, touched to the quick by the ridicule, would fly into fury, and his fury would not be easily appeased. The fact that he did not deign to accept the customary welcome at the gates showed it clearly. No wonder, then, that the night of the 15th to the 16th of Iyar passed in fearful anticipation. For many, it was to be the last night of their lives.

After entering the city, the procurator occupied the former palace of King Herod the Great. It was a large and well-equipped complex of buildings set in artificially irrigated gardens. On one side, it was adjacent to the city wall, which protected it from that direction, and on the other, it had its own high, massive wall. It was also protected by three large towers, each of which was practically a fortress in its own right. Fragments of the biggest, once called Phasael, remain to our times and are known as the Tower of David. Roman governors visiting Jerusalem usually stayed in this palace, which was beautiful and comfortable, and at the same time, easy to defend. Sometimes, however, they also stayed in the fortress called Antonia, at the northern corner of the temple precinct.

Florus was probably accompanied by his wife. We may assume this because coastal Caesarea had recently witnessed violent clashes between Jews on the one hand and Syrians and Greeks on the other, and it would not have been safe to leave a woman there. And it wasn't just a matter of love and affection. There was a more specific reason to protect *this* wife. Namely, the viceroy *owed* his office, so lucrative and so honorable, to her. She had earned him his nomination thanks to her friendship with Poppaea Sabina, the wife of emperor Nero.

But had Florus brought her with him? Had he not left her in Italy?

CONCERNING THE WIVES OF VICEROYS

In the olden days of the Roman Republic, commanders and senior officials going on business beyond the borders of Italy were not allowed to take their wives with them. Emperor Augustus lifted this ban, but under his successor, Tiberius, the matter was debated again in the Senate. The debate was heated and very interesting—on the grounds of public morals.

Severus Caecina proposed a law that no provincial governor should be allowed to travel to his assignment with his wife. In his speech, he first clarified that he lived in peace and harmony with his wife and that they already had six children. He then added that he himself had always followed what he now proposed as a general rule. For though he had served in various provinces for forty years, he had never allowed his wife to leave Italy.

He went on to say:

"Not without reason was this once the established Roman practice that the wives of officials were not be taken along to allied or neighboring countries. Their mere presence causes undesirable phenomena. Women hinder peacemaking through their love of luxury and warfare through their timidity. Their sex is weak and incapable of enduring hardships, and yet, if only left unsupervised—cruel, ambitious, and power-hungry. Some women dare to stroll freely among soldiers and have officers at their service. It happened recently that a woman sat on a tribune to review cohort exercises. Also, consider this: whenever any of the governors is accused of extortion, it is their wives who are accused of facilitating most of the crimes. For it is to them, to the women, that the worst elements of the population of each province find their way, and it is the wives who undertake to represent their husbands in their most nefarious interests. And in the final analysis, it comes to this: if a viceroy travels with his wife, two persons are now publicly respected, and each is a nexus of power. And it is known that women are more stubborn and more uncontrollable than men. Our old laws kept women in check; in our time, when these restrictions have been lifted, their sex governs both domestic and public affairs, and recently even the army!"

However, Ceacina's speech did not meet with the approval of the majority. Numerous voices of opposition were raised at once. Valerius Messalinus made a sharp polemic. First, he recalled that the austerity of the old times had already, in many cases, given way to better and more enlightened practices. And rightly so. After all, the city was no longer threatened by war, and the provinces were at peace. Of course, when fighting in the field, one should only have a sword at one's side; but for those who return home after the hardships of war, what could be more honorable than to take comfort in his wife's embrace? It is said that some wives are overly ambitious and greedy. But don't most of the governors themselves succumb to various temptations? And yet no one suggests that no man should be entrusted with the administration of a province! It is also said that wicked wives corrupt their husbands. But are single men blameless? It is the husband's responsibility if his wife behaves inappropriately! It would be highly injurious to deprive the husbands of their companions for good and bad just because this or that man had proven to be weak of character and unable to control his wife. At the same time, such a law would mean that the inherently weaker sex would be doomed to loneliness and left to the mercy of both their own love of splendor and the lust of others. Even with constant, vigilant, personal supervision, one defends the purity of his marriage with difficulty. How much more difficult it is during the many years of separation, while the husband is away on duty and the shared life is forgotten as if a divorce had already taken place?"

Caecina's law has been rejected, leaving the provincial

governors of different ranks free to bring their wives along. As did Gesius Florus.

And his wife bore the name of Cleopatra.

CLEOPATRA OF POMPEII

Because of the tragic fate of the famous last queen of Egypt, her name was rarely given to girls in the Roman Empire. Evidently, some considered it unlucky, others too pretentious—precisely because of the fame of the woman who had played such an extraordinary role in history. Therefore, the name of Florus' wife is notable as very rare for its time. And therefore, when it was found in an inscription dating from this period but located in a place thousands of miles away from Jerusalem, the question naturally arose whether it did not refer to the same Cleopatra.

In 1928, and later between 1930 and 1932, excavations took place in Pompeii—yes, that well-known Pompeii, buried as a result of the eruption of Vesuvius in AD 79. They were carried out in the so-called first district, until then, hardly explored. And now a large complex of buildings came to light, surrounded by broad streets on all sides. It was what the Romans called an "insula," literally an island and, in our modern terms, a city block. Today, the main house of the group is conventionally called *casa del Menandro* because a fresco depicting this famous comedy writer was found there. The house, the seat of a very wealthy family, had been decorated with many works of art and many valuable objects. Most had been stolen in antiquity—not long after the catastrophe that destroyed the city. Former inhabitants of Pompeii, or perhaps just robbers, broke in by digging wells and tunneling through heaps of congealed lava and compressed ash. Fortunately for us, they didn't find everything. In the cellar, where the jugs of wine were normally kept, just below the bathhouse, a wonderful treasure was now discovered, probably hidden there at the last moment by the owner or his faithful house manager. It is a set of silver tableware consisting of one hundred and eighteen vessels. These plates, bowls, cups, spoons, and scoops weigh twenty-four kilograms in all. Of the five treasure hoards excavated so far in Pompeii, this one is the most complete and the most valuable. It testifies convincingly to the size of the household, which needed so many vessels, and to the wealth of the master of the house who could afford it. The layout of the building itself is quite typical. Rooms of various sizes are grouped around a large peristyle, or inner garden, surrounded by a colonnade. In a separate part of the house are the utility rooms and apartments of the servants, who used to sleep here and then walk to work in the suburban estates of their master.

Who were the owners of the house? Inscriptions answer the question. There are a lot of them in the *casa del Menandro,* just as in many other Pompeian houses. Mostly, they are very short, random, scraped, or sketched in haste to commemorate what had seemed important to the writer at the time, important, interesting, amusing, or outrageous; most entries are just names.

These inscriptions indicate that the *casa del Menandro* belonged to one of the branches of the Poppaeus Sabinus family. They also owned other real estate in Pompeii, for they were among the wealthiest of its residents and had been settled there for a long time. The wife of Emperor Nero, the famous Poppaea Sabina, came from Pompeii. It's no surprise that both she and her husband were very popular in that city. This is evidenced by numerous inscriptions on the buildings, not official inscriptions but *graffiti* drawn by ordinary, simple people who wanted to express their sincere sympathy for the imperial couple.

Some representatives of the Poppeans held high state offices. The wealth of the family and its social position meant that their Pompeian residence was visited by many eminent personalities. Such visits remain recorded to this day by inscriptions giving the names of distinguished guests; they are probably the work of servants.

On one of the columns of the peristyle, we find this name: "Neratius Pansa Cleopatra." Could this be our Cleopatra, wife of

Gesius Florus? Such a suggestion has been made by some scholars. [6]

These scholars remind us that the family of the masters of the house was related to Nero's wife, and Cleopatra, wife of Florus, was, as is known from other sources, one of her friends. The inscription, however, was written not long before the eruption of Vesuvius, that is, in the year AD 79. And if our Cleopatra visited the house of the Poppaeus Sabinus as the wife of Neratius Pansa, and thus as the widow of Florus, or divorced from him, the bloody events of Jerusalem thirteen years earlier, on the 16th Iyar in the year AD 66, were by then only a distant memory.

THE BAREFOOT QUEEN

On the morning of the 16th Iyar, soldiers built a platform of planks in the square in front of Herod's palace. Proconsul Gesius Florus sat upon it, surrounded by officers in shiny armor and plumed helmets. The Roman dignitary looked on with contempt at the long-robed, bearded men crowded below; they were representatives of the local population, high priests and citizens, intimidated, trembling with fear, humble. In a threatening voice, Florus ordered them—he probably spoke Latin, and an interpreter repeated his words in Aramaic [7]

---

[6] Matreo della Corte, *Cace ed abitanti di Pompei*, Roma 1954, s. 246

[7] Originally, Aramaic was the language of the Arameans, a Semitic-speaking people of the region between the northern Levant and the northern Tigris valley. Aramaic rose to prominence under the Neo-Assyrian Empire (911–605 BC), under whose influence it became a lingua franca of the empire and its use spread throughout the Middle East. At its height, Aramaic, gradually replaced many earlier fellow Semitic languages.

According to the Babylonian Talmud (*Sanhedrin* 38b), the language spoken by Adam — the Bible's first human — was Aramaic.

Aramaic was the language of Jesus, who spoke its Galilean dialect during his public ministry, as well as the language of several sections of the Hebrew Bible, including parts of the books of Daniel and Ezra, and also the language of the *Targum*, because this was the common language spoken in Palestine at that time—to immediately bring in the criminals who had so brazenly insulted him a few days earlier in the temple courtyard. He cried out that if they did not hurry, his righteous wrath would be upon them and upon the whole city.

They tried to defend their compatriots. They swore, shouting past one another and raising their hands to the sky, that the inhabitants of Jerusalem were peaceful, loyal to the Romans, and full of good intentions. They begged for mercy for the youthful fools. True, they admitted that a crime had been committed, but only in words! It is hardly surprising that among the countless crowds of pilgrims who come to the holy city from all over the country, and even from outside Palestine, there are bold and stupid individuals, bold and stupid because they are young. But how to find the real culprits now? At the moment, everyone sincerely regrets what had happened. But who will voluntarily admit to having taken part in the excesses?

The tearful speeches infuriated Florus. He shouted at the soldiers to search the High City; this was the name for the district between Herod's palace and the Tyropoean Gorge,[8] beyond which the walls of the temple rose.

Before the Roman cordon sealed the whole district, its inhabitants, realizing what was afoot, tried to flee in panic. However, the streets were narrow and winding, and most of those who ran—ran straight into the swords of the soldiers. And the soldiers killed anyone they could lay their hands on: men, women, children. The wealthier citizens remained in their houses, hoping thereby to save their dignity and fortune, and thinking that the Romans would spare the members of their party, which had from the beginning strongly condemned any

---

the Aramaic translation of the Hebrew Bible. It is also the language of the Jerusalem Talmud, Babylonian Talmud and *Zohar*.

[8] Tyropoeon Valley (i.e., "Valley of the Cheesemakers") is the name given by Josephus the historian (*Jewish War* 5.140) to the rugged ravine in the Old City of Jerusalem, which in ancient times separated Mount Moriah from Mount Zion and emptied into the valley of Hinnom.

dissension against the authorities and had always fully cooperated with them. But they were sorely disappointed. The soldiers dragged them out of their houses and brought them before the governor, where the same verdict was invariably pronounced:

"Flog and crucify him!"

To streamline the action, everything was done immediately, in front of Florus, right in front of the palace. Among those crucified that day were many Roman citizens—or so the governor's enemies later claimed.

But the main purpose of the attack on the High City was to loot. Every house was searched thoroughly. And it could not have been otherwise: the soldiers had to find something not only for themselves but also for their officers and for the governor himself.

Berenice, terrified by the screams of the people being tortured and murdered, sent the commander of her bodyguard to Florus several times, demanding that he cease the slaughter. But since her messengers achieved nothing, she left the palace herself and stood before the dais in the square. She came barefoot—perhaps because it was the custom of those who had taken the Nazarite vow. Or perhaps simply to show her humility, naively thinking that she would be able to arouse the Roman's pity.

However, neither the queen's entreaties nor her bare feet moved Florus. As they spoke, soldiers within their sight continued with their bloody work. They tortured, crucified, and murdered. And—Berenice reported later—they nearly attacked her, too. And who knows, perhaps the procurator, irritated by the moaning and pleading of the woman he did not dare harm, quietly said to his men:

"Spook her a little. Make sure she stays away."

Berenice fled to her palace. She spent a sleepless night under guard. She trembled for fear that the legionaries might burst in swords bared at any moment.

Because the proximity of human corpses defiled her, she had to undergo ritual purification. She offered very costly gifts at the temple, as the Law commanded, and then began the thirty-day period of Nazarite abstinence and mortification anew.

Berenice

THE GREAT-GRANDFATHER AND GRANDFATHER OF BERENICE

And all this happened in Jerusalem to a woman who could rightly boast of being the great-granddaughter of the king of that city, the daughter of a king, the sister, and the wife of kings!

Berenice's great-grandfather had been King Herod the Great, a brilliant politician, a strict ruler, and an excellent administrator. For the price of complete and total submission to Rome, he gradually acquired, by the grace of her emperors, dominion over the greater part of Palestine. He gave peace to the country, enriched it, adorned it, and strengthened it with a great number of construction projects. He founded Caesarea Maritima—a city which later became the informal capital of the country—and the city of Sebaste on the site of former Samaria. He raised powerful strongholds in all parts of the kingdom, the most fearsome of which was Masada at the western shore of the Dead Sea, hanging high up on a vertical rock like an eagle's nest.

But Herod's greatest and most famous work was the expansion of the Temple in Jerusalem. The king carried it out with incredible panache, not sparing costs. But all that remains of the magnificence and vastness of that temple today are the boulders of its wall facing the Valley of Tyropoeon. It is known as the West Wall today.[9]

And yet all these admirable works and achievements of the king did not bring him popularity among his subjects. On the contrary, they hated him with all their soul and all their heart. Both the king and his people were at fault. Herod ruled ruthlessly and tyrannically; he did not shrink from any crime to achieve his goals; he favored Greeks and Greek culture; and above all, he ostentatiously manifested at every turn the most subservient loyalty to the Empire and the Emperor. His people, on the other hand, fanatically attached to the idea of independence—confirmed and reinforced by Messianic

---

[9] Formerly referred to as the Wailing Wall.

prophecies—did not understand Herod's political rationale. They did not understand that under the circumstances in which they found themselves, giving up external independence and showing humble submission before the Empire offered the only hope to retain some autonomy, a small, limited degree of freedom. This lack of understanding caused constant conflicts between the ruler and his subjects. Herod, suspicious and cruel by nature, repressed all signs of opposition mercilessly. He could, however, justify himself by saying that he treated his closest family and even his own sons with the same brutality. Three of his sons paid with their lives for real or alleged plots against their father.

One of them was Berenice's grandfather, Prince Aristobulus. He died a victim of a palace intrigue, strangled on the orders of Herod. He had three sons and a daughter, Herodias. This last was the same Herodias, whose daughter Salome, many years later, danced at a feast before her stepfather, Herod Antipas, as he celebrated his birthday. The prince liked the dance so much that he said in front of everyone:

"Ask me whatever you want, and I will not refuse you!"

The girl consulted with her mother, Herodias, and, returning to the hall, said:

"I want you to hand me on a tray the head of John the Baptist!"

For Herodias hated John because he had openly condemned her marriage to Herod Antipas. And he did so because she had previously been married to Herod Antipas' half-brother and had had Salome with him.

And so, the girl's wish was fulfilled.

Of the three sons of the tragically murdered Aristobulus, one bore his grandfather's name and was thus called Herod; he later became the prince of the city and county of Chalcis in southern Syria. [10] His second son received his father's name—Aristobulus. He never attained a princely title but was a very influential man of great wealth. Little is

[10] Modern Qinnasrin in Syria.

known about his fate. Finally, the third son bore two names, Herod Agrippa. The latter was given to him in honor of Marcus Agrippa, the closest friend and ally of Emperor Augustus. In history, he is known as Herod Agrippa I or simply Agrippa I.

Berenice was his daughter.

THE FATHER OF BERENICE
AND THE DEATH OF CALIGULA

The biography of Agrippa I reads like a romance, full of extraordinary adventures and unexpected twists of fate. The scenery is varied—Italy and Egypt, various cities of Syria, Greece, and Palestine. He found himself in all sorts of circumstances. He was once the star of the imperial court in Rome and, later, its prisoner, chained in irons. He prided himself on the friendship of the emperors of Rome and miraculously evaded death at their hands. Sometimes he squandered millions. At other times, he lived at the mercy of his relatives on meager jobs in provincial towns. And then he regained princely fortunes again.

Thanks to the extraordinary favor of emperor Caligula, he obtained huge grants in AD 37 and 39: first, the territory to the east of the Sea of Galilee and the River Jordan, and later—the whole of Galilee itself. However, he managed to remain in his Palestinian estates only for a short time. Already by AD 40, he had returned to Rome, where a plot against his benefactor was maturing.

The plot arose among the officers of the Praetorian Guard and, to some extent, involved their prefect, Marcus Arrecinus Clemens. These men violated their military oath but justified it by Caligula's growing madness, especially dangerous for those closest to him. The conscience of Clemens and his officers was ultimately shaken by the case of Quintilla.

She was a well-known and handsome Roman theater actress, always surrounded by a swarm of admirers. Among them was also a

Senator Pomponius, a man prudently avoiding all politics and instead enjoying life of Epicurean pleasure. And yet, he managed to expose himself to danger. A certain Timidius accused him of publicly insulting the emperor's majesty. Timidius, of course, made this denunciation in the hope that—as a reward for his vigilance and zeal—he would receive a share of his victim's enormous fortune.

Quintilla was the first witness called by the prosecution. Usually, in such cases, the witnesses immediately confirmed everything that was demanded of them, thus trying to redeem the inexcusable guilt of not having been the first person to report the alleged crime. And especially so if the witness was a woman and, what is more, a woman of loose morals. Timidius had reasons to be pleased with his idea and confident of his success.

Meanwhile, things turned out differently. On the first interrogation, Quintilia denied everything. The emperor ordered torture. Led to torture and knowing what awaited her, the girl still had enough presence of mind to step meaningfully on the foot of one of the witnesses. In this way, she made him understand that she could be counted on—that she would not betray anyone. And, actually, unbelievably, she endured the torture. And the torture must have been terrible since the sight of the tortured girl moved even Caligula when she was dragged before him. He dismissed the accusation and rewarded Quintilla generously to compensate her for her suffering and her courage.

The torture had been overseen by the praetorian tribune Chaerea. The emperor often entrusted him with such tasks. However, Chaerea's endurance had its limits. After this business, he entered into a conversation with his commander, Prefect Clemens. He began seemingly ambiguously:

"We guard our emperor well. We slaughter all conspirators, and we torture innocents so well that Caligula himself takes pity on them. We're good soldiers."

Clemens didn't answer—he only blushed. This emboldened Chaerea. He uttered openly and with some violence all that had long been on his mind:

"People accuse the emperor. But if you think about it, the real perpetrators of all the evil are we, the officers of the Praetorian Guard, and you above all. After all, it is up to us to put an end to the injustice. But we prefer to obey the madman's orders. All orders. We are no longer soldiers—we've become executioners! Why exactly do we carry these weapons? We do not protect the Empire or its government but a man who had enslaved Rome! Every day, we are splattered with the blood of the tortured. But only until the emperor comes after us."

The rhetoric of these words alone would probably never have convinced Clemens were it not for the fact that he had some personal reasons not to trust the emperor. So, he dared to agree with Chaerea *a little*. But he advised him not to share his thoughts with others. For if, by any chance, the case would become public, they would both pay for it with their lives before their conspiracy had a chance to mature. So, it was best to wait for a lucky opportunity. He himself, in any case, could not take part because of his advanced age.

They parted, and from then on, both lived in constant fear that they had said too much. Each asked himself whether the other one would not inform on him, and if so, should he not beat him to the punch by informing on him first? But after a while, they both came to the conclusion that they could trust each other. Although Chaerea made no further attempts to talk to Clemens, he informed his friends that the prefect was with them. They began to prepare for the assassination. However, a good opportunity did not come until January 24, AD 41. By then, Herod Agrippa had already been in Rome for several months.

Chaerea drew his sword at Caligula in a narrow, covered passage in the palace. He struck him between the collarbone and the neck. Then the other conspirators caught up with the wounded emperor, inflicting a total of thirty wounds with daggers and swords. Prefect Clemens was not among the assailants, but he did them a great favor anyway. For when, in the first hours of general confusion, the Praetorian Guard, not privy to the coup, captured one of the conspirators, he ordered him released. Moreover, he publicly acknowledged him and justified his and his companions' actions:

"In fact, it was Caligula himself who plotted against himself. He committed crimes and broke the laws. These men are only technically killers because, in fact, he himself had sharpened their swords against himself!"

But mere words were not enough for Chaerea. He believed that the Prefect should declare himself more clearly on the side of the tyrannicides. Since he could not force Clemens to do it, he chose his close relative. This was Julius Lupus, a praetorian tribune. Chaerea ordered him to kill Empress Caesonia and her daughter. Admittedly, opinions among the conspirators on this matter were divided. Some believed that Caligula alone was responsible for all his crimes and follies, so it would be wrong and unworthy of them to take vengeance on a defenseless woman. Others argued that Caesonia was the emperor's evil spirit; they blamed her for giving Caligula a love potion that had caused his madness. Chaerea himself settled the dispute firmly and ruthlessly:

"We must finish the job. No one from the Emperor's family should survive!"

Julius Lupus found Caesonia lying on the ground and hugging her husband's corpse, weeping and despairing, her dress stained with the blood pouring from his wounds. Her daughter was with her. The woman sobbed and repeated the same words over and over:

"Have I not said this would happen? Have I not warned you?"

What was she thinking about? Had she been admonishing her husband to act differently, more wisely? Or had she advised him to purge all suspects in time?

At first, Caesonia didn't realize why Lupus had come. She thought that he wanted to help her lift the corpse of Caligula. She beckoned him and asked him to come closer. But he walked towards her silently, with a strange look in his eyes. And then she understood and exposed her neck. The little girl also died.

King Herod Agrippa took care of the emperor's body. It was he who picked it up with his own hands and placed it on a bed. Covering it carefully, he announced to the guards:

"The Emperor is alive. He received many wounds and is in

great pain, but I have already sent for doctors."

BERENICE'S FATHER AND EMPEROR CLAUDIUS

Agrippa said so because the situation was unclear. No one knew what the conspirators would do next or what the Senate would do. A revolt of the Praetorians was feared, acts of blind vengeance, anarchy, and general mayhem. Agrippa felt it was necessary to appease and even lie to the soldiers in order to keep them under control for as long as possible. News soon came that the Senate was prepared to return to the old republican form of government. Alas, in the meantime, in the praetorian camp, a new emperor has already been acclaimed. He was Claudius, the uncle of the murdered Caligula, an elderly man generally despised and ridiculed because he was an amateur historian. One of the soldiers, while plundering the imperial house on the Palatine, pulled him out from behind a curtain where he had been hiding in fear.

Herod Agrippa understood at once how events would unfold. He also realized what he had to do in order to emerge from this confusion with the greatest possible personal gain. He showed up immediately at the Praetorian Barracks and held a confidential conversation with Claudius, who—frightened, helpless, lost—was about to renounce all political power in favor of the Senate. But Herod Agrippa was of a different opinion and spoke frankly. Then he returned home, where he ordered his hair to be anointed as if he had just left the table. He guessed what would happen now: the senators already knew that he had spoken to Claudius, and they would want to see how things were going and what position to take. Soon a delegation came to him, begging him to come to the Senate and express his opinion. The king went immediately. His speech, skillful and persuasive, pointed to a clear conclusion.

"I would give my life," Agrippa said, "to defend the dignity of the Senate. But one should evaluate the situation calmly and not succumb to emotions or pious wishes. Suppose you want to take power in your hands. A beautiful and worthy thing. Where are the weapons with which you will defend it? Where are your soldiers? You say there are enough men in the city and that the money will be found. Indeed, apparently, you are even ready to free your slaves and staff new units with them! I wish you luck. I consider it my duty, though, to warn you that the soldiers who elected Claudius are a very experienced lot. And you—on whom can you count? On the city rabble, some nerds who can't even draw a sword! I think there is only one course of action. The best thing we can do is to send envoys to Claudius immediately, asking him to relinquish the powers given to him by the soldiers. As for myself, if necessary, I would not refuse to undertake such a mission."

And when he arrived again at the praetorian camp, this time as a member of the official legation, he found an opportunity to inform Claudius confidentially that the Senators were incapable of any effective action, quarreling among themselves, chattering about the lofty ideals of freedom and making unrealistic plans to seize power. Therefore he, Claudius, should take a firm stance and reject the suggestion that he abdicate—and without entering into any discussions. Instead, he should promise that his reign would not be tyrannical, that he would not permit any violations of the rule of law or the sort of cruelty Rome had experienced during recent reigns, especially since he himself had suffered from its horrors. And that he was willing to share power with the Senate.

In the face of the firm attitude of the Praetorians and the message of Claudius, the Senate had to give way. The new emperor arrived on the Palatine. His first act was to convene his privy council. This decreed that Caligula's killers must be put to death as soon as possible, for even though what they had done was commendable, as soldiers, they had broken their oath. In fact, the point was to scare off any would-be imitators.

Guided to the place of execution, Chaerea did not even turn pale, whereas Julius Lupus wept and trembled—though supposedly only from cold for he didn't have a coat, and it was January. Chaerea joked:

"Wolves don't care about the cold."

Which was a pun because, in Latin, *lupus* means wolf. Then Chaerea matter-of-factly asked the soldier who was about to behead him whether he was any good at it. And he asked that the execution be carried out with the same sword with which he had killed Caligula. He exposed his neck boldly and died from the first blow. Lupus, on the other hand, instinctively kept pulling his head back so that the executioner had to hack at it several times.

Nothing happened to the praetorian prefect, Arrecinus Clemens. And rightly so, for he had not raised his sword against his emperor. For all we know, he died peacefully, and in any case, history is silent about his further fate. He left two children. His son, bearing the same name and surname as his father, later rose to very high offices. His daughter, Arrecina Tertulla, was probably still a tiny girl in AD 41. Twenty years later, around AD 60, she married the young son of the senator Flavius Vespasian, Titus. It was the same Titus who, in the year AD 75, welcomed in Rome and hosted on the Palatine Berenice, the daughter of that Agrippa, who had served emperor Claudius so well.

THE RULE AND DEATH OF THE FATHER OF BERENICE

Almost immediately after he assumed power, Claudius rewarded Herod Agrippa in a truly imperial manner. To the lands which Herod Agrippa had previously obtained from Caligula, he now added all the lands west of the Jordan and the Dead Sea, that is: Samaria, Judea, Idumea, and the coastal plain. Thanks to this grant, Herod Agrippa became the ruler of nearly the whole of Palestine—nearly everything which had once belonged to his grandfather, Herod the Great.

Unlike his grandfather, however, he managed to win the favor of his subjects, even though he pursued the same policy of total loyalty and submission to the Empire. He achieved this mainly with the help of empty gestures. He was generous, personally kind to his subjects, and showed an attachment to Jewish traditions. He won the support of the powerful party of the Pharisees. And, unlike his grandfather, he treated Syrians, Greeks, Samaritans, and all the other assorted religious dissenters harshly. This was felt especially painfully by the sect of the followers of Jesus—the tiny group who believed that He had been the Messiah. Suddenly, they found themselves in grave danger. One of their leaders, James, son of the fisherman Zebedee, was beheaded on the king's orders. Another, Peter, was imprisoned and escaped death only by a miracle.

After three years' reign over Palestine, in the year AD 44, Herod Agrippa held magnificent games in honor of emperor Claudius at Caesarea Maritima. He appeared in a robe woven of silver threads. When he stood in the theater in the morning, he gleamed in the rays of the rising sun like a celestial being. Immediately, the voices of flatterers rose up, crying:

"You shine like a god!"

Reportedly, just at that moment, the king saw an owl perched on a wire stretched over his head. His heart skipped a beat with a bad premonition. Years earlier, when—in the times of Emperor Tiberius—he had been held in an Italian prison, he was led out of the dungeon one day for a walk and, at one point, leaned against a tree on which an owl sat. One of the inmates, a German by birth, noticed it. He approached him and said:

"Today, this bird bodes you imminent release and prosperity. But when you see him the next time, you will die within five days."

And indeed, the king was gripped by sudden and violent stomach pains. Brought back to the palace, he suffered for five more days. His chamber was on a high floor of the palace, so he could see from his bed how the Jewish population of Caesarea—men, women, and children—put on penitential robes and went out into the streets of the city, weeping and praying for the health of their king. And, says a historian, at the sight, tears flowed from the king's eyes.

He died aged fifty-four. He left a seventeen-year-old son, Agrippa II, and three daughters. The eldest, Berenice, was sixteen, the middle, Marianne, ten, and the youngest, Drusilla, only six.

How much the king was hated by his gentile subjects was shown on the same day. In the two cities of his kingdom, which had the largest number of Greeks and Syrians, that is, in Caesarea Maritima and Samaria-Sebaste, crowds went out into the streets. People sang and shouted for joy, cursed the memory of the king, and hurled the foulest abuses at him. They feasted in public squares, in their temples, and in front of their houses. Crowned with flowers and fragrant with perfumes, they toasted each other again and again, shouting and laughing:

"Cheers! The king is dead!"

Also, his own soldiers joined the festivities, which surprised no one, as they had been recruited mainly from among gentiles. They broke into the royal houses and stole the gilded statues of the princesses. They carried them to brothels and placed them on flat roofs; from there, they showed with vulgar gestures, to the delight of the people in the streets, what obscenities could be done with Berenice, Marianne, and Drusilla.

TEMPLES AND SEX

And speaking of brothels, let us return to the story contained in the teachings of Simon the Magus, that *Ennoia*-Helen ended up in a brothel—and not as a statue or some other likeness, but in person. By what logic, by what association, could one imagine a scene so shocking and blasphemous?

Well, dear reader, consider this: to the people of the time, especially in the Middle East, the thought did not seem at all unusual. Indeed, in many countries of the East, it would have been completely in keeping with ancient religious customs. Berenice, who so often traveled through the lands of Syria and Phoenicia, was familiar with these practices. And later, Titus also heard about them when he visited the temple of Aphrodite in Paphos, Cyprus.

The statue of Aphrodite of Paphos, if it deserved this name at all, looks odd. The images on the coins minted in Paphos and our ancient sources confirm and complement each other: it was a tall, round stone pillar, tapering towards the top, and it stood near the altar, in the open air, in the temple courtyard. Ancient legends would lead us to believe that not a drop of rain had ever touched the altar, nor was it ever drenched with the blood of sacrificial animals: only the purest flame burned upon it. As for the offerings, only males were sacrificed to the Lady of the Shrine, preferably young goats. From their entrails, her priests predicted the future of pious pilgrims.

But what was the nature of the cult in Paphos? Was it an ancient survivor of the cult of sacred stones, a cult so widespread in the countries of the ancient East from the times of the Neolithic? Was it perhaps a meteor fallen from the sky? On some coins, the likeness of a crescent moon and a star is seen above the stone and the temple; however, this does not tell us much because the Lady of Love was often associated with the Moon.

The cult of Aphrodite was said to have come to Cyprus from the Palestinian city of Ashkelon. The legend placed her first temple on Cyprus at the site in Paphos and referred to the goddess by many different names. Her Cypriot shrines—for eventually, many other temples to her arose on the island besides Paphos—soon eclipsed in fame the site of Ashkelon. That is why it became so common in the Greek world to call her Aphrodite of Cyprus and to say that she had emerged from sea foam on the shores of the island.

There are, however, interesting connections of her cult on Cyprus not only to Palestine but even to distant Babylonia. For example:

It was the custom in Cyprus that girls of pre-nuptial age would sit on the shore on certain days of the year and wait for men; they offered themselves for money which they saved for their dowry. By acting in this way, it was said, young Cypriot women made a sacrifice of themselves to their goddess. Once married, however, they remained unwaveringly faithful to their husbands. And similar temple services were practiced in the various religious centers of Babylonia and Syria from very ancient times to the very end of antiquity.

When Herodotus, the famous Greek historian who lived five centuries before the time of Titus, passed through the cities of Babylonia, he saw in the shrines of the goddess of love—he identified her with Aphrodite—a custom which he found extremely scandalous:

> Every woman must go to the temple once in her life and sell herself to a man from a foreign country. Even very wealthy women follow this practice. They come in covered litters, followed by a procession of servants, and do like all the others. They sit on the ground in the sacred grove of the goddess, wearing a wreath of hempen rope on their heads which signifies that they are slaves of the goddess. At times there are very many of them, and they sit on both sides of an aisle where foreigners walk. Once a woman has entered the grove, she cannot return home until a stranger throws her a silver coin and utter these words:
>
> "I summon the goddess against you!"
>
> The coin can be quite small, but the woman is not allowed to refuse it, nor is she allowed to refuse the man who throws it. She gives herself to him outside the tabernacle. Only after fulfilling this sacred duty, can she return to her ordinary life. And from then on, she lives an exemplary life, unavailable for any money. Of course, good-looking women fulfill their duty very quickly, but ugly women sometimes sit and wait for years until someone willing turns up.

And in connection with this story, Herodotus says that the same custom existed in some places on Cyprus.[11]

And consider Syria. In the city of Heliopolis, today called Baalbek, girls had to give themselves to anyone who wished in the temple of Aphrodite before they got married. Only the administrative victory of Christianity in the fourth century AD put an end to this practice. But, the local population saw this as a violation of their most sacred religious tradition, waited for an opportune moment, and took their revenge on the local nuns in an exceptionally cruel manner.

And here is another land of the East: Phoenicia. There, in the city of Byblos, stood the shrine of the goddess in whom the Greeks saw

---

[11] Herodot, *Histories*, I 199.

their Aphrodite. Every year, Byblos celebrated the death of Adonis, the lover of Aphrodite, killed by a wild boar but then resurrected. During the ceremony, there was deep mourning throughout the city, weeping, wailing, groaning. All the women cut their hair as if they had lost a loved one, and she who would not do so had to go to the market on the appointed day and sell herself there—but only to foreigners. And the money thus earned she donated to the temple.

On the Armenian border, on the upper Euphrates, the house of the goddess Anaitis enjoyed great reverence. Among her temple prostitutes, there were, in addition to ordinary slaves, also free-born girls, some from the most illustrious families of neighboring lands, and some remained in service for many years. They served their goddess with their bodies, giving themselves to pious pilgrims. Later, they left, married, and everyone considered it an honor that his wife had once served in the sanctuary of Anaitis. True, they had the right to choose their lovers, and therefore, they usually took on only young men of their rank. They took only a symbolic payment from them, but in return, they hosted them beautifully in their rooms and showered them with expensive gifts.

But let's return to the temple in Paphos on Cyprus. The temple also held special ceremonies for men, a kind of mystical initiation. Those who passed it received a pinch of salt from the hands of the priest—as a reminder of their Lady's birth from the waves of the sea and a small image of a phallus. In turn, they offered Aphrodite a small coin in thanks, "as a man gives to his beloved," wrote one of the ancient writers.

But how should we understand the origin and meaning of such practices? Today, one might advance the learned argument that it was a survival from prehistorical times when certain tribes willingly lent their women to foreigners; they did this both as a form of hospitality and to diversify the gene pool. In antiquity, however, a rather different, mystical explanation became popular: a man who takes a woman dedicated to the goddess in the acts of love, in fact, connects with the goddess herself, for the woman embodies the life-giving forces of nature. Such were perhaps the teachings of Simon and his disciples—or at least that seems to follow from the accusations of debauchery we read in the works of the enemies of the Samaritan magician.

TEMPLE PROSTITUTION

Simon's enemies attacked him virulently, him, his successors, and his followers, presenting their teaching and conduct in very shocking terms:

> This impudent crook showed off his Helen everywhere and called her his ewe lamb, a ewe lamb that had gone missing but had been recovered. What had really happened was that he fell in love with the girl and bought her out of a brothel, then made up a fairy tale to justify himself in front of his own disciples. But they faithfully follow in the footsteps of this juggler! According to them, everyone has the right to live with whatever woman he desires. And they say shamelessly:
>
> "All soil is soil, and it matters nothing who plants his seed in it, what matters is that the seed be planted."
>
> Then they boast of their debauchery and call it perfect love! Truly, their disgusting and unbridled ingenuity surpasses all imaginable boundaries of decency. But if someone accuses them of debauchery, he will hear an arrogant reply:
>
> "We should not allow ourselves to be convinced that something is evil when that evil is merely apparent and conventional."
>
> So, they do whatever they please, claiming that they are the only truly liberated people. For, as they teach it, only the grace of the Supreme Godhead saves, and righteous deeds are of no help. And why is it so? They have a ready answer to that:
>
> The evil angels (who made this world) formulated its customary laws in order to enslave men and keep them in awe. Your prophets of old prophesied not from the inspiration of the Supreme Godhead but only from the prompting of those angels!
>
> They also claim that when the end of the world comes, only those who

believe in Simon and Helen will be saved and thus freed from the power of the evil creator angels. [12]

Their priests serve all base lusts. They practice magic, know spells and charms, prepare love potions, summon the spirits of the dead, interpret dreams. They also have statues of Simon and Helen. He is like Zeus, and she is like Athena. They invoke them as Lord and Lady. They prostrate themselves before them, offer them sacrifices, pour out libations. But when someone calls these statues by their proper names, they immediately condemn him as uninformed and uninitiated.

APOLLONIUS OF TYANA

Among the famous personalities who visited Paphos on Cyprus and took an interest in the local rites, there was another contemporary of Berenice and Titus, although much older than either of them—a Greek sage and prophet, a miracle worker and ascetic, and perhaps also a bit of a charlatan: Apollonius of Tyana. His *Life*, written a century and a half later by Philostratus on the basis of some earlier texts, preserves the following note:

> At Syrian Seleucia, Apollonius and his companions found themselves on a ship bound for Cyprus. They landed in the city of Paphos, famous for the temple of Aphrodite. There is a symbolic statue of the goddess there. Apollonius admired it and gave many instructions to its priests in the matter of its worship, and then sailed for the shores of Asia Minor. [13]

We invoke the figure of the holy man not because, while traveling in various lands, he also happened to stumble upon Cyprus. Nor because he later came close to the House of the Flavians (of which Vespasian, the father of Titus, was the founder). The reason why we invoke Apollonius is because we wish to illuminate the historical epoch of our story from many different angles. We devoted a lot of space to the

---

[12] Compare to Luther's claim, contested by the Roman Church, that "[Christians] are justified by faith alone." (see *Letter to the Romans* 3:28)
[13] Philostratus, *Life Apollonius of Tyana*, III 58.

surreal—that's how some people describe them!—ideas of Simon the Magus; we recalled the erotic practices of both his sect and many other Eastern cults. Therefore, it seems appropriate to present someone who stood in a certain opposition to these views and customs. However, here too, apart from contrasts, we will find similarities because both Simon and Apollonius were both the children and the creators of their age.

Apollonius was born in the Cappadocian town of Tyana, which is today's eastern Turkey, sometime during the reign of Emperor Augustus. He attended schools first in the Cilician city of Tarsus—the same city in which his contemporary, Saul, later called Paul, was born and spent his youth. Perhaps the two met? Or at least knew of each other?

Later, Apollonius studied at Aegae. For several years during the reign of Tiberius, he wandered around various lands of Asia Minor and Syria, from Ephesus to Antioch. Finally, he decided to make a pilgrimage to the very source of secret wisdom: he went to Assyria and Babylonia and from there to India, where he met and argued with the Brahmins. These journeys took a long time. Meanwhile, emperor Caligula reigned in Rome, then Claudius. Apollonius returned west through Babylonia. At the borders of the Empire, on the banks of the Euphrates, he learned that Rome had a new emperor—Nero.

By way of the cities of Syria, he reached Antioch and, from there, the port city of Seleucia. There, as has been said, he found a ship bound for Cyprus and landed on the shores of the island at Paphos. Of some of his later adventures, there will be occasion to talk again more broadly. But to understand the views and practices of Apollonius and the reasons for the sage's fame, we must go back to his youth. This is what he himself said about it:

"When I was fourteen, my father took me to Tarsus and sent me to the school of the rhetorician Euthydemus, a native of Phoenicia. I started learning from him and became very attached to him. But I did not like the atmosphere of the city. It's hard to study seriously there. The people there think only of pleasure and enjoyment of life. They mock and laugh at everything, they behave insolently. They love fine clothes more than the wisdom of the Athenians. They sit by their river, the Cydnus, like some water birds. That's why, many years later, I wrote to them in a letter: 'Stop getting drunk on your river water!' I finally managed to get my father to take me away from there. I moved to the city of Aegae, also in Cilicia, but a little further east, by the sea. The tranquility of this town is very conducive to anyone who really desires to devote himself to philosophy. People cultivate their studies over there with real enthusiasm.

"Aegae is also home to the famous temple of Asclepius, in which the god shows himself to pilgrims. I met supporters of various schools of philosophy in that town. The followers of Plato were the most numerous, but there were also Stoics, Aristotelians, and even Epicureans. I listened to all of them very carefully, but I was most interested in Pythagorean philosophy. Its teacher in Aegae was a certain Euxenos. Admittedly, he did not command much respect because he did not practice his philosophy in his personal life. Yes, he knew the teachings of Pythagoras, but in a way in which birds learn the speech of man. So, they say: "Good morning," and "Farewell," and "God bless you," and similar things, but they themselves do not understand anything, and the words they utter do not prove that they have somehow become men. All they can do is pronounce a few words.

"Nevertheless, I studied with Euxenos attentively for almost two years—until my sixteenth year. Only then did I decide that I must seriously implement the Pythagorean way of life. Of course, I did not stop showing respect to my teacher. I even convinced my father to give him a suburban estate with a pleasant garden and springs. But, at the same time, I said to him: 'You stay here and live in your own way, and I will go out and look for Pythagoras!'

"He asked how I was going to go about it. I replied that I would do it like the doctors, for they first cleanse the patients' stomachs and thus achieve it that some never get sick while others recover fully. It was then that I completely gave up eating meat, and then, one by one, I reduced my needs and practiced more and more abstinence."

42

THE ASCETIC PRACTICES OF APOLLONIUS

Pythagoras, an influential sage of six centuries earlier, whom Apollonius especially adored and wished to follow, had given his students the following commandment:

"A man should not associate with any woman; an exception can only be made for his wife."

Apollonius, however, stated authoritatively that Pythagoras was thinking of others when he said those words, for he himself had never married. Apollonius resolved to follow his example as faithfully as possible. He never married and shunned all love affairs. And he made this decision while still a very young, healthy, and robust man. But the enemies of Apollonius claimed that he, too, was subject to lust and that he had left his homeland because of a disappointment in love and moved for a whole year to the land of the Scythians. His disciples rejected these claims as slanderous and fictitious. They averred that their master had always controlled his passions and never visited the land of the Scythians. They also pointed out that Apollonius' most vociferous critic, Euphrates, never accused him of succumbing to sexual desire, although he wrote many other mendacious things about him. And the cause of Euphrates' hatred is said to have been this: Apollonius had once rebuked him for his willingness do anything for money and publicly exhorted him to stop selling secret knowledge.

Apollonius himself gave away almost all the property he had inherited from his parents. First, he gave half of his share to his elder brother, and later he distributed the rest, little by little, to various relatives, leaving almost nothing for himself. He said that in doing so, he acted significantly wiser than some very famous philosophers of centuries ago: for some of them left their lands and houses to chance, while others threw their money into the sea. In this way, although they got rid of the encumbrance of wealth, they did not help anyone and thus wasted the assets entrusted to them by fate.

Returning, however, to the issues of asceticism and abstinence: Apollonius did not practice strict self-discipline in matters

43

of sexual love alone. Following the teaching of Pythagoras, he ate no meat at all; he said that there was something impure about it and that it dulled the clarity of thought. He was content with bread, fruit, and vegetables. He didn't drink wine. Although he admitted that as a fruit of the earth, it was a pure and wholesome beverage, he nevertheless thought that it obscured the ethereal element of the soul and threatened the peace of mind. He went about barefoot. He wore only linen clothes. He never cut his hair. He took only cold baths because he was of the opinion that warm water promoted disease and premature aging of the body. On one occasion, he arrived in Syrian Antioch just after the emperor had ordered its great baths to be closed for a time as a punishment for some offenses of the city's citizens against the Roman authorities. Hearing of this, Apollonius declared:

"You do him wrong, and yet the emperor rewards you by prolonging your life!"

On another occasion, the Ephesians wanted to stone to death the chief official of their city because he allegedly did not keep the bathhouse properly heated. Apollonius came to his defense. He said:

"You accuse this man of poor management of the bathhouse, and I accuse you of bathing in a wrong way!"

But he anointed his body with oil and resorted to massages.

The greatest ascetic achievement of Apollonius, however, was the preservation of complete silence for a period of five years. In this case, too, he faithfully followed the express recommendation of Pythagoras, who ordered that all students wishing to join his community observe a five-year period of silence. The final stimulus for this heroic decision was a question Euxenus, his teacher at Aegae, once asked him:

"Why do not you write? After all, you have many interesting thoughts, and you speak beautifully!"

To this, Apollonius replied:

"I have not yet undergone the trial of silence."

And he started immediately. However, he did not give up human company. Those who got to know him at that time claimed that although he did not say a word, communing with him had a special appeal. He took part in discussions, expressing his thoughts with his eyes, gestures, movements of the head. He was not one of those gloomy and introverted wise men. He socialized freely, was always cheerful, and showed kindness to people. Later, he admitted the period of silence had been the most difficult in his life:

"How many times have I had something very important to say, but I was not allowed to open my mouth! And how many times have I had to pretend that I did not hear insulting, rude, irritating words! But every time, when it seemed to me that I was about to break my silence, I repeated to myself this line from the Odyssey:

Endure this, too, my heart![14]

Apollonius spent those difficult years in the lands where he had previously studied, that is, on the south coast of Asia Minor, in Cilicia and Pamphylia. And there, in the Pamphylian city of Aspendos, an extraordinary thing happened.

It was a year of crop failure. Great landowners and merchants hoarded grain, kept it off the market, or exported it to places where the prices were even higher. When Apollonius entered the city, he could see only bitter vetch in the market;[15] the common people were reduced to eating such weed. There was a riot. An angry mob snatched up burning faggots and attacked the council building. They wanted to burn alive the chief magistrate because the scoundrel, in league with the rich, did nothing to remedy the misery of the people. The unfortunate looked for asylum, wrapping his arms around the statue of Emperor Tiberius. If he were torn away by force or the statue damaged, a terrible punishment would inevitably befall the city, for the Romans would consider it a sacrilege and an insult to the sovereign's majesty. (A story was widely repeated across the Empire that a certain Senator had been dragged before court because he had struck his slave, who happened to hold a coin with the likeness of

---

[14] Odyssey, 20:1

[15] *Vicia ervilia*, commonly known as ervil or bitter vetch, is an ancient grain legume crop of the Mediterranean region.

Tiberius in his hand). Fortunately, both for the wretched city official and for the mob, Apollonius managed to stop the advancing crowd at the last moment. He blocked its way with his body. He stood motionless, silent, with his arms crossed over his chest. And then (it was said with great admiration) he performed a real miracle—he arranged a settlement with the city's grain merchants, and all without opening his mouth, without breaking his silence! His posture, gestures, seriousness, the expression of his eyes, and the fame of his divine wisdom were enough. It is true that he later admitted that there was a moment when he almost spoke—and in a loud and menacing voice, too: namely, when the grain speculators were brought to the square.

About the time when Apollonius practiced his five-year silence and enjoyed a great rise in fame and popularity on its account in the countries of Asia Minor, Berenice lived in Palestine and was still a little girl. And by the time she lost her father in AD 44, the ascetic was already in Babylonia or perhaps even farther east.

THE FIRST TWO HUSBANDS OF BERENICE

Although at the time of her father's death, Berenice was only sixteen, she was already a widow and married for the second time.

She had first married when she was thirteen. Her husband was Marcus Julius Alexander. Despite his Roman name, he was a Jew. He came from a Jewish family long settled in Alexandria, enriched and Hellenized there. Ever since Egypt had come under Roman rule, the family had served their new masters faithfully, exercising practically hereditary oversight over the collection of customs dues by land and sea. As a reward for these services, Marcus's father received Roman citizenship and, with it, a Roman name.

But Berenice's first marriage was a mere formality, for Marcus died shortly after its conclusion and before it could be consummated. The young virgin widow soon remarried thanks to her father's efforts.

Agrippa I married her to... his brother Herod; in other words, she married her own uncle. However, this did not surprise or scandalize anyone because marriages within the same family were common in the East at that time, and in the Herodian dynasty, they were almost a rule. Agrippa I obtained from emperor Claudius for the husband of Berenice the duchy of Chalcis, in southern Syria, between the mountain ranges of Lebanon and Anti-Lebanon.

From this marriage, two sons came into the world. They were still little boys when their father died. This happened in AD 48. Herod thus outlived his elder brother, King Agrippa I, by only four years, and Berenice, by then twenty years old, was widowed for a second time. She and her sons ought to have inherited the principality of Chalcis, but Emperor Claudius decreed otherwise. He gave it instead to Berenice's brother, Agrippa II. This was intended to compensate him, however modestly, for the loss of his father's inheritance, that is, the whole of Palestine, which, immediately after the unexpected death of Herod Agrippa in Cesarea Maritima, reverted to direct Roman rule, exercised by governors with the title of procurators. Because of this change of regime, those who had so brazenly mocked the dead king and had so lewdly ridiculed his daughters did not suffer the punishment they may well have expected. Who knows—perhaps those very ugly incidents influenced the imperial decision to restore Roman rule in Palestine. Perhaps the advisors of Claudius feared that the irreconcilable hostility of Jews and Gentiles might lead to the unleashing of bloody riots with which the very young Agrippa II might not be able to cope? But to make up to the young prince for the loss of his vast inheritance, the emperor offered him the little principality of Chalcis, then without a ruler, for the sons of Berenice were still too young to inherit.

THE BUILDING PROJECTS OF THE BROTHER OF BERENICE

Having lived in Rome for many years and made many friends there,

Agrippa II enjoyed the complete trust, perhaps even friendship, of Emperor Claudius—as had his father. No wonder then that after some time, he received an extraordinary gift: he gave up to Rome the small principality of Chalcis and, in return, received much more extensive lands located to the east and north of the Sea of Galilee—the former possessions of Prince Philip, son of Herod the Great. He also received the small kingdom of Abilene near Damascus. Emperor Nero, the successor of Claudius, also proved generous to Agrippa II. He gave him two cities on the western—Galilee—shore of the lake: Tiberias and Tarichaea, and a small district in the south of the country, at the mouth of the Jordan, where it entered the Dead Sea. Moved by this kindness, the king renamed his beautiful residence at the source of the Jordan, Caesarea Philippi: henceforth, it was officially called "Neronias." And he splendidly expanded the city so that it could bear such an honorable name with proper dignity.

In Judea proper, which was now governed by Roman procurators based in Caesarea Maritima, Agrippa retained only one privilege: the custody of the temple in Jerusalem. This meant that he was entitled to appoint and depose its high priests. He did it often, under various pretexts, with obvious satisfaction, happy to demonstrate his power. In religious matters, he was rather indifferent, like all members of his family, but formally and ostensibly, he adhered to the provisions of the Law. Therefore, when he gave his younger sister, Drusilla, in marriage to the king of Emesa in Syria, he demanded that the bridegroom be circumcised first. (A few years later, when the same Drusilla, having divorced the ruler of Emesa, married the then Procurator of Judea, the Roman Felix, the king did not make such a stipulation). At the same time, Agrippa adorned the Phoenician city of Berytus, today's Beirut, with a multitude of public statues and all kinds of works of art, many of which depicted living beings—in flagrant violation of the Jewish Law.

Agrippa II liked Berytus and felt at home there. Already his great-grandfather, King Herod the Great, had built halls, porticos, temples, and market squares in that city. In this way, he courted Roman favor because Berytus had been refounded as a Roman colony and settled by the veterans of two legions. When some of those Heriodian buildings required restoration, Agrippa II expanded and improved them. Sometime in the late 1950s, a damaged Latin inscription was found in Beirut:

QUEEN BERENICE,
DAUGHTER OF THE GREAT KING AGRIPPA,
AND KING AGRIPPA
RESTORED THIS BUILDING WHICH
THEIR GREAT-GRANDFATHER, KING HEROD, HAD BUILT
AND WHICH HAD COLLAPSED DUE TO OLD AGE.
THEY DECORATED IT WITH MARBLE AND SIX PILLARS.[16]

Note that their father, Herod Agrippa, is also called "great" in the inscription. Indeed, he did a lot for the city. He built a theatre, an amphitheater, baths, and porticoes, decorating all these buildings wonderfully. He staged musical and poetic performances at his own expense as well as bloody gladiator fights. And once—and this extraordinary event was remembered for many years—he set upon each other two squads of gladiators, each numbering seven hundred men. The fighters were all criminals sentenced to death. By murdering each other, they gave delight and joy to the spectators and, at the same time, dealt each other the punishment they deserved. The idea of this mass and public execution, combining the beautiful and the useful, met with general approval.

Following in his father's footsteps, Agrippa II held games at the Beirut theater every year, and on each occasion, he distributed grain and oil worth tens of thousands of drachmas among the people. Of course, this caused sincere indignation among the king's subjects: the city lay beyond the borders of his kingdom, so they felt that foreigners were being fed at their expense. As was indeed the case.

In Jerusalem itself, the king expanded the former Hasmonean palace in the High City, now serving as his Jerusalem residence (since Herod's much grander and more modern palace now served Roman

---

[16] E. M. Smallwood, *Documents illustrating the principles of Gaius, Claudius and Nero*, Cambridge 1967, No. 212 b.

procurators). Meanwhile, work on enlarging and beautifying the temple, begun in the time of Herod the Great, was completed. This caused widespread unrest in the city, as these works had provided employment to many thousands of craftsmen, especially stonemasons: there were reportedly eighteen thousand of them in Jerusalem. The number is undoubtedly exaggerated, even if we assume that it included their families, but certainly, the crowd of stonemasons was a real army. And let us bear in mind that the wages and work conditions at the Temple were excellent: it was enough to work just an hour to qualify for a full day's pay! The immensely rich temple treasury paid well, as it well could—for it received gifts and contributions from all the lands of the Mediterranean and the Middle East.

Now, when the Temple works came to a completion, the king was asked to undertake the restoration of the Great Portico, which enclosed the outer courtyard from the east. (That courtyard was called the Court of the Gentiles because everyone, not only Jews, was allowed to enter it). But Agrippa declared that it would cost too much and take too long. He remarked sententiously if a little cryptically:

"To build is difficult, but to demolish is easy!"

Instead, he very graciously allowed some streets of Jerusalem to be paved with cobblestones at his expense. The remains of this cobblestone pavement have been preserved in several places, several meters below the surface of the modern city.

Now, regarding the portico, which will often be mentioned on these pages, it was also called Solomon's Gate, wrongly assuming that it had been built by the famous sage-king who had reigned ten centuries earlier. It was gigantic: by our measures, it was more than four hundred meters long; two rows of columns—each monolithic, each over twelve meters high—supported a roof of cedar beams. It was a huge avenue of columns, the longest of all the temple porticoes, for the southern one, called the Royal, although wider and taller, and with three rows of columns instead of two, was only half the length; and neither the opposite, western one, reached the length of Solomon's portico.

This portico was the favorite place for meetings and

promenades, especially on winter days, when the afternoon sun warmed it with its rays, but the external wall protected it from the irritating blasts of the cold wind from the east. Standing here, one could see the whole vast Gentile's Courtyard and, in the middle of it, on a low dais, the dazzling white edifice of the Tabernacle, surrounded by its own wall behind which were the inner courts, glistening with gilded roofs and bronze gates. And the most splendid of those gates opened towards Solomon's Portico. The outer wall of the portico, built of closely-fitted mighty boulders, rose on a sheer vertical rock which plummeted down into the valley of Cedron.[17] Those who stood on the roof of the portico (there were stairs to the top) found themselves looking down as if into an abyss. The impression was particularly strong—some people suffered vertigo when they got there—when one entered from the south balcony. Small wonder that the followers of Jesus said that when Satan tempted Christ, he took Him there and said to him:

"If you really are the son of God, why don't you jump?"

AQUILA: I WAS A STUDENT OF SIMON THE MAGUS

"I can hurl myself from the top of the highest mountain into the deepest abyss, and I'll not be hurt. I will land on the ground without any injuries as if angels carried me in their hands."

Simon Magus often makes this claim. His countrymen in Samaria are overawed by his miracles. And most are inclined to believe that he is some sort of a god who had descended from Heaven to save humankind. As for me, I think I, too, could easily be carried away and persuaded by his magnetic charm—if I didn't know him so well and didn't take part in his affairs. But because I did, we were able—my brother Niketas and me—to break away from him. We reconsidered

---

[17] Kidron Valley (classical transliteration, *Cedron*) is the modern name of the valley originating slightly northeast of the Old City of Jerusalem, which separates the Temple Mount from the Mount of Olives, and ends at the Dead Sea.

all his magic tricks and his highly suspicious ideas. Do you want to know what kind of man he is, where he comes from, how he does his business, how he deceives people? Just listen!

His father was a certain Antonius, and his mother was named Rachel. He was born in Samaria, in the village of Gitta, six miles outside of the city. He was an expert magician, but he also mastered the Greek authors. He had mastered both these fields during his long stay in Egypt. He desired fame and glory more than any man I know. He wanted his followers to believe that he was the Supreme Godhead, the god who stands above the creator of the world![18] He also claimed to be the Messiah. He was called in Greek by the title *Hestos*, meaning *Constant* or, perhaps, you might say, *Everlasting*. This was supposed to mean that he could never be destroyed, as, thanks to his power, his body was uniform and compact and, therefore, immortal.

This was shortly after the death of John, called the Baptist, the one who was beheaded on the orders of Herod Antipas. You know that Salome asked for John's head, persuaded by her mother, Herodias. At that time, Dositheus preached in Samaria and had thirty disciples. He also had a woman named Helen or Selene with him, "Selene" meaning the Moon. These thirty were said to symbolize the thirty days of the month. According to some, Selene was included among the thirty. In that case, the number would not be full because, after all, as everyone knows, a woman is only half a man, and this again would correctly point to the fact that the lunar month does not really have thirty days but twenty-nine and a half.

In any case, he had a rule against increasing the number of his followers, and he never accepted as a disciple anyone not thoroughly tested. Therefore, whoever wanted to occupy an honorable place, tried with all his might to gain merit—of course, according to the principles of their faith. But even so, one could count on advancement only after

---

[18] One of the ideas common to the age was that an aloof Supreme Godhead had a subsidiary deity, whom some called in Greek "the Demiurge," and who was responsible for the creation of the universe. Many read the Biblical line, "Let us create man in our image" (*Genesis* 1:26-28) as an indication that that was indeed the case.

the death of one of the thirty.

Now, Simon, who had just returned to Samaria from Egypt, approached Dositheus. He pretended to be friends and begged to be taken in as a disciple when one of them died. And all because he lusted after Helen/Selena. Since we had known him before, he told us frankly that he was a sorcerer. That he loved Selena. That above all, he wanted fame, that he would refuse to win the girl by trickery but would patiently wait for a worthy opportunity to win her. And that such an opportunity would surely come if only we would conspire with him and help him in everything. He swore that he would reward us well for our services. We would receive the highest honor: our followers would regard us as gods. Truth be told, he sounded a little deranged:

"If only you would always give priority to me! I can make signs and miracles that will strengthen our fame and our followers' faith in us. For example, I can disappear from people's sight should they want to capture me—and reappear at any moment. Running away, I will pass through the very middle of a mountain or a cliff, as if they were made of clay. If they bind me, the ropes and shackles will fall of their own accord and bind those who have bound me instead. Should someone throw me in jail, the locks will open by themselves. When I want, I can breathe life into dead statues so that they will appear as people of flesh and blood. At my command, trees and bushes spring up in the blink of an eye. I walk into a fire, and the fire does not dare touch me. I change my face so that no one can recognize me. I appear to two different people at once but to each with a different face. I'll say a word, and little boys will grow beards. I fly in the air, I deceive the greedy with heaps of illusory gold, I raise kings to their thrones or overthrow them. Whole nations will pray to me. In cities, they will raise my statues.

"But why use so many words? Suffice it to say briefly: I can do anything I want. I have tested this. For example, my mother, Rachel, once ordered me to go into the field and mow hay. I went and saw a sickle on the ground. I said: Get up and do it for me! It obeyed immediately and mowed more hay than ten peasants could ever do in a day. And look at that thicket and that tall tree! I brought them out of the ground in an instant. And I had come here through the center of that mountain."

Hearing this nonsense, we were amazed by his impudence. He had opened himself to us, and yet he could not stop himself from telling us tall tales. We were familiar with the area and knew that those bushes, and the tree, and the cave had existed in the time of our grandfathers!

And so, we looked indifferently at his misdeeds. We have allowed him to deceive others. Moreover, we lied in his interest, even though he still showed nothing of the things he so clearly had promised to do to astonish the world.

Finally, he became one of the thirty disciples of Dositheus. Barely did he find himself in their number, but he set out to undermine the authority of their leader. He said that the master's teachings were flawed, and not because he jealously refused to reveal to his followers everything he knew, but because he did not know anything! Dositheus finally realized what was going on and who was plotting against him. How the final showdown between the two came about, I know only from the reports of others; of course, I could not have witnessed the scene since I was not one of the thirty. Apparently, this is what happened:

Once, when everyone was gathered in their tabernacle, as usual, Dositheus suddenly appeared, grabbed a rod, and started laying it about on Simon. But the rod passed through Simon's body as if he were only smoke and mist! Dositheus was dumbfounded, dropped the rod from his hand, and asked in a trembling voice:

"Tell me, are you *hestos*, and if you are, I shall submit to you!" To which Simon replied:

"I am He!"

So Dositheus threw himself on the ground and touched it with his forehead. He immediately resigned from the leadership of the community, relinquished his office, and ordered the thirty to obey Simon. He himself took his place as one of the disciples, and he died soon thereafter. It was only then that Simon took possession of Selene, also called Helen, and since then, she has been with him.

54

CLEMENS, SON OF FAUSTUS

The preceding chapter is taken from a third-century novel[19] whose action begins in Rome. Clemens is its main character and narrator. As he himself says, he was born in a wealthy and illustrious house, the son of Faustus and Mattidia, their third son. His older brothers were twins. Shortly after Clemens's birth, his mother had a strange dream. In it, she received a warning that she must leave Rome with her elder sons, or else all three would die soon. His father, very devoted to his family but also a little superstitious, agreed, and Mattidia and the twins left for Athens: the boys were to attend the famous local schools there. Little Clemens remained with his father in Rome. Months and years passed, and no news came from Athens, although Faustus sent people and money. It was not until four years later that he learned definitively that Mattidia and her sons never reached Athens: all trace of them had been lost. It seemed obvious that they had been lost at sea. Distraught, the father decided to go in search of them. He boarded a ship and sailed away, and no one heard of him ever again.

Many years passed. Clemens, still living in Rome, grew up thinking about the great and fundamental problems of philosophy. He thought about death: was it really the end of life? Or the beginning of its new chapter? He pondered the creation of the world: if earth and heaven had come into being at some point, then what had existed before? If they were to come to an end, what would follow? He was prepared to pay any price to find answers to these troubling questions.

He studied philosophy with various masters, but this only brought him disappointment: each of his teachers was chiefly concerned with refuting the views of his learned colleagues and constructing learned syllogisms. Their point was not to discover the truth but to show off their own skill at argumentation. Even matters

---

[19] *Clementine Literature* (also called *Clementina, Pseudo-Clementine Writings, Kerygmata Petrou, Clementine Romance*).

as important and sensitive for Clemens as the question of the immortality of the soul were only the subject of rhetorical arguments, either for or against. This pained him and depressed him.

One day, he saw a crowd in one of the squares of the city. He came closer and heard a foreigner speaking of these great matters, and he saw the crowd jeering the orator as if he were a madman. However, certain words of the sermon gave Clemens food for thought. So, he first defended the foreigner and then invited him to his house and hosted him for several days, diligently learning more from him about his message. But the man—his name was Barnabas—did not want to explain everything. He claimed that religious duties required him to return to his homeland as quickly as possible. Clemens would have liked to go with him, but first, he had to collect money from his debtors. So, he saw Barnabas off, inquired where to look for him in the Levant, and after a cordial farewell, returned to Rome.

He left as soon as the most urgent matters were taken care of. After fifteen days of sailing, his ship arrived at the port of Caesarea Maritima. While looking for an inn in the city, Clemens learned from a conversation overheard by chance that the following day a great disputation would take place between two famous men: on the one hand, Simon, born in Samaria, in the village of Gitta, and on the other, Peter, a student of a man who at one time had performed great miracles in various locations of Palestine.

Clemens began to inquire where that Peter lived. He was shown the house, and when he presented himself at the door and explained to the doorman who he was, and whence he came, Barnabas came out and, weeping for joy, threw himself into his arms. He invited the visitor inside. Peter had already heard much about Clemens, so he greeted the visitor from Rome with great cordiality. From then on, the men remained constantly together. There were about a dozen in Peter's entourage, and among them, two brothers, very similar to each other, Aquila and Niketas.

This is the plot of the first book of the novel. The work has survived to our times in two versions: one Greek, entitled "Homilies," and one Latin, entitled *recognitiones*, or "Recognitions." Both date to late antiquity, but both are paraphrases of a common source, which was probably written in Greek at the beginning of the third century, during the reign of the Severan dynasty. But even that work had its earlier source, for, beyond any doubt, some of its themes and motifs date back to yet earlier times, when early Christianity took shape in Palestine and had to contend with such opponents as Simon the Magus and his followers.

HELEN AND SELENE

The story of Aquila seems to support our hypothesis that Simon was associated with the temple of *Kore* in Samaria-Sebaste. While holding the dignity of a priest there, he was honored by the members of his community as the incarnation of the Supreme Godhead; he was nicknamed *hestos*, or "Constant," or perhaps "Everlasting," and he had with him a woman said to be the incarnation of the divine *Ennoia*. His predecessor—perhaps even the founder of the cult—was one Dositheus.

Here, some organizational outlines of the community are described. Its leadership consisted of thirty disciples. They were appointed from among the most ardent and most tried believers and held their office for life. It also seems that the cult attached special importance to the practice of magic. Fantastic stories were deliberately spread about the miraculous power of each priest. It was evidently believed that this was the most effective way to win believers. Many other religious movements of the time did the same.

There remains one thing to clarify: *Ennoia*'s double name. In contemporary testimonies, she is sometimes called Helen, sometimes Selene. What is the reason for this variation?

It should be recalled that ancient Greeks often associated these two names with each other—the former was a personal name, the latter meant "The Moon." Whether the name "Helen" truly derived from "Selene" is irrelevant: what is important is that it was generally thought to do so at the time. Soon, a myth was born that derived Helen herself, the heroine of the Trojan War, from—the Moon.

According to a story often told, Helen was born not of Leda but of a great egg. But where did the egg come from? There were various answers to this, but the most common was that Leda had laid it—because Zeus had approached her in the form of a swan. However, there was another, much more interesting and almost surreal version of the myth:

The egg had fallen from the Moon.

Women on the Moon did not give birth but laid eggs, and out of them hatched the residents of the planet. They were a lot taller than earthlings, as much as fifteen times because the Moon was like the Earth: it had mountains and seas, forests and fields, people, animals, and plants, but everything there grew incomparably grander and richer than with us, for the obvious reason that the Moon lies higher than the Earth, in the first celestial sphere.

In antiquity, it was commonly believed that there were several concentric celestial circles or spheres around the Earth. The Earth lay at the center of the universe, of course, but also at its lowest point. The first of the surrounding spheres—counting upwards from the level of the Earth—was the one in which the Moon moved. Next came the sphere of the Sun. Then came the spheres of the individual planets and, finally, the sphere of the fixed stars. Thus, if, as Simon taught, *Ennoia* had fallen from the highest heavens downwards toward the Earth, then her last step before her arrival on Earth was—the Moon. And as a Moonling, of course, she had to have hatched out of an egg. Then, however, a strange thing happened—and the egg fell down to Earth. In this way, thanks to a miraculous chance, everything was accomplished: both the complete humiliation of *Ennoia* and the subsequent salvation of all mankind.

But it was also held by some in antiquity that the souls of the elect, after the death of the body, flew to the Moon and lived there in eternal happiness; for, some said, the Elysian Fields were not located in the dark and cold underground, and not somewhere across the Western Ocean, but on the Moon, in celestial radiance and transparency.

In many countries of the East, the goddess of the Moon was considered the sister of the god of the Sun, for it seemed obvious that the sky was ruled by these two planets in perfect harmony.

THE THIRD HUSBAND OF BERENICE

The loving siblings, Berenice and Agrippa II, had been inseparable ever since the king had returned from Rome. It was then that the rumor began that the widowed queen lived with her brother as man and wife. She first brushed it off as slander, but in the end, she decided to counteract the gossip. She concluded that the best way to suppress it was to get married again. But it was not so easy to find a candidate since he had to match the queen not only by birth and wealth but also in religious rite. For Berenice, so persistently and unjustifiably accused of debauchery, was, in fact, distinguished by exemplary piety and sincere interest in the matters of faith. Because the Jewish Law explicitly forbade intermarriage with pagans, a pagan was out of the question. With what contempt must Berenice have thought of her younger sister Drusilla, who had dared to take the wicked step of marrying a Roman official!

Eventually, the right candidate turned up, though in a rather distant land. King Polemon ruled in Cilicia, in Asia Minor, previously part of the Kingdom of Pontus. Of course, he only reigned by the grace of Rome, just like King Agrippa II reigned in his kingdom. We do not know how the two met—perhaps in one of the cities of Syria or Phoenicia. Whether Polemon succumbed to Berenice's charms or to her persuasion, we do not know, but he had himself circumcised in order to marry her. Of course, he spread it about his court "confidentially" that he did this only for the sake of her dowry. Whatever the reasons, Berenice had a moment of triumph in her competition with her sister Drusilla, who, though supposedly more beautiful, yet did not manage to persuade her Roman to submit to the commandments of the Jewish Law.

Virtually nothing is known about Polemon as a human being. It is worth noting, though, that he wrote poems for entertainment. Two, possibly three surviving epigrams appear under his name in an ancient anthology—the latest critical editions ascribe them to Berenice's husband and not, as previously, to his father, also named Polemon. One of these epigrams, perhaps the most successful, explains the symbolic meaning of a bas-relief depicting a still life: a human skull lying next to a wreath, a loaf of bread, and a bottle of wine:

> Here's the graceful beggars' gear: a loaf of bread and a bottle.
> And here—a wreath of flowers fresh-sprinkled with dew.
> And here the dead bone, the bulwark of the mind
> Now lifeless, the highest tower of the soul.
> The sculpture says: Drink, eat, and crown yourself with flowers
> For soon this shall be you. [20]

The couple soon became disillusioned with each other. If Berenice moved to Cilicia—which is not certain—she must have felt bad so far away from the cities and people she was used to. But whether she was there or in Palestine, she behaved very freely, as her temperament dictated. Maybe even more freely than usual since she didn't have her beloved brother at her side—the only man she truly cared about. In any case, she ended up returning to Agrippa after a short time, either voluntarily or at her husband's behest.

And thus, the attempt to combat scandalous rumor by remarrying—failed. On the contrary, the brevity of the marriage to Polemon and the queen's speedy return to Agrippa convinced many that Berenice loved her brother too much. But from then on, the siblings cared little about gossip. They always appeared together, officially, publicly, and openly.

---

[20] *Anthologia Palatina*, II 38, cf. See also A. S. F. Gow, D.L. Page, *The Greek Anthology, The Garland of Philip*, Cambridge 1968.

And Polemon? After parting from Berenice, the king-poet abandoned the Jewish rite.

THE GOD OF APOLLONIUS

Were Polemon minded to return to pagan gods, he would have had plenty of religious centers in his native Cilicia to choose from. One of the most famous was in Aegae, the city where young Apollonius had once studied. Crowds of pilgrims flocked to the local temple of Asclepius, some from very far away. Apollonius had a special reverence for the physician-god, and whenever he was in Aegae, he stayed in the temple precinct. For his part, the god revealed to one of the priests in a dream that he was pleased to have Apollonius as a witness to the many miraculous healings that took place in his temple.

Once (it was before his five years' silence, but when he was already a practicing ascetic), a young man came to the temple from Assyria. He suffered from dropsy and begged the god for relief. He prayed and made sacrifices, but at the same time, he made a truly barbaric use of his immense wealth: he lived in splendor, spending his days and nights intoxicated with wine. For this, Asclepius despised him and refused to appear to him in a dream. [21] The Assyrian was indignant and angry until one night, the god appeared by his bedside and said:

"You will find relief only after you talk to Apollonius."

So, in the morning, the young pilgrim came to Apollonius and asked:

"Asclepius has ordered me to see you. How can I benefit from your knowledge?"

To this, Apollonius replied:

"I can give you a piece of useful advice. You want to recover,

---

[21] The practice at the various temples of Asclepius was for the pilgrim seeking a miraculous healing to make sacrifices then sleep in the temple precinct in the hope of seeing a dream which would guide him to a cure.

yes?"

"Of course. But Asclepius only heralds the return of health. He doesn't really grant it, does he?"

Apollonius became outraged:

"Be silent! Asclepius does grant good health, but only to those who really want to get well. But you do everything you can to make your sickness worse. You lead a dissolute life and stuff your bowels, watery and weakened as they are already, with food you cannot digest. It's like throwing mud into water."[22]

On another occasion, Apollonius saw rivers of blood flowing from the altar during a splendid sacrifice. Whole herds of sacrificial animals lay about in profusion, Egyptian oxen and fat Syrian pigs, some only just butchered, others already being skinned. Soon, he learned that someone had donated to the treasury of the temple two gold cups studded with the finest stones that could only have been imported from India. Apollonius approached the priest and asked:

"Who is this donor?"

And the priest replied:

"I wondered about this man. He didn't pray to the god, he didn't sleep in the temple, he wasn't healed. It seems to me that he only arrived yesterday—and yet he is already making offerings worthy of a king. And he promises that this is just the beginning. What will happen when Asclepius hears him? He's a rich man. He has more property in Cilicia than all the rest of our countrymen put together. He asks our god to restore a lost eye."

Apollonius, as was his habit all his life, stood motionless during the conversation, his eyes fixed on the ground. He asked the name of the rich man and then remarked:

"It seems to me that it would be better not to receive this man at our temple. He is cursed. And the suffering that has touched him will not end well. If he makes such sacrifices now, before he obtains anything from our god, he must be seeking forgiveness for some heinous and repulsive crime."

---

[22] No one is quite sure what that means.

That night, Asclepius showed himself to the high priest in a dream and said:

"The rich man must leave the temple with everything that he has given me. He is unworthy of keeping even the one eye he has left."

It was later learned that the man had once married a woman who had an adolescent daughter from her first marriage. He liked the girl so much that he seduced her and continued the affair. The wife eventually caught them in bed; she put out both of her daughter's eyes with a hairpin and one of her husband's.

Apollonius preached always and everywhere that, as a rule, sacrifices, and gifts to gods should not exceed a reasonable measure. This was in keeping with the ancient teaching of the Pythagoreans, who said that one ought not to stain gods' altars with blood, for cakes with honey, incense, and laudatory hymns are more pleasing to the gods than a hundred fat animals slaughtered with a knife. Pythagoras did offer an ox to Zeus in Olympia once—but it was an ox made of dough.

Apollonius also taught that everyone who entered a temple should pray: "Gods, give me what I deserve!" An evil man had no hope at the altars of the gods, even if he bought with him all the gold of India. He laid out his treasures not out of reverence for the gods but out of the desire to redeem himself from some just punishment. Gods, being fair, would never stoop to such a trade.

Although Apollonius treated Asclepius with special reverence, he worshipped all other deities, too, both Greek and barbarian. Wherever he visited, he took a keen interest in the local cults.

His daily routine during his travels was as follows:

He stayed in the temple precincts. At sunrise, he performed his secret rites alone. He revealed their content and form only to selected disciples—namely, those who successfully passed the test of at least four years of silence. Then, if he was in a Greek city, he called upon the priests of the various temples, discussed their gods with them, and pointed out where their time-honored methods of worship had gone astray. If, on the other hand, the local cults were foreign, barbarian, and bizarre—such as the cult of Aphrodite in Paphos—he inquired who established them, why, how the rites were performed, and on occasion, expressed his own opinion as to the possibility of a deeper understanding of them.

Afterward, he met with his disciples, they asked him all sorts of questions, and he gave them clear and well-argued answers.

This was because, as he used to say, one should always stick to this order: talk to gods at dawn, talk about gods in the morning, and during the day, talk to people about everything that interested them. After he had talked with his favorite disciples, other people had access to him for the rest of the day—but never before noon. In the evening, he took a bath in cold water, rubbed his body with oil, and massaged it.

And sometimes, he performed miracles.

BIRDS AND DEMONS IN EPHESUS

Having taken leave of the temple of Aphrodite in Paphos, Apollonius sailed for the coast of Asia Minor. Everywhere he went, he met with the praise of local oracles and solemn deputations of the local citizens.

First, he stopped at Ephesus, famous for the great shrine of Artemis. Standing on the high wall that ran around the temple courtyard, he gave a speech—today, we would say that he "delivered a sermon." He encouraged his listeners to study philosophy and to take their life seriously and scolded them for indulging in laziness, games, and pleasures. He condemned the fact that dances and pantomimes consumed their attention and that the shrill sounds of flutes and the dull thud of drums were heard everywhere in their city.

The following day, he spoke in a grove beside the city portico and preached that all property should be held in common (for this, too, belonged to Pythagoras' commandments). Accordingly, Apollonius taught that men should help one another. As he spoke, a flock of sparrows perched on the branches of the tree above him.

"Antiochus" (King Agrippa)

Suddenly, a lone sparrow came flying towards them and chirped: it seemed to be summoning the others. And then all the birds flew away with loud screeching and lots of fluttering of wings. Apollonius seemed not to pay attention to this and continued to develop his thoughts. But when he saw that his listeners were looking in the direction in which the birds had flown, he interrupted the course of his argument and said:

"In that street over there—you can't see it from here because of the trees—a boy carrying a basket of wheat has slipped and fallen. He got up and collected what he had spilled, but not everything. The solitary sparrow, which noticed this, flew at once to those perched in the tree above me and summoned them to feed together."

Some listeners immediately ran to see if, indeed, things had happened that way. But Apollonius returned to his speech about the advantages of communal property:

"See how the birds of the sky take care of each other and rejoice when they can be of help to others. But we humans do not approve of such a way of life. If a very wealthy person shares his food with others, we call him a spendthrift, and his guests—spongers. If so, we should probably lock ourselves up in cages like poultry for fattening; they are kept in the dark, and their stomachs are forcibly stuffed so that they almost burst with excess fat."

From Ephesus, Apollonius went to nearby Smyrna. Meanwhile, news came that a plague had broken out in Ephesus (as Apollonius had predicted) and was claiming hundreds and thousands of victims. Soon, an Ephesian delegation arrived in Smyrna. Its members begged Apollonius to return to their city and help them fight the epidemic. He decided that he must not delay for a moment. He said briefly:

"Let us go right away!"

Saying these words, he disappeared from sight—and simultaneously appeared in Ephesus, miraculously transported there. Soon a crowd of people gathered around him, begging him for help. At the head of this huge crowd, he started in the direction of the theater. There, at the entrance, they all saw an old blind man. His face was ugly and worn, his clothes were in rags, and his bag was filled with bits of dried, half-chewed bread. Apollonius raised his hand to stop the crowd and motioned, still silent, for everyone to form a wide circle around the beggar. And when this was done, he suddenly cried out in a loud voice:

"Take up stones and stone this enemy of the gods!"

The crowd hesitated, not ready to commit a homicide. Doubtful voices arose:

"Why put this miserable pauper to death? He arouses only pity!"

The beggar, for his part, also burst into weeping and moaning. Pitifully, he begged for mercy, asking why they should kill a man who had not done anything wrong and had not hurt anyone.

Nevertheless, there were a few daredevils who trusted the words of Apollonius. They picked up stones and started throwing them at the old man—not to kill him, but rather to frighten him. But at that moment, something astonishing happened. The supposedly blind man suddenly regained sight. He looked at the crowd with angry, hateful eyes: a living fire seemed to spring forth from them. Then, the Ephesians understood that a dangerous demon—the perpetrator of the plague—was sitting before them in the form of a wretched beggar. And now a hail of stones fell upon him, and soon, the man's body was buried under their pile. After a while, Apollonius asked for the pile to be uncovered. He said:

"You will see with your own eyes whom you have killed!"

To everyone's amazement, a dead dog was found under the stones. It was huge, the size of a lion, with froth around its mouth, as rabid animals have.

PAUL BEFORE AGRIPPA AND BERENICE

After this digression concerning Apollonius' miracles, it is time to return to Berenice. Having separated from Polemon, she returned to her brother and henceforth accompanied him everywhere, faithfully and openly, perhaps even ostentatiously. One spring, they came together to Caesarea Maritima to welcome the new Roman procurator. This was Porcius Festus, the successor of Felix. Of course, Berenice was happy with this change. Finally, she was rid of her dearly hated sister, Drusilla, who left for Italy with her Roman husband.

King Agrippa and his sister stayed in Caesarea for a while. One day, Festus related to them the following matter:

"I have a man here in prison, a man named Paul. He was left to me as an inheritance from Felix. When I was in Jerusalem a few days ago, the chief priest and the elders there demanded that I put him to death. I told them that we were Romans and, therefore, never passed a sentence on anyone until the accused had had the opportunity to confront his accuser and defend himself against the accusations. I returned to Caesarea, and as soon as I took my seat in the tribunal, I ordered Paul brought in. His accusers also showed up. I thought they were going to impute some serious crimes. But their accusations were all about some obscure issue of their religion and some Jesus who is already dead, but Paul claims is alive. I know nothing about any of this, so I asked Paul if he would not prefer to be tried in Jerusalem. But he demanded that the matter be examined by the emperor. He is a Roman citizen and has the right to appeal. So, he's here under guard for the time being, but soon I will send him to Rome."

Agrippa expressed the desire to hear Paul. Berenice, a woman of great piety, was also interested in this man: she may have heard of him before. The procurator said he wanted to know their opinion on his case: the whole thing was too esoteric for him. He promised to present the prisoner to them on the following morning.

The next day, the procurator took a seat in the audience hall of the governor's palace—it was the former palace of Herod the Great, the great-grandfather of Agrippa and Berenice. The king and his sister also came in, as always, together. The Greek text of the *Book of the Acts of the Apostles* uses an interesting Greek term: *meta polles phantasias*, which, freely translated, may mean something like "they entered with great panache." Senior Roman officers and the leading citizens of the city were also present. Paul was brought in immediately. Festus addressed the king and all those present:

"This is the man that a great multitude of Jews have complained about, both here and in Jerusalem. They said that he did not deserve to live, but I came to the conclusion that he did nothing punishable by death under Roman law. I will send him to Rome for the emperor to judge him because he has made this appeal and is entitled to it. However, I have nothing definite to write about his case. That is why I put this matter before you—and above all, before you, King Agrippa!—so that after our interrogation, you may give me some background on the matter."

The king allowed Paul to speak. Paul described at length how he, an orthodox Jew and a ruthless persecutor of the followers of Jesus, had an extraordinary vision on his way to Damascus and thenceforth became the preacher of the Messiah who had already come, died, and risen again.

However, the procurator was unable to understand the meaning of the whole story and did not hide his confusion at all. He said:

"You're out of your mind, Paul. Your learning has driven you mad."

To which the prisoner replied humbly:

"I am not mad, most illustrious Festus! I only speak the words of truth and reason. The king, present here, knows about these matters. Nothing I speak of is foreign to him. None of this happened in some untold backwater, but here, among the Jews, who have seen it."

And turning to Agrippa, he asked:

"O king! Do you not believe the prophets? I know you do!"

Agrippa answered him politely:

"A little more if your preaching, Paul, and you will convince me to become a follower of Christ."

But Paul answered him gravely:

"I pray to God, O King, that not only you but all listening to me here may become just what I am now—in all respects except these fetters!"

And he raised his chained wrists into the air.

At this, the king, the governor, Berenice, and all the others stood up. As they left, they said to each other:

"This man has done nothing to deserve either death or prison!"

And Agrippa said to Festus:

"Except for the appeal he has made to the emperor, you might well release him outright!"[23]

This story brings to your author's mind Pieter Breughel's famous painting *Saint Paul On The Road To Damascus*.[24] If you look at it closely, you will see a figure in a blue robe somewhere in the background, lying on a stony path, and a bright beam of sunlight shining upon him from behind a cloud. But in the foreground are bright yellow and dark green jackets of horsemen, tawny gray haunches of their horses, infantrymen laden with bundles and weapons, and—above them—dark-green cypresses shooting up into the sky like bristling spear points. This is the Spanish army of the Duke of Alba marching through the Alpine passes toward Breughel's homeland to lay waste to it.

The Roman army, too, would soon begin a similar march on Jerusalem.

SIMON THE MAGUS AND CHRISTIANS

As far as we know, Paul never met Simon or any of his disciples. And yet he sparked a confrontation in Samaria between the incarnation of the "Supreme Godhead" and the followers of Jesus.

This happened several years before Paul's conversation with

---

[23] *Acts*, 25.

[24] *The Coversion of Paul* is an oil-on-wood painting by the Netherlandish Renaissance artist Pieter Bruegel the Elder, painted in 1567. It is currently held at the Kunsthistorisches Museum in Vienna. For a very large reproduction see: https://tinyurl.com/DamascusWien.

Agrippa and Berenice. Paul was still called Saul then and a rabid persecutor of Christians, seeing them as blasphemers and apostates. And they, fleeing from Saul's persecution in Jerusalem, sought refuge in various places in Palestine, including Samaria. Among the refugees in Samaria was a young and especially zealous follower of Jesus named Philip. The *Book of Acts* says that he preached, performed miracles, expelled impure spirits, and healed the lame. Therefore, many Samaritans were baptized, Simon among them. The *Book of Acts* characterizes Simon as follows:

"He engaged in magic and astonished the people of Samaria by claiming that he was someone great. He was worshiped by many, from the greatest to the least, who said that he was the Power of God himself!"[25]

After receiving his baptism, Simon accompanied Philip everywhere, admiring the miracles performed by him. Then, the apostles Peter and John came to Samaria to give the faithful the gift of the Holy Spirit through the laying of hands. Simon also stood before them. He brought money and asked that they give him the same power. But on hearing this, Peter rebuked him sternly:

"Let your money perish with you if you think you can buy God's sacraments! You have no part in this business, for your heart is not pure before God. You must repent for this and beseech the Lord, and perhaps the impure intention of your heart will be forgiven."

And Simon asked them to pray for him.

This account of *The Book of Acts* raises some interesting questions.

Why did Simon convert so easily and without any apparent resistance as soon as the first disciples of Jesus arrived in Samaria? After all, Samaria was his native land, and he was considered the incarnation of the Supreme Godhead and widely revered there; while the apostles spoke of a Messiah from Judea, a land hated by the Samaritans.

The author of *The Book of Acts* makes no attempt to explain this sudden and astonishing change. It is, therefore, difficult to resist

---

[25] *Acts* 8:9

the conclusion that the whole story is made up for propaganda purposes. It's designed to show as clearly as possible the superiority of Christianity over the teachings of Simon. Here is the master himself, supposedly the Supreme Godhead, bowing and humbling himself! And though he was an accomplished magician, he tried to buy with money a sacrament that only true Christians can access.

Simon and his followers were a serious competition to the young religious movement because the worshipers of the Supreme Godhead and his *Ennoia* were able to parry all attacks and undermine the most important tenets of Christianity in a very surprising way. They simply said:

"Simon appeared as a man, but he was not really a man. In Judea, he apparently suffered under Pontius Pilate and died on the cross. The Jews recognized him as the Messiah. Now, the Samaritans recognize him as the Supreme Godhead. He allows other foreign peoples to call him by other names still."

Thus, early Christians saw in Simon their most dangerous opponent and came in time to call him the "father of all heresies." For this reason, they had to show that even he had bowed his head before the apostles of Jesus. Interestingly, they did not deny that he performed extraordinary miracles—only they attributed them to horrific magical practices.

AQUILA: SIMON THE NECROMANCER

Simon has deceived many, both by his words and by the miracles he performs–though they are not real miracles. Amazed by these signs, his people believe that he is the Supreme Godhead. One day, Niketas and I asked him directly:

"How are you able to perform such miraculous works? Where does your power come from?"

Believing us to be his allies, he explained:

"The soul of a murdered boy is always at my service. I use

arcane spells to make it serve me. Everything I command happens through the agency of that soul."

To which I replied with a question:

"How can a boy's soul have such power?"

He replied:

"Surely, you know that the human soul is the second most powerful thing in the world, right after God, but it realizes its full powers only after it frees itself from the prison of the body. At that point, it gains knowledge of the things to come. That's why it can be summoned by necromancy."

I asked:

"Then why would the souls of the murdered not take revenge on their killers?"

"Have you forgotten what I told you, that when the soul leaves the body, it receives the knowledge of the future?"

"I remember that," I replied.

"Well, having this knowledge, the soul understands that fair judgment awaits everybody after death and that everyone will be punished for what they have done while alive. Therefore, the soul does not need to take revenge for its wrongs because it sees that those evildoers will not escape the most terrible torments which they have coming to them. And besides, the angels who watch over the souls of the dead do not let them go out and act in the world according to their will."

"But if the angels do not allow souls to return to earth, how can you summon that soul?"

"It's simple," he replied. "If you can bind those angels by a power more powerful than they are, they are released from their guard duty over the souls of the dead and will release whomever you wish."

Hearing this, Niketas could no longer contain himself and said what I would have said, though I wanted to question Simon more thoroughly first. Beating me to the question, Niketas asked:

"And you? Are you not afraid of the Judgment Day? You enslave angels, you summon the souls of the dead, you deceive people, you command them to worship you! Or do you mean to convince us that there will be no judgment, as some Jews believe, or that souls are not immortal? After all, you see these souls with your own eyes and receive warnings from them!"

When Niketas said this, Simon turned pale but soon took hold of himself and replied:

"Ha! Do not think that I am human! For I am neither a sorcerer, nor a lover of Helen, nor the son of Antony, my mother's husband. My mother, Rachel, conceived me a virgin even before she married Antony. You see, I had decided to reveal myself among men as a man, and now I took you on as my disciples as a test. I am giving you the opportunity to sit with me in heaven. What I have just told you about the soul of the dead boy, I made up on the spot to test you, to see whether you truly loved me."

I now understood that Simon was a lost soul. I was so amazed by his insolence that I blushed for him. But at the same time, I was afraid that he might somehow harm us. So, I made a sign to Niketas and said:

"Do not be angry with us, who are just frail men, O God the Indestructible. Graciously accept our submission and our honest readiness to learn the true nature of God. For we have not until now understood that you are the one we seek!"

And we talked more nonsense like this, making appropriate faces. And he, the vainest man in the world, believed that he had deceived us. Satisfied, he answered us at once:

"I appreciate the honesty of your intentions. You loved me, but you did not know me. You looked for me, but you didn't realize that I was here. But surely you do not doubt that Divinity can incarnate in any being—even the humblest—whenever It wants to. After all, how else could I have revealed myself to mortal men?

"I will now reveal to you the whole truth about this allegedly murdered boy. It happened once that I turned air into water and then that water—into flesh and blood. In this way, I formed a new human being: a boy. I have thereby performed a work incomparably greater than that of which the creator of the world boasts. For he fashioned man from clay, and I fashioned man from air—which is incomparably more difficult. Then I spoke a magic word again, and he vanished with the breeze. I keep only his likeness in the most secret room of the house so that a permanent proof of my deed would remain."

We looked at each other, fully understanding what those words meant. He had murdered the boy and kept his remains in his house, using them in terrible necromantic practices. And he told us about some "likeness," just in case we should come across some evidence of his crime.

In fact, we were playing a double game of deception. For all his obsession and morbid ambition, Simon was too clever not to understand that we guessed everything and that we only pretended to be gullible. But since he pretended to think that we were, we pretended not to guess that he didn't.

But such a game could not last long, so we fled from Samaria and went to Caesarea Maritima.

THE DEMANDS OF FLORUS AND THE TEMPLE PROCESSION

Paul left Caesarea Maritima shortly after his interview with Agrippa and Berenice. Since he had appealed to the emperor, he was taken to Rome. Meanwhile, some two years later, Procurator Festus died in Palestine before his term expired. After him, Albinus served two years, and then came Gesius Florus, Cleopatra's husband and the perpetrator of the bloody events of the 16th of Iyar of AD 66.

On the day following the events, there were lamentations and moans and curses against Florus throughout the city. There would probably have been riots had it not been for the high priests and the leading citizens. These, rending their robes, threw themselves weeping at the feet of the angry people, begging them to remain calm and not to provoke Florus. The procurator, for his part, summoned the city elders. He stated bluntly what he would consider sufficient proof that the people of Jerusalem would never allow themselves further unfriendly acts: the inhabitants of Jerusalem should go outside city walls to welcome two Roman cohorts arriving from Caesarea. But some later said that the procurator had simultaneously sent a secret messenger to the officers of these cohorts with strict instructions that the soldiers should not respond in any way to a friendly welcome. But if any insulting words were to come from the crowd, they were immediately to draw their weapons and attack.

When the demand of Florus was communicated to the people gathered in the courtyard of the temple, loud cries of indignation arose all around. The leaders of the extremists, the so-called Zealots, opposed Florus's demands. They thereby gained respect and support, especially among the young and the poor, which is hardly surprising since everyone still had before their eyes the corpses of those murdered the day before. On the other hand, the rich and the high priests who stood to lose much in the event of new riots were terrified by the specter of a catastrophe. So, they quickly prepared an extraordinary spectacle:

The priests, dressed in their precious, colorful robes, left the Temple in a procession, carrying the sacred Temple vessels and utensils. They were accompanied by temple servants, *kithara* players, and singers. They knelt on the paving stones of the courtyard and, weeping, begged the people to have mercy on themselves and on the temple, for the Romans would inevitably strip it of all its treasures. The members of the Sanhedrin poured dust upon their heads, tore their robes, and called upon everyone they knew by name, even the common people. They exclaimed that welcoming the cohorts was a shameful but trivial business; in fact, it was just a matter of not giving Florus a pretext for a new slaughter.

Eventually, by pleading and dire warnings, they succeeded in persuading both the people and even some of the Zealots. The inhabitants of Jerusalem, led by the dignitaries, came out to the gates of the city to welcome the approaching troops just as they had recently greeted Florus himself.

FIGHTING IN THE NEW AND IN THE UPPER CITY

The Romans marched with a measured step and in total silence, not saying a word. Probably, this contemptuous silence caused hostile cries to be raised here and there. The cohorts immediately struck out at the crowd. At first, they only struck with the shafts of their spears, but even so, there were many casualties. For when the crowd began to retreat in panic, and the Roman cavalry pressed it with their horses, many people were strangled and trampled in the stampede. The scariest scenes, of course, were played out in the cramped quarters of the gate. When the corpses were collected on the following day, some of them were so crushed that even their relatives could not recognize them.

The two cohorts entered the city, mercilessly beating the crowd in the narrow streets of the New City. The New City stretched north of the Temple, between the so-called Third and Second Walls. The Romans wanted to make their way to the fortress of Antonia at all costs. The fortress stood in the northwestern corner of the temple and completely dominated it. Upon hearing of this, the procurator Florus set out from Herod's palace. Leading his own cohort, he made his way toward Antonia through the streets of the Upper City. But by now, the population in both neighborhoods attacked the soldiers, barricaded the streets, and threw missiles at the Romans from the rooftops. In this situation, Florus ordered his men to turn back. Nor did the two new cohorts manage to break through to Antonia.

The leaders of the Zealots now feared that the Romans would soon renew their attack. As a precaution, therefore, they demolished the two temple porticoes, which adjoined Antonia from the north and from the west. In this way, the fortress was cut off from the buildings and courtyards of the Temple itself so that even if the Romans were to enter Antonia, the Temple itself would not be threatened.

After these clashes, there came regrets. Florus summoned the Sanhedrin to his palace. He announced that he must leave the city for now to attend to other pressing business but would leave behind such garrison as they, the members of the Sanhedrin, saw fit. He knew very well that the people he was talking to feared the Zealots—the most extremist group among the insurrectionists—no less than he did himself.

The Sanhedrin replied that they would do everything in their power to prevent a new riot. They said that it was enough to leave just one cohort in Jerusalem, but they asked that it should not be one of those that had taken part in the massacre in the Upper City. Very conciliatory, Florus agreed to everything. He set out for Caesarea Maritima with two cohorts but promised that he would be back.

THE ARRIVAL OF THE KING

Supervision over Judea and its procurator lay in the hands of the governor of the neighboring province of Syria, who bore the title of Imperial Legate. At the time, this was one Cestius Gallus. Reports of the events in Jerusalem now began to come to him. They were sent by Florus on the one hand and by the Jerusalem Sanhedrin and Berenice on the other. For the queen wrote together with the elders, accusing the procurator of a shameful, unprovoked attack on the civilian population. The queen declared herself in full solidarity with the cause of her coreligionists.

In view of the contradictory nature of the two accounts, it was impossible to arrive at the truth or form a clear picture of the situation. Cestius held council with his senior officials and officers in Antioch. Some suggested that he should go to Palestine personally as soon as possible, leading a considerable military force. The argument went as follows: if the Jews had really committed crimes, they should be punished promptly; but if, on the other hand, they had been loyal, their loyalty would only be strengthened by a proper display of Roman power. The viceroy, however, was not that energetic and decided to send one of his officers on a fact-finding mission first to assess the mood of the population. A tribune named Neapolitanus was dispatched.

Meanwhile, King Agrippa, summoned by Berenice, left Alexandria and hastened to Jerusalem along the coastal road through Gaza, Ashkelon, and Jamnia. [26] Here he met the tribune, who had gone out of his way just for this purpose. The elders of the Jews also came to Jamnia to pay their respects and report their misfortunes. Agrippa listened to their complaints and lamentations, and then publicly rebuked them in harsh words for their insufficiently solicitous loyalty to the procurator. He did this not so much because of the presence of the tribune as to dissuade his countrymen from any notion of resistance. The members of the delegation, very wealthy and peace-loving men, understood at once the reasons for the king's rebuke. It went down differently with the people of Jerusalem.

The crowd went out to meet the king and the tribune a mile before the city walls. The wives of those murdered in the last incidents ran ahead, moaning and wailing, while the whole crowd begged for mercy and justice in a loud voice. Screams and lamentations resounded everywhere, everyone trying to express the enormity of his suffering. When they entered the city walls, the arrivals were shown the ravaged districts and private homes stripped of all possessions.

Later, the tribune was asked to tour the whole city alone—and that with only one servant—as far as the Pool of Siloam [27] at the southern end of Jerusalem. In this way, the city elders wanted to demonstrate that the inhabitants of Jerusalem were completely loyal and friendly to the Romans and only hated Florus. As he walked through the streets, the officer found everything in exemplary peace and order.

Then there was a meeting of the people in the first (outer) courtyard of the temple, that is, in the spacious Court of the Gentiles, surrounded by vast porticoes, including Solomon's Portico. Neapolitanus praised the loyalty of the citizens of Jerusalem and called

---

[26] Modern Yavneh.

[27] During the Second Temple period, the Pool of Siloam was centrally located in the Jerusalem suburb of Acra, also known as the Lower City.

on them to preserve peace and order; to win over his listeners, he ostentatiously bowed down to the Temple. Then he went back to Syria to report to Cestius. But Agrippa and Berenice chose to stay in the city to watch over the affairs.

The most important question now was to establish who had started the fighting. If, as Florus maintained, the Jews had behaved in a provocative manner, they could be severely punished by the emperor. Therefore, some in Jerusalem suggested that envoys should be sent to Emperor Nero to present the course of events from the Jewish point of view and thus forestall or at least refute the procurator's reports. Agrippa found himself before an embarrassing decision. Should he follow the demands of the people and go to the emperor with the mission? This would mean making an enemy of Florus and exposing himself to the implacable hate of his wife, Cleopatra. And while Empress Poppaea Sabina had died, Cleopatra retained many former friends and contacts in Rome. But then, on the other hand, could he defy the demands of his own people? This threatened to fuel a turbulent mood and could lead to new riots. The Zealots, though recently cooperative, did not intend to back down and did not give up their agitation.

The king decided to try persuasion. He called a meeting in the square adjacent to the Hasmonean palace where he lived with his sister. Only men were allowed to attend the assembly. An exception was made for just one woman: Berenice. Even though she was not allowed to stand in the square by her brother's side, she did find a way to observe the course of the proceedings. She went out onto the flat roof of the palace, and from there, she heard every word spoken by the king.

AGRIPPA ON THE POWER OF ROME

The king started out by saying that only a minority were agitating for war. Because who wanted it? First, inexperienced, volatile, mindless youth. Then there were those few who—completely irrationally—

believed that they could win independence. Finally, there were greedy criminals who wished to stir turmoil intending to enrich themselves at the expense of the weak and helpless in any general disorder.

In order to justify an armed insurrection, the king continued, the war party advanced two slogans. The first was vengeance for the wrongs suffered at the hands of the procurator's men. Yes, such wrongs did happen. However, they had to be endured with humility, for Jews should remember that not all Romans were cruel. The emperor certainly wasn't. Alas, he couldn't possibly know what had happened in Jerusalem. But to raise arms against the procurator would mean to declare war not only on Florus but on the entire Empire!

The second slogan was "Independence." What a silly and outdated notion! Independence could perhaps have been defended one hundred and twenty years ago when the Roman general Pompey first stood in Judea with a relatively small army. But the rulers and inhabitants of Judea failed to oppose him then.

Now, Judea was not the only land that had had to accept the Roman yoke. The same fate had befallen other once famous and powerful nations: Athens, Sparta, Macedonia. The mighty Empire has subjugated a great multitude of peoples. Do the Jews consider themselves richer than the Gauls, braver than the Germans, more numerous than all the peoples of the world put together?

And with what feeble forces did the Romans hold their subject lands in check! There were no troops in Greece at all; its viceroy had only a few ushers. Same in Macedonia. Similarly, in the western reaches of Asia Minor, though its towns numbered over five hundred. The entire shore around the Black Sea was defended by three thousand men and forty ships. In Thrace, vast and mountainous, the Roman garrison numbered only two thousand! There were two legions in Illyria on the middle Danube and one in Dalmatia. Gaul was vast, rich, and populous; three hundred and fifty tribes dwelled in its territory, and yet one thousand two hundred soldiers were enough to keep the peace! In Spain, there was one legion. The border on the Rhine was defended by a mere eight legions against the vast multitude of Germans who were wild, brave, and terrifying. Britain had only recently been conquered, but four legions were enough to keep it under control. North Africa covered vast areas from the Atlantic to Libya; it was inhabited by numerous and valiant peoples, and these lands were so rich that they fed the city of Rome for eight months of every year. And only one legion was stationed there! In Egypt, outside of Alexandria, there were seven and a half million people, and its military garrison was just two legions!

Or maybe the insurgents expected some help from outside? Dream on! The only bigger cluster of Jews beyond the borders of the Empire lived in Mesopotamia, in the state of the Parthians. But if those Jews decided to take part in the war—and, seriously, why would they care?—the Parthians would not let them; for in such a case, they would violate their peace treaty with Rome.

So, only God could help the Jews. But God was clearly on the side of the Romans! For how else could they have created an Empire so great and glorious? What was worse, in the event of a war, Jewish religious observance would be a serious obstacle. That goes especially for the prohibition to work and, therefore, to fight on the Sabbath. This had already proved fatal once when Pompey besieged the Temple one hundred and twenty years ago and captured it *precisely* because the defenders chose to observe the Sabbath. But breaking the commandment to keep the Sabbath would be breaking the covenant with God! More than that, it would go completely against the whole purpose and sense of the fight because freedom was presumably desired so that Jews could live fully and freely according to the Law of their fathers! Should they violate the Law in order to serve it?

Thus, left to their own devices, deprived of the support of both men and God, the war party was doomed to inevitable disaster. They might as well kill themselves with their own hands, their wives and children, and then burn this beautiful country to the ground. Such an act, mad as it was, would at least spare them the disgrace of defeat. For the Romans will destroy the whole country, exterminate its inhabitants, and spare no one. And an equally terrible fate awaits those Jews who live in diaspora in different provinces of the empire. The Temple, the only Tabernacle in the world where sacrifices can be made to God, will be destroyed. And once it is ruined, never again will sacrifices be resumed anywhere.

And saying these words, Agrippa began to cry. On her balcony, Berenice cried also.

CONCERNING THE SPEECH OF AGRIPPA

The king presented the disposition of the Roman armed forces relatively accurately and in accordance with the current state of affairs. This can be demonstrated by comparing the data contained in his speech with information from many other sources. Yet, we should remember that Agrippa did not intend to give a complete list of all the armed forces of the Empire. He did not name all twenty-seven legions that defended the frontiers at the time. He only wanted to make the inhabitants of Jerusalem aware of the power they were going against; and so, he passed over in silence certain less important or well-known facts. He didn't mention the two legions stationed on the lower Danube. Nor did he mention the mighty army of four legions on the upper Euphrates. In Syria, just on the borders of Palestine, there were three further legions; this last fact was so widely known in Jerusalem that there was no need to mention it at all.

At the same time, Agrippa wanted to emphasize how small armed forces were required to keep populous, valiant, and rich peoples in subjugation. This is indeed a matter worthy of our attention—even more worthy than the king realized. Indeed, to this day, many learned historians dwell in the same ignorance as the king's listeners. Books devoted to the history of Rome discuss *ad nauseam* the enormity and excellent organization of the Roman army, various details of wars waged by various Roman commanders, and examples of the bloody suppression of any and all attempts at resistance. Which is all true and relevant, and yet, at the same time—one-sided and superficial. Of course, no one denies that the Romans, while making their conquests, terrified their enemies with their superb military machine. And no one denies that, whenever necessary, they were ready to carry out cruel mass slaughters among many peoples of many lands with absolute and total ruthlessness. But it is also a fact that a few generations later, when the memory of those wars had faded, and thus some revival of the spirit of resistance could have been expected, there prevailed instead in most provinces of the empire a blissful, profound peace and complete contentment with the present state of affairs. There were, indeed, governors of vast and populous provinces who performed their tasks very efficiently with literally only a few ushers at their disposal. This was the case in Greece, Macedonia, and Asia Minor. Today's France—the then Four Gauls—was inhabited in antiquity by at least five, and perhaps even ten million people, but peace and security were kept there—as Agrippa rightly pointed out—by twelve hundred men stationed in Lyon! Of course, the Rhine legions could be called upon as a last resort; these, however, had other tasks, vigilantly pointing their spears against the warlike Germans. So, in fact, twelve hundred men made up the entire military and police force of Gaul, and it was sufficient for the task: the population remained calm and loyal to the authorities for generations.

The reasons for this are easy to see. The people of the provinces had an important say in the local government whose decisions mattered most to them. They cared little for national politics, willingly leaving it to the emperor and the senators. They benefited at every step of their life from the public order and the rule of law and from the blissful sense of political stability. And this was the source of the greatness, durability, and power of Rome. The real foundation of the Empire was not the iron fist of its legions—their job was principally to defend the empire against external threats—but something much more solid: the unwavering daily acceptance by millions of ordinary citizens of a political system governed by law and reason.

THE EDUCATION OF TITUS

But in order to deliver such a satisfying government to his subjects, a Roman had to learn how to govern and learn it by practice in the hard school of life and in different provinces of the empire. Of course, this duty fell primarily to young people from distinguished and wealthy families because they were predestined to occupy higher posts.

What were the stages of this school of government? The life of any son of a senatorial or knightly family could serve as our example. But we will use that of a man whose name was to be inextricably intertwined with the history of Palestine and the adventures of Berenice.

Titus Flavius Vespasian began military service in the year 57 in one of the eight Rhine legions mentioned by King Agrippa in his speech. On entering the army, he was immediately promoted to the high rank of tribune, though he was only eighteen. (He had been born on December 30, AD 39, just as his father Vespasian entered his thirty-first year of life). Since Titus was the son of a senator, he had the privilege of skipping over the lower military ranks. On the other hand, a year's military service was an obligation for all senators' sons if they intended to hold higher offices and become members of the Senate. Such rules had been introduced by Emperor Augustus.

The army must have benefited little from these spoiled brats accustomed to the comforts and luxury of big-city life. They showed up at the legion camps every year and usually only stayed for a year. In terms of rank, they belonged to the highest officers, that is, to the staff of the commander, who bore the title of legate, but of course, they had no experience. In practice, life in the camp, drills, and combat operations were managed by professional officers, i.e., centurions of various ranks. The young sons of senators paraded around in their tunics with a wide purple stripe—to distinguish them from the tribunes of the equite (knightly) class who were entitled only to a narrow stripe. They represented the legate and performed various functions assigned to them, mainly administrative or secretarial; for all army formations had extensive administrative and auxiliary services. But even this was an excellent school of military life. Provided they applied themselves, the tribunes had the opportunity to learn a great deal, both of the military matters and of the country where they were stationed. Titus did not let his military service go to waste. He was an excellent soldier, both then and later in life.

By the time he arrived on the Rhine, Titus had already learned various skills—and with the best teachers, too. He owed it not only to the fact that he came from a wealthy family but also to a special circumstance: as a boy, he was assigned as a companion to Britannicus, son of Emperor Claudius, and grew up and studied with him. We can even guess who obtained this honor for him: a special friend of Vespasian was one Antonia Caenis, a freedwoman of Claudius's late mother. She was a person of great influence at court because of her connections with other imperial freedmen.

Had Britannicus succeeded his father, Titus would have been assured of a dazzling career. However, it happened otherwise. After Claudius' death in AD 54, his stepson Nero was proclaimed emperor, largely by the efforts of Nero's mother, Agrippina. A few months later, still in the same AD 54, Britannicus suddenly died during a feast in front of the entire court and the imperial family. A drink was brought to him from the kitchen; it was too hot, the boy refused it, and the slave tasting his food, added a cup of cold water. Only then did Britannicus drink it. Titus was lying next to him. He was already putting the same cup to his lips when he pulled it away at the last moment, seeing his friend fall to the ground. Some later said that he did drink a small sip of the drink and paid for it with a severe, long-lasting illness.

Titus never forgot the unfortunate Britannicus. Many, many years later, he erected a golden statue of him on the Palatine and had another statue of Britannicus—on horseback—carried around the stadium during the solemn processions opening chariot races.

Following the prince's death, Titus and his family dreamt of only one thing: to be forgotten. First of all, no one had any doubts concerning the true causes of Britannicus's death or the identity of the perpetrators of the tragedy. Titus's father had another reason to fear, too—Agrippina hated him personally. And thus, the whole Flavian family left Rome and moved to one of their country estates. At the time, the family had just five members; apart from the parents, Vespasian and Domitilla, there were three children: Titus, Domitian, born in AD 51, and Flavia Domitilla, perhaps the eldest of the siblings.

Eventually, the situation changed in their favor because Nero quarreled with his mother. And now, those hitherto persecuted by Agrippina could count on the emperor's favor. Of course, no one cared about the death of Britannicus anymore. Since Titus had just turned seventeen, his father decided that he should complete his military service and thus open the door to a future political career. Titus was assigned to one of the Rhine legions.

The young man was in great physical shape. Though not very tall, he was well-built, handsome, strong, and agile. He excelled in swordplay and horseback riding, and these were the most important skills in the army. However, his general education also left nothing to be desired. He was well-read, not just in Latin but also in Greek. He used both languages fluently, composing not only speeches but also verses; he could even improvise poetry. He was interested in music, sang beautifully, and played the *kithara*. He mastered the art of shorthand so well that he later competed with his own secretaries for fun.

Our sources say that Titus also served in Britain. So, either he moved in one year from one province to another—for no legion relocated at the time—or he repeated his tribunate, this time in another province with another legion. We know of other such cases, though they were rather rare. Why did he do it? The answer seems clear. Several years earlier, his father, Vespasian, had fought in that province, commanding the IInd legion nicknamed *Augusta*. He fought three victorious battles and captured the island of Vectis, which is today's Isle of Wight. It seems likely that Titus now served in his father's legion in order to renew old connections. The legion was then stationed at a camp in the town of Glevum, i.e., in present-day Gloucester.

It was later said that Titus-the-tribune managed to make a positive and lasting impression on the inhabitants of Rhineland and Britain. This was supposedly evidenced by the multitude of statues and honorary inscriptions in his honor in various places of these lands. However, these monuments were erected much later when Titus was already emperor; by then, every town where Titus had stayed as a tribune, even if only in passing, wanted to commemorate the fact of his visit for centuries to come.

By AD 59, Titus was back in Rome. It was an unlucky year: the year in which Nero murdered Agrippina, and the Senate and the people of Rome congratulated him on having done so. Indeed, they proclaimed *boundless joy* at the fact that their beloved emperor had managed to preserve his precious life in such a miraculous way and thwart his mother's criminal designs. Titus's father was obliged to participate in the meeting of the Senate, during which these resolutions were passed, expressing sincere gratitude to the immortal gods for having preserved the beloved ruler of Rome. What's more, Vespasian most certainly voted yea and—who knows—perhaps even spoke in support of these resolutions. We know that only one Senator, Thrasea Paetus, remained silent throughout and, at one point, left the hall ostentatiously.

Titus was almost certainly not yet part of the august assembly, but he had the right to listen to its deliberations—a privilege Emperor Augustus had granted to the sons of Senators. The idea was that they should thus gain familiarity with the great political problems of their day and the way the Senate handled them. But if Titus was already in Rome, he must have taken part in another ceremony along with all the people of the capital: he must have stood outside the city walls and enthusiastically greeted the emperor, returning from the Bay of Naples, where he had murdered his mother.

Life went on unchanged. Agrippina was slowly forgotten. The following years brought new developments, joys, and troubles. As befitted a young man of his estate who had already completed his military service, Titus now devoted himself to the study of law. This combined both theory and practice. He took advantage of the lectures, advice, and guidance of one of the luminaries of the jurisprudence of his age and, at the same time, appeared in person before the tribunals, in certain trials, usually as for the defense. Of course, initially, these were minor matters. And if anyone turned to Titus for help, it was not because they believed in his profound knowledge of the laws or extraordinary oratory skills. Other considerations guided them. They simply proceeded on the correct assumption that the decision of the courts may well be influenced by a famous Senator's name. It is possible that Titus also participated in important, high-profile, serious trials; in such cases, however, he was only one of the speakers, as they would have been presided over by one of the older, well-known jurists.

But Titus never gave any political speeches, such as the speech of King Agrippa in Xystus Square in Jerusalem. [28] There was no genuine political life in Rome at that time, and no need to persuade or convince the agitated masses of the people; it was enough to flatter the autocrat.

FAREWELL TO JERUSALEM

The king's speech did not only move him and Berenice but also many other listeners. Among the crowd gathered in Xystus Square, new shouts could be heard now:

"Let us not fight the Romans! Only Florus!"

To which the King replied:

"But how do we justify your refusal to pay tribute? And that you demolished the porticos leading to Fortress Antonia? What more conclusive proof of your hostility towards Rome can one possibly ask for? If you really wish for peace to return, you must collect and pay back taxes and rebuild what you have destroyed! Because both Fortress Antonia and these taxes constitute the property of Rome, not of Florus!"

---

[28] The Xystus of Jerusalem was a famous building erected in the Judaeo-Hellenistic period probably under Herodian rule.

Next, many of those gathered followed Agrippa and Berenice to the temple district—from Xystus Square, there was a bridge over the valley—and began the symbolic work of rebuilding the ruined porticoes. And the members of the Sanhedrin went about the city and personally collected the unpaid taxes, and soon the whole overdue amount—forty talents—was deposited in the treasury.

It seemed that the threat of an uprising and war had been averted. But it was only an illusion and dissipated a few days later when Agrippa openly stated his view of the situation: that the people should submit without grumbling to Florus's rule and wait patiently until the emperor, in his goodness, appointed a new governor.

The Zealots protested against this view with an unheard-of vehemence. There were sharp quarrels and disagreements between the king and their leaders. They did not mince words. They flung at the ruler all kinds of insults. They demanded that he leave the city immediately. Finally, a mob incited by them threw stones at him.

And now Agrippa, angered and deeply offended, realized that he was no longer able to direct the course of events and decided to leave Jerusalem. He refused further intercession and told the elders to communicate with Florus directly: he did not want to have anything to do with any further tax collection and declared:

"Let the procurator decide who and how shall collect the tribute across the country!"

And the country was poor. It did not have any natural resources, and only in a few areas did the land yield a surplus. The population made a living mainly from farm work and small workshops. The situation was aggravated by an unhealthy income distribution. A small layer of high priests, great landowners, and bankers held immense wealth in their hands, while the majority of the population were peasants who rented small pieces of land and lived in extreme poverty. To make things worse, feuds smoldered between different ethnic groups in Palestine. Jews and Samaritans, Greeks and Syrians, Phoenicians and Arabs lived side by side in this small, poor country. All this fueled religious fanaticism, especially Jewish fanaticism. This latest found its expression in the widely held expectation of the arrival of the Messiah—the Anointed One—who could come (or so it was taught and promised) any day, defeat and humiliate the enemies of the Lord, and give the Chosen People liberty, and dominion over the world, and eternal enjoyment of all material goods and pleasures.

And therefore, it was hardly surprising that even though the Roman province of Palestine had only about half a million inhabitants—one-tenth, perhaps even one-twentieth of that of Gaul—yet, its governor had at his command forces greater than those stationed on the Rhône. He had five cohorts of infantry and a squadron of cavalry: a total of perhaps three thousand men. And these troops were kept busy because, among other things, the individual administrative districts of Roman Judea (there were eleven of them) were generally in arrears with their tax payments. But Romans strictly enforced their dues. Every year at least six hundred talents were expected to come into the treasury from all over Roman Palestine on top of the revenue from customs duties. One talent, a unit of accounting, counted six thousand Roman denarii, each weighing almost four grams of silver. For comparison, a hired farmhand received an average of a denarius per day.[29]

These ordinary burdens would have been bearable if it were not for the extortion, looting, and abuse on the part of officers, soldiers, and officials. Some of them were ashamed of their work. This is well illustrated by the well-known Gospel story told about John called the Baptist: even if it is not literally true, it at least reflects the atmosphere of those times, the fears and hopes of the people. And so, when John called upon all people to repent and amend, tax collectors came to him, asking:

"Teacher! And we, what shall we do?"

And he replied to them:

"Do not collect more than is due!"

Similarly, he spoke to soldiers:

---

[29] About $3.20 in 2023 money, making the total tax burden of Palestine about $11.5 million.

"Do not abuse the people. Be satisfied with your pay!"

But what could be expected of simple soldiers and ordinary collectors when their superiors, the procurators, did not refrain from corruption? After all, Felix, Drusilla's husband, kept Paul in prison with the secret hope of extracting from his followers a ransom—which is why he treated him relatively leniently.

The emperors knew perfectly well how their officials behaved, but they accepted it with surprising forbearance. Emperor Tiberius openly stated that corruption was an inherent feature of the state. Therefore, he reasoned, one should not rotate these people too often because each new one committed extortion with redoubled zeal; but he who has been sated was inclined to a certain restraint. He illustrated this theorem with the following parable:

"A wounded man was lying by the roadside, and swarms of flies crawled all over him. A passer-by, moved by pity, approached to drive away the flies. But the wounded man asked to be left alone:

"'If you drive away these flies, I will suffer even more. These flies are already sated, so they are not very annoying. But if new ones come, they'll drain a lot more blood, and I'll die sooner!'"

That was the Roman version of the parable of the Good Samaritan.

King Agrippa washed his hands of the thorny tax matters and everything else that went on in Judea. He left Jerusalem with Berenice and returned to the capital of his kingdom—to Caesarea Philippi on the slopes of Mount Hermon, near the source of the Jordan. From that point on, neither he nor his beloved sister were eyewitnesses to the events in the city, even though they closely followed the developments. They did try to preserve as much as they could of the work of their great-grandfather, King Herod the Great, but for all their efforts, they would never see either Jerusalem or the Tabernacle in their glory again.

THE PALACE OF BERENICE ON FIRE

Soon after the departure of the royal siblings from Jerusalem, a bloodless and seemingly insignificant event took place there, which nevertheless became the formal beginning of a war with Rome.

Eleazar—son of the high priest Ananias and the young commander of the temple guard—managed to convince the lower-ranking priests that they should no longer accept offerings from Gentiles. In practice, this meant that sacrifices for the prosperity of the emperor and the Roman people would henceforth be forbidden. Hitherto, they had been offered in the temple twice a day, each time by offering a bull and two rams. This custom had been introduced many years ago at the request of Emperor Augustus. The cost of purchasing the animals, which was not insignificant, had been covered by the emperor—most likely by deducting the appropriate amount from taxes due to the state treasury. But this meant that the donor of the animals was a Gentile.

The cessation of these sacrifices amounted to an open declaration of hostility towards Rome and its ruler. Therefore, the leaders of the peace party—members of the Sanhedrin, prominent Pharisees, rich men—made every effort to reverse the provocatory decision. They called an assembly of the people. It took place in the outer courtyard, between the portico of Solomon and the great bronze gate—"The Beautiful Gate" as it was called—that led to the inner courts of the Tabernacle. There were many speakers. They pointed out that unleashing a war was madness, that gifts and offerings from foreigners had been accepted at the Temple for generations, that interrupting them now would offend Rome and the emperor. They called for calm and reason and the earliest possible resumption of the sacrifices. Even the most learned priests were summoned, who publicly declared that the forefathers had never forbidden foreigners from offering sacrifices to the Lord.

However, all this was to no avail—especially since the leaders of the insurgents did not deign to attend the assembly in front of the bronze gate. They felt very confident: just recently, they had managed to seize by a sudden foray the mighty fortress of Masada. Masada lay on the shores of the Dead Sea in a deserted, secluded, wild region; it had been expanded and strengthened by Herod the Great. And now, the insurgents murdered the Roman garrison of the fortress and fortified themselves inside.

The Jerusalem Sanhedrin and their allies realized that they would not be able to control the situation by persuasion alone. They foresaw that if things continued unchecked, they themselves—perceived allies of the Romans—would soon fall victim to the hatred of the masses; or else be punished by the same Romans as responsible for the disturbances in Jerusalem. So, they sent two embassies, one to Florus in Caesarea Maritima and the other to Agrippa and Berenice in Caesarea Philippi. In both places, the delegates begged for troops to be sent to Jerusalem to restore order. The procurator did not respond to the request at all—perhaps he wanted to make things worse? But the king sent two thousand horsemen under the command of Darius and Philip; the latter was the governor of the fortress of Gamala. [30]

Thanks to these troops, the peace party managed to stay in control of the Upper City while the insurgents controlled the temple district and the Lower City. There were constant street fights between the two forces. They fought with melee weapons, they shot at each other with slings and arrows. Many died. For several days, the forces of the two sides seemed about even; neither managed to supplant the other. This changed only on the 14th of Ab—that is, in August— when the Feast of Bringing Wood was celebrated. On that day, the faithful placed logs of wood in front of the altar so that the eternal flame would not run out of fuel. On that occasion, pilgrims from all over the country flocked to the temple. Among them were the most fanatical Zealots. They were the so-called *Sicarii*, or Knifemen, for they carried knives concealed under their clothes and used them to deal suddenly with all whom they considered enemies of the people and of the holy cause.

---

[30] Situated at the southern part of the Golan.

Now vastly outnumbering their opponents, the insurgents managed to take over the Upper City. They seized the house of the high priest Ananias and the palace of Agrippa and Berenice—the former palace of the Hasmoneans. They burned both, as well as the archive building, where all the land titles, promissory notes, contracts, and lists of taxpayers were stored. The fire was started deliberately, not merely out of blind hatred of the rich: the insurgents wanted to gain the support and trust of those in debt—and there were huge crowds of them in poor Judea.

Agrippa's soldiers retreated to Herod's palace, where the procurator Gesius Florus had stayed a few months before. They locked themselves within its mighty walls along with the Roman cohort and several leaders of the peace party. Among them were the high priest Ananias, son of Nedebeus, and his brother Hezekiah. Other members of the Sanhedrin and nobles who failed to get through to the Palace sought refuge in the sewers of the Upper City.

MESSIAH MENAHEM

Although the history of the so-called Jewish War is not the main subject of our book, it does connect here with the story of Titus and Berenice, and therefore, it is appropriate to recount certain events both because of their historical significance and because they characterize the atmosphere of the times and the mood of the people. For example, here is what happened in Jerusalem after the burning of the palace of Agrippa and Berenice:

On the next day—the 15th of Ab—the insurgents attacked Fortress Antonia. It was now the only point of resistance besides the Palace of Herod, but it was the more important of the two because it towered over the courtyards and buildings of the Temple. A handful of Roman soldiers defended it for two days, but eventually, they were overcome. They were slaughtered, and the fortress was partially destroyed. Only afterward did the insurgents attack Herod's palace. It was attacked from all four sides at once, with unheard-of ferocity, and without any concern for casualties. The defenders, however, put up a stiff resistance, protected as they were by their mighty walls.

During these bloody fights, a team of insurgents secretly left the city and headed south. Their destination was the recently conquered fortress of Masada. Menahem of Galilee, son (or grandson?) of Judas, commanded this force. That Judas had been considered the founder of the Zealot movement and had led it for many years. The men of Judas had made sudden raids from their hiding places on Roman soldiers and officials, the rich, the foreigners, and the infidels. They conducted a small guerrilla war mainly in the frontier lands: in Galilee, beyond the Jordan, and in Idumea. These elusive and formidable fanatics remained at work continuously since the days of Judas, though not always with the same intensity. They were hated and hunted by the Romans, by high priests and nobles, who called them *bandits* and imprisoned and punished them by crucifixion. On the other hand, poor peasants, shepherds, craftsmen, and even lower-ranking priests had boundless admiration for the Zealots and provided them with all kinds of help, seeing them as fearless defenders of the faith who, in the name of the Lord, punished foreign invaders and rich Jews living unworthy and frivolous lives.

Thus, his descent made the young Menahem one of the leading figures of Judea of the day. And now, by going to Masada, he proved that he had also inherited Judas's energy, courage, and ingenuity, for, having entered the fortress, he broke into Herod's armory and seized all the weapons along with the ceremonial garments of the great ruler. He now returned with his company to Jerusalem like a king. Dressed in purple, shining with silver and jewels, he led a retinue of knights in splendid armor, eye-catching with the bright colors of their cloaks. Great crowds poured into the streets of the city and out of its gates, hailing Menahem not only as a victor but as the true and rightful king of the Jews. And what is more, some greeted him enthusiastically and rapturously as the long-awaited *Messiah*: the one whose coming had been foretold by the prophets centuries ago. Here, at last, came that great historical moment when He would lead His people out of the house of slavery, put an end to their sufferings, give them victory, peace, dominion, and heavenly bliss on earth!

There were probably very few people in all of Jerusalem at that time who would have had enough independence of thought, discernment, and courage to treat these messianic hopes as they deserved: as a kind of collective madness. If we accept the Schopenhauerian notion that the history of humanity is primarily a history of mental illnesses and malfunction, this phenomenon can, of course, be understood, analyzed, and justified. We should add, however, that like any disease, this one, too, has tended to appear in countries and times very distant from Menahem's Palestine.

CONCERNING POLISH MESSIANISM

I've always been of this opinion, and I didn't hesitate to say it to Krasiński's face. I remember one conversation I had with him about it. It was in Paris in 1858. I lived at Quai d'Orléans, not where the Polish Library was, but a bit further on, in the direction of Notre Dame. Krasiński used to visit me there. Well, once we talked about messianism in general and his messianism in particular. Not wanting to beat about the bush, I simply told him, when he questioned me on the matter, that while I adored him as a poet, I was opposed to his messianic theories.

Why should we tell a people who are unhappy, broken, troubled, demoralized, losing ground, surrounded on all sides by enemies, deprived of political existence, that they are a chosen people, that they are the Christ of nations, that in them and their suffering lies the salvation humanity? We will only mislead them because instead of working, instead of thinking about improving their fate, instead of learning and striving to be useful citizens, trying to make themselves better than their fathers had been, who had lost their homeland and political independence, they will stand with folded arms proud of their Christhood, their role as God's Chosen People, their moral superiority over other nations, their "super-European" virtue. That is why I believe that this theory of messianism is a demoralizing theory: it tells a people something that should not be told to any nation, and to us, Poles, in particular.

Th people should be told the naked, honest truth, may it hurt ever so much, for the truth is always the most effective remedy for all vices and imperfections. The people should always have their faults pointed out to them so that they try to get rid of them because only by knowing their faults can they improve morally and hope to raise themselves from their misery.

These words, spoken with all sincerity and force of conviction, made a greater impression on Krasiński than I could have supposed. He heard me out sitting, but when I had finished, he got up, and you could see how deeply he was agitated because he began to pace the room nervously as if struggling with himself, until finally he came to me, took my hand and said in a voice that betrayed strong emotion:

'You're wrong! It is not so! If to a fallen, vicious, perverted, corrupt, and reckless woman, but one not completely corrupted, not utterly corrupted, sometimes grieved by her frivolity, often repenting of her sins which she would like to amend, you begin to preach her fall, you begin to enumerate her sins and vices by dwelling on her wicked and immoral life, what effect will you have? What effect will you have on her by telling her the naked and brutal truth in this way? Why, you will demoralize her completely, corrupt her completely, and instead of saving her from the abyss, you will push her to the very bottom of her downfall and disgrace. For when you reveal to her all the horror of her position, all the abomination of dirt and mud into which she has fallen, all the disgrace she has covered herself with, then she will doubt herself, she will believe that having fallen so low, she can only sink even deeper, that having found herself on this slippery slope she has no chance of turning back, and she is lost forever. And she will not improve because she will doubt the possibility of improvement. She will become incapable of repentance.

But if to such a fallen woman, but one not completely devoid of noble instincts, you say that there is great holiness in her, which she has only soiled with her reckless and vicious conduct, that she is an angel, though with mud-bespattered wings, that if she has fallen, it was only because she has been driven to her fall by those worse than she, more vicious, people not possessed of that holiness and virtue, which are in her and have not yet entirely died out in her heart, which are still smoldering under the ashes of corruption, but blown up by repentance and atonement, are capable of bursting with the purest flame of holiness... When you talk to her like that, then you will lead her on the path of improvement, then you will not arouse self-doubts in her, then you will appeal to her nobler instincts: she will believe in her virtue, believe that she can yet become an honest woman, that she can still whiten her angel wings, and that she can still be saved. [31]

This is how Julian Kłaczko described his Paris conversation with Zygmunt Krasiński. He related it in the afternoon of February 27, 1897: the day was sunny, cloudless, the sky was blue, the breath of spring was already felt in his Kraków home. That palace still stands today on the corner of Smoleńsk and Straszewski Streets, a bit set back, surrounded by a tiny garden, and serving after recent renovations as a wedding hall. [32] Kłaczko's guest was Ferdynand Hoesick. What he heard from the old man, he faithfully wrote down years later in his biography.

RELOCATION TO PELLA

And what was Messiah Menahem's view of people who believed that the *real* Messiah had already revealed himself long ago, during the life of the previous generation? And what did they think about him?

For Jesus—also called Christ in Greek—was born when Herod the Great, the great-grandfather of Agrippa II and Berenice, was king in Judea, and Augustus was emperor of Rome; and was crucified when Pontius Pilate was governor of Judea, and Tiberius reigned in Rome.

During the thirty years since the death of Messiah Jesus, the

---

[31] F. Hoesick, *Julian Kłaczko*, Warsaw 1934, pp. 345–346. The two men in the conversation are Zygmunt Krasiński (1812-1859), a Polish poet traditionally ranked among Poland's Three Bards—the Romantic poets who influenced national consciousness in the period of Partitions of Poland (1795-1918); and Julian Kłaczko (1825-1906), a Polish-Jewish writer, activist, and politician. And the topic of their discussion is Polish Messianism, a doctrine which referred to Poland as *the Christ of Europe* or as *the Christ of Nations* "crucified" in the course of the foreign partitions of Poland (1772–1795). During the period of partitions, the territory of former Poland was home to most of Europe's Jews, it was only natural that Jewish ideas filtered into Polish intellectual life, and especially that of the coming of the Messiah who would one day restore the nation's former glory.

[32] A branch of mBank in 2023.

number of his followers grew steadily, especially outside of Judea, thanks to their strenuous missionary activity. But in Jerusalem itself, their situation was precarious. Its members suffered frequent persecutions, both by the high priests and the common people. Yet here, in Jerusalem, Christians observed all the commandments of the Jewish Law with exemplary zeal. Despite this, they were considered apostates. Their critics said that they deserved severe punishment and expulsion from the Jewish community as blasphemers.

James, son of Zebedee, was beheaded on the orders of King Agrippa I, father of Berenice, most likely in AD 42. Some twenty years later, an even more severe blow fell upon the Jerusalem church: its leader at that time, James the Greater, called the Righteous, brother of Jesus, was arrested by the high priest Ananus ben Ananus. It was probably the year 62. Procurator Festus—the man who once questioned Paul in Caesarea Maritima in the presence of Agrippa and Berenice—had just died, and the new governor had not yet arrived. This moment was used by the high priest to deal at last with the head of the schismatic movement. He was all the more eager to do so since James was known throughout the city as a man of great holiness. The old man had lived much of his life as if he had made an eternal Nazirite vow in its most severe form. He didn't drink wine; he did not eat meat; he did not shave, he did not anoint himself with oil, he did not wash; he wore only linen robes and spent all days on his knees in the Temple It was said that from constant prayer his knees became as thick as those of a camel.

Brought before the high priest, James did not deny his Messiah despite all attempts at persuasion and despite increasingly dire threats. At last, he was led to the balcony above Solomon's portico and pushed over the precipitous cliff of Cedron. But he did not die immediately. He was still trying to get up. Stones rained down on him, and then someone from the crowd jumped down and finished him off with a rolling pin.

By murdering James, Ananus acted not only cruelly and against Jewish Law but also against Roman law because the Romans had forbidden anyone to be put to death without the consent of the governor. But the high priest assumed that the death of James would be long forgotten by the time the new procurator arrived. And if the matter were ever raised, he was going to explain simply that he had had no one to appeal to at that moment yet had to act quickly to prevent a dangerous riot. But he proved mistaken in his calculations. The new procurator—his name was Albinus—was already on his way from Alexandria. Enemies of the high priest, of which there was no shortage in Jerusalem, made sure that the Roman would learn about the circumstances of James's death. At the same time, they sent a secret complaint to King Agrippa. Albinus rebuked Ananus severely, and the king deposed him from his high priesthood, even though he had held the office for only three months.

The small Jewish-Christian community—because that's what it really was, unlike the Christian communities emerging outside of Palestine, which rejected the burden of the Mosaic Law—never recovered after the martyrdom of James.

Then in AD 66 came new shocking political developments: turmoil and bloodshed in the streets of Jerusalem, clashes with the Romans, the specter of a great war, and general fear of a universal disaster. Simultaneously, there flocked to the holy city great crowds of fanatics from all over the country welcomed with open arms by Messiah Menahem.

His reign was to last a very short time, but for the followers of the Messiah Jesus, all these events were a clear warning not to place any more hope in Jerusalem, a city that had rejected them. And thus, it happened that in the same year, the community's elders decided that it was God's will that all true believers should leave the doomed city and move to Pella, a Greek settlement across the Jordan.

And so it happened.

THE BATTLE FOR HEROD'S PALACE

After his triumphant return from Masada, Menahem became the *de facto* leader of the uprising, overshadowing everyone else, even Eleazar, who had led the Zealots up to that point. Menahem would soon pay dearly for this moment of glory, for he was as widely hated by his ambitious rivals as he was idolatrously admired by the masses.

Meanwhile, the continual attacks on Herod's palace yielded no results. The mighty walls could only be broken with siege machines, and there were none in Jerusalem. Menahem, however, came up with the idea of tunneling under the walls. A long subterranean passage was dug under the foundations of one of the towers. It was held up by wooden beams, which were then set on fire to collapse it. The tower wobbled and fell, but to the amazement and fury of the besiegers, as soon as the dust cloud cleared, a new wall appeared just beyond the rubble! The defenders had built it in feverish haste just as Menahem's men dug their tunnel; for the tremors of the ground, the sounds of hammering, and the shaking of the walls, all inevitable in all such work, had forewarned them what was going to happen.

So, to the despair of the insurgents, the whole process had to start anew. Fortunately for them, King Agrippa's soldiers were exhausted from fighting; they did not believe further resistance made any sense, suffered severe shortages of supplies, and many of them, being Jews, sympathized with their opponents anyway. Talks began. Menahem swore a solemn oath that he would let Agrippa's men leave the palace safely, for they were all Jews and countrymen. He made only one reservation: that the promise of safety covered only them. And indeed, when Agrippa's soldiers came out from behind the walls, no one raised a hand against them.

Left to their own devices, the Romans now found themselves in great danger. There were only a few hundred of them, so they could not even think about defending the entire palace. They hastily retreated from their positions to its three most powerful towers, called Hippicos, Phasael, and Mariamme. All this happened so quickly and in such great disorder, with the enemy already rushing in, that many of the soldiers had no time to retreat. The insurgents killed them on the spot. They also looted the supply depots and set fire to the former

Roman quarters.

The next day, Menahem's men began a thorough search of the entire palace grounds. They even looked into the underground channels that carried water to the garden pools and fountains. And from them, they dragged out the high priest Ananias, son of Nedebeus. He was now killed along with his brother Hezekiah.

It was the 7th of Elul, which is to say the end of August or the beginning of September, according to our calendar.

TYRANT MENAHEM

Menahem claimed the merit of the victory to himself alone. He acted like a tyrant; he ruled the city with a firm hand, mercilessly persecuting all those suspected of favoring the Romans. Among the suspects was also Joseph, son of Matthias, later a historian of the war, known to us as Josephus Flavius, although he would acquire that name only several years later.

Josephus came from a distinguished priestly family and, through his mother, was even related to the royal dynasty of the Hasmoneans—the family that had reigned over Judea for a whole century until the time of Herod the Great. Josephus was still relatively young, barely in his thirties, but he had already made some important contributions. In AD 64, he went to Rome on his own initiative. There, he found access to Empress Poppaea Sabina and, thanks to her support, obtained from Nero the release of several priests who had been imprisoned and sent to Italy by Felix, Berenice's brother-in-law. The empress, always favorable to the Jews and apparently God-fearing,[33] gave him generous gifts. When he returned to Jerusalem in the spring of 66, he became an eyewitness to the events which we know mainly on the basis of his later account. About what he himself experienced at the time, Josephus wrote in his autobiography:

---

[33] A term for Gentiles who performed minor acts of piety towards the God of Israel without embracing the Mosaic Law.

I saw the start of the revolt when a lot of people wanted to liberate our country from the Empire. I tried to restrain them. I urged them to consider carefully against whom they were going to war. No one could equal the Romans—neither in military skill nor in fortune's favor. I told them that they had no business exposing so rashly their cities, families, and themselves to mortal danger. But I achieved nothing. Those people were completely desperate. They were like madmen.

Because I kept repeating my views, I began to fear that I would attract hatred and accusations of treason. If the insurgents decided to go against me, I would face possible death. So, I hid in the Temple (because Fortress Antonia had already been captured)." [34]

Menahem's main supporters were simple peasants and shepherds who had come to Jerusalem from the countryside, some from very distant parts. The arrogant behavior of these uncouth fanatics, prone to quarrels, fights, and robberies, aroused the resentment and anger of both the townspeople and the priests. Messiah Menahem, triumphantly returning from Masada, had been at first greeted enthusiastically; but after a couple of weeks, the mood started to turn against him and, in some circles, became outright hostile. Eleazar, displaced by Menahem, hated him especially.

Eleazar had done nothing to defend his father, the high priest Ananias, son of Nebedeus, or his uncle Hezekiah. He remained silent as they were pulled out from the water pipes in Herod's palace. He watched their execution with a stony calm. He would not have been able to save them anyway, but through this apparent indifference to their fate, he showed that he was ready to sacrifice everything for the sake of the cause and, in consequence, the word spread about the city that he was an unyielding warrior, the most zealous of the Zealots, but one of their own number: a man from Jerusalem. Almost all the priests and the entire native population of the capital stood behind Eleazar. Even the great landlords, who were fundamentally opposed to war, thought he was less dangerous than Menahem.

In secret meetings, people said that, surely, they had not risen

---

[34] Josephus Flavius, *My Life*, 17–19.

against the Romans in order to bow slavishly before a Jewish tyrant—
and a country bumpkin to boot. Some said openly:

"If the good of the cause requires one man to lead, let anyone
lead, anyone but Menahem!"

Soon, a plot was hatched to attack the tyrant when he least
expected it.

The coup took place a few days after the capture of Herod's
palace, before the middle of the month of Elul. Menahem, dressed in
his royal robes, went with his company to the Temple for prayers.
When the procession reached the outer courtyard in front of the
entrance to the Tabernacle, that is, between Solomon's Portico and the
Beautiful Gate, and walked into the midst of the huge throng usually
assembled there, the men of Eleazar struck suddenly, sword in hand.
The bodyguard tried to resist. But when the crowd, too, turned on
them and began pelting them with stones, they fled at once. Those
captured were killed on the spot. Those hiding were hunted down like
animals. Only a few managed to escape from Jerusalem and flee to
Masada. Eleazar, son of Jairus, a relative of Menahem, commanded
them.

Menahem himself, the king and Messiah, hid cowardly for a
while in the crevices of the Temple Mount. He was eventually
captured and killed after horrific torture. And Joseph, son of Matthias,
was able to leave the Temple and rejoin the company of high priests
and leaders of the party of the Pharisees.

THE THREE TOWERS

If some of those who attacked Menahem and his party had secretly
hoped that, by overthrowing the tyranny of the self-proclaimed king,
they would put down the rebellion, they were now sorely
disappointed. The victorious faction grouped around Eleazar called
for even more radical measures against the Romans, wishing to show
that they could "out-radical" the radical "fake Messiah." So, while the

opinion was often expressed in the city that the siege of the three towers should be lifted and the remaining Roman garrison allowed to go free, Eleazar's men, deaf to all words of reason, stormed the towers all the fiercer. After a few days, the defenders, having no more food and water, understood that the end of their resistance was near. They started negotiations. They asked only to be allowed to go free and offered to abandon all their weapons and all their possessions. The representatives of the insurgents agreed to these terms, swore an oath, and shook the hand of the Roman commander, Metilius, to seal the bargain. The Romans came out of their towers. As long as they held their weapons in hand, the insurgents stood around in deafening silence. The soldiers laid down their swords and shields in the indicated place and were already looking around for a way to leave the city, but at just that moment, on a single command, the people of Eleazar fell on them from all sides. The Romans, defenseless and surprised, shouted desperately with their last breath:

"We had a deal! You swore an oath!"

All were massacred, several hundred men. Only one survived—Metilius. He humiliated himself by begging for his life. He cried out loud that he wanted to become a Jew and would be circumcised. But that was not why Eleazar's men spared his life. The reason was something else: it was his hand that their plenipotentiaries had shaken as they swore their oath. Formally, therefore—they claimed brazenly—they had honored the oath because the one man whose hand they had shaken was left alive and unharmed.

The argument convinced no one, not even among the Jews. In fact, the people all realized that something terrible and irreversible had just happened. There wasn't a man in town who didn't now realize that there was no more turning back. Defenseless Roman soldiers had been treacherously murdered—and they were not even the ones who had "pacified" the Upper City in May. The Roman Empire had been challenged. It was inconceivable that it would not exact revenge.

War was inevitable. Everyone understood it. In many houses, especially the more affluent ones, the mood was not of joy and triumph but—of mournful gloom. And the devout lamented that the murder of the unarmed had been committed *on a Sabbath* when only prayer was allowed, and all work and exercise of any kind was strictly forbidden; and even fighting was a sin unless one fought to defend his own life from imminent danger. But what could justify the attack in this case—since the Romans had laid down their arms?

Some now prophesied that this violation of the Sabbath would bring down a terrible calamity on the city and on the whole nation.

POGROMS FROM SYRIA TO EGYPT

The massacre of the Roman cohort took place on the 17th of Elul, so already in September. From then on, the situation began to develop very quickly.

First, bloody riots broke out in the cities of Palestine, Syria, Phoenicia, and even Alexandria in Egypt.

They started in Caesarea Maritima. It is reported that already on the 17th of Elul, the local Syrian and Greek population attacked the Jewish quarter, murdering many thousands. Those who managed to escape with their life fell into the hands of the soldiers of Florus, were shackled and imprisoned in the shipyard docks to be sold into slavery.

To avenge the pogrom in Caesarea, the Jews in Palestine rushed to the nearby towns and villages inhabited by Greeks and Syrians. They burned houses and estates and murdered the population. This happened in cities east of the Jordan, west of the Jordan, and even on the coastal plain—in Gaza, Antedon, Ashkelon, and around Phoenician Tyre. But, where the Greek and Syrian populations prevailed, it was the Jews who suffered more. Old scores were settled, land and possessions were seized. Each settlement was suddenly divided into two warring camps, both burning with hatred for each other and trembling with fear and seeing the only hope of survival in attacking the other party first.

Josephus, son of Matthias, writes:

The cities were full of unburied bodies. The corpses of old men and children lay abandoned side by side, and the corpses of women with their private parts uncovered. In all parts of the province, untold horrors took place, and the only thing worse than what had already happened was the fear of what might happen next. [35]

Only a few large urban centers managed to prevent riots: in Syria, Antioch and Apamea; in Phoenicia—Sidon; and to the east of the Jordan—Jerash. But very dangerous disturbances took place in Alexandria.

The Jewish colony there was huge, numbering well over a hundred thousand. Skirmishes between Jews and Greeks had often taken place over the centuries, and it was impossible to determine which side was more responsible for the mutual and ever-increasing hostility. News of the events in Palestine and Syria naturally fueled mutual suspicions and fears.

And yet, it was during these days of tension that the Greeks called a great rally in the city's amphitheater.

The purpose of the assembly was to dispatch deputies to Emperor Nero. Details of the emperor's upcoming trip to Greece were already known, and it was also no secret that he wanted to visit Egypt as well. Now it was proposed that a delegation should go to Greece and invite the emperor to Alexandria. The Jews, however, suspected that the matter of the embassy to Nero was only a pretext and that the real subject of the meeting would be something quite different, namely, an impending attack on the Jewish quarter. Because of these fears, there slipped into the amphitheater—although it had been officially announced that the meeting was for Greeks only—many young Jews. When they were recognized, a hue and cry went up that they were spies. The crowd threw itself on the intruders, and though most successfully escaped, the Greeks captured three and wanted to burn them alive. A great crowd of Jews rushed to their rescue, shouting and howling, waving burning torches and throwing stones. If the

---

[35] Josephus Flavius, *The Jewish War*, II 465.

amphitheater—built of stone but with a lot of wooden elements—were to be set on fire, an incredible catastrophe would occur, which in turn would lead to mutual slaughter and huge destruction throughout the city.

The office of the prefect of Egypt was then held by one Tiberius Julius Alexander. He was a brother of Marcus Julius Alexander—the man who years earlier had married Berenice, then a young girl, as her first husband but who soon thereafter died, leaving behind a virgin widow. Like Marcus, Tiberius was a Jew by birth, a Greek by education, and a Roman by citizenship and conviction. He had served in the Roman army, held various titles and offices, and, for some time, even the governorship of Palestine in the days of Claudius. He had been made Prefect of Egypt a few months ago, in May. King Agrippa congratulated him in person, having traveled to Alexandria for this purpose (and, you will remember, having left Berenice in Jerusalem to fulfill her Nazarite vow).

And now, by order of this prefect, several high officials blocked the way of the crowd of Jews, calling on the attackers to come to their senses and not to bring terrible misfortune upon themselves. However, these words were greeted with ridicule and mockery, not sparing even the viceroy himself.

Alexander then put into action the two legions garrisoned near the city, as well as two thousand auxiliaries who had recently arrived from Libya. These troops stormed the Jewish Quarter. They had been explicitly ordered to kill Jews and to loot and burn houses, all in order to strike terror in the population. The Jews initially tried to put up resistance in the streets, and many were killed on both sides. However, it was not so difficult for the well-armed and well-trained soldiers to break the desperate resistance of the chaotic mob, who fought only with sticks and stones. The Romans proceeded to "pacify," sparing no one along the way. Thousands of people were murdered, most of them completely innocent. Only then was it possible to appease the prefect and order the soldiers to return to their camps. The legionaries immediately wiped the blood off their swords, but the Greek mob raged on for days among the ruined houses and in the streets littered with corpses, looting whatever they could and tormenting the wounded.

THE MISADVENTURES OF PHILIP

But where were Agrippa and Berenice during all this? And how did they react to the events in their country? After all, their possessions were located on the Galilean/Syrian border and were inhabited by a mixed population with different languages and different religions, and riots must have taken place there, too. Information about this is limited but informative: we have a story about the adventures of a man who, by extraordinary coincidence, played an important role in several critical events in Palestine.

His name was Philip. It was that same Philip who had brought Agrippa's soldiers to Jerusalem to help the moderates in their fight against the insurgents and who later took part in the defense of Herod's palace but made a deal with Menahem and left with his men, abandoning the Roman contingent to their own devices.

Despite having struck a deal with the insurgents, Philip soon found himself in danger: some revolutionaries openly demanded his head. He survived only with the help of his relatives from Babylonia, who happened to be in Jerusalem: on the fifth day after abandoning his defense of the palace, Philip managed to escape Jerusalem in disguise and wearing a wig. He headed straight north, up the Jordan in the direction of Gamala, a fortress east of the Sea of Galilee, in the land of Batanea, of which he was the titular commander. (The surrounding countryside was also under his authority).

However, before he reached Gamala, shocked by all the events he had witnessed, weary from the journey, and weakened by fever, he stopped in a small village already within his territory, thinking he could rest safely there. He then sent two trusted men with letters: one to Gamala itself, asking for an escort to take him back to the fort, and the other to Caesarea Philippi, to Agrippa and Berenice.

However, the king and queen had left their capital by then. They had first gone to Phoenician Berytus and from there to Antioch: they wanted to join forces with the governor of Syria. But before his departure, Agrippa had entrusted the management of his lands to a certain Varus. He was a Syrian of high birth and supposedly related to some princely dynasty. He was ambitious, and the turmoil unfolding throughout Palestine encouraged him to entertain the wildest of hopes. He began to imagine that he could carve out a principality for himself—of course, at the expense of Agrippa and Berenice, whom he had secretly hated for a long time.

Now, this viceroy—as we should probably call him—became convinced that Philip and his men had died in Jerusalem or had been taken prisoner there. The unexpected arrival of a messenger with a letter from Philip, alive and so near, threatened to destroy his well-wrought plans. Philip, a high dignitary, commander of an important fortress, trusted by the king, would know how to prevent the impending coup. Varus did not lose a moment. He placed the bearer of the letter before an assembly of the people of Caesarea Philippi. Then he cried out in a loud voice and with the most holy indignation that a peddler of forgeries had been caught:

"The impudent author of this letter says that Philip joined the Jewish rebels in Jerusalem and now fights with them against the Romans!"

In this way, Varus achieved two goals at once: by allegedly denying a non-existent slanderous rumor, he aroused the suspicion that Philip had betrayed the king and stirred animosity towards him among the Caesareans because they were largely pro-Roman. He then ordered the messenger to be killed on the spot. The seed of the false rumor, skillfully planted in good soil, sprouted beautifully; soon, no one knew what was true and what was not, all the more so because news from Jerusalem came delayed, incomplete, and distorted. Philip, still bedridden in his small village, grew impatient. He sent another messenger to Caesarea with another letter. This, too, fell into the hands of Varus and disappeared without a trace because the viceroy had already entered into an agreement with the Syrian citizens of the city, who were largely opposed to Agrippa. They assured him that a regime change in their kingdom was due at any moment since Agrippa had to fall: either the Romans would overthrow him as a Jew, or the insurgents would overthrow him as an ally of Rome.

The gates of Caesarea Philippi were closed, and all contacts with Antioch were cut off. Many people loyal to the king were killed. An attempt was made to capture another city in Batanea but failed: the population, warned in time, fled to Gamala.

Finally, Philip arrived in the fortress of Gamala—and just in time: had he stayed in the village longer, Varus's assassins would probably have discovered him there.

Some in Gamala advised him to go to Caesarea Philippi immediately, join Varus, and kill all the supporters of King Agrippa. But Philip resisted these urgings. Meanwhile, news of these events reached Antioch and the ears of Agrippa and Berenice. Varus was immediately deposed, and a certain Modius, a Roman, was appointed in his place.

THE PUNITIVE EXPEDITION OF CESTIUS GALLUS

King Agrippa and Berenice had first stayed in Berytus in Phoenicia and then went on to Antioch in Syria. There, during stormy discussions with the governor, Cestius Gallus, a decision was made that armed intervention in Palestine was necessary—and the sooner, the better. Rioting and pogroms had taken place in almost every town in the country. The procurator of Judea, Gesius Florus, discredited and incompetent, had been completely unable to control the situation, and his forces were too small anyway: he only had five cohorts.

And thus, in the fall of AD 66, the governor of Syria decided to move south. He led a large army, the core of which was the entire XIIth legion—about six thousand men—and two thousand soldiers drawn from the other Syrian legions, as well as six independent infantry cohorts and four cavalry squadrons. Troops of allied Syrian kings joined in; King Agrippa alone contributed three thousand foot and nearly two thousand horse. And when Cestius reached the city of Ptolemais in southern Phoenicia, many volunteers from the local population joined in. Though they were not trained, they were eager to fight, both because of their hatred for their Jewish neighbors and of the hope of plunder.

King Agrippa took part in the expedition. Because he knew the country and its inhabitants well, he was able to offer valuable advice. He was entrusted with the management of the food supplies for the army.

The first operation was carried out by selected units under the command of Cestius. They entered a territory of Galilee bordering southern Phoenicia. The chief town in that region was Habulon. Although its people managed to escape in time and take refuge in the mountains, they left all their belongings behind. Habulon had been a beautiful and rich town, with tall houses like those of Tyre and Sidon, but now it was plundered and burned. The same fate befell the surrounding villages. Then the governor returned to Ptolemais, but his Syrian troops remained behind in order to loot. The local population unexpectedly attacked them, emerging from their hiding places, and inflicted heavy losses on them.

In response, Cestius moved his quarters further south to Caesarea Maritima. Its citizens greeted him enthusiastically. At the same time, his troops, sent ahead, attacked Joppa[36] by land and sea. The attack was so sudden and unexpected that the inhabitants did not even try to fight back. The Romans killed eight thousand there—men, women, and children. The city was plundered and burned. They also looted and "pacified" the villages of the neighboring district of Narbata.

Simultaneously, another corps returned to Galilee. Its chief city, Sepphoris,[37] welcomed the Romans. Several others followed its example, and the insurgents retreated into the mountains. Pursued,

---

[36] Today Jaffa

[37] Modern Tzippori.

they defended themselves valiantly, but were beaten, losing two thousand dead; only a handful of combatants managed to escape and hide in the wilderness.

Marching steadily further south, the governor took the city of Antipatris on the coastal plain and the neighboring Lydda[38] on the all-important road to Jerusalem. Both towns and their surroundings had been completely deserted, as all their inhabitants were in Jerusalem to celebrate *Sukkot* (The Feast of Tabernacles). Only fifty were found— all were promptly killed. Lydda and the nearby villages were burned.

The road to Jerusalem led uphill from the plain through a gorge called Beth-Horon. The landscape and the procession probably looked a lot like the scene in the painting by Breugel *Saint Paul on the Road to Damascus*, which portrays the Spanish army traversing the Alpine passes. Tawny rocks, dark green cypresses shooting high into the sky, helmeted infantrymen laden with baggage and carrying spears, horsemen in shining armor, and colorful robes.

The Romans negotiated the difficult passage without any resistance and took the city of Gibeon—they were now, at most, a two hours' march from Jerusalem. But since it was a Saturday, they were not vigilant: they were already familiar with Jewish customs.

And now, something completely unexpected happened: suddenly, out of the blue, thousands of Jews fell on the column of troops just beginning to lay their camp. Masses of young men charged them, howling and screaming, flailing all kinds of weapons without any order or discipline but driving forward like a mighty tidal wave. Taking advantage of the element of surprise, they managed to penetrate deep into the Roman ranks. They killed several hundred soldiers. Only a last-minute charge of the Roman cavalry forced them to retreat.

At the same time, a unit of insurgents led by Simon, son of Gorias,[39] attacked the Roman rear and its wagon train, still working

---

[38] Modern Lod.

[39] Also known as Simon bar Giora

its way through Beth-Horon Gorge. They seized many pack mules and took them to Jerusalem.

A STEP SHORT OF VICTORY

Nine years later, Josephus, son of Matthias, stood in Rome before Berenice and King Agrippa. Over and over, he repeated stubbornly:

> I was in Jerusalem at the time, so I know what I am saying. Cestius had only to advance, and he would have won. How many misfortunes would have been averted if he had!

And King Agrippa, who had been a member of the expedition and one of its leaders, seemed to agree with these words. He spoke as if he wanted to justify himself:

> I was still hoping for a negotiated settlement. Since Cestius decided to camp near Gibeon for three days, I sent two of my men ahead to the walls of Jerusalem. They were supposed to deliver the message that anyone who laid down their arms and passed over to our side would be pardoned. But what answer did my men receive? One I never saw again because the Jerusalemites killed him. The other was badly wounded and barely escaped with his life.

Josephus, however—always ready to exonerate the people of Jerusalem and to blame the outsiders for everything—immediately interjected:

> True, I saw the crime myself. But I also saw that the people of Jerusalem were willing to listen to what your representatives were saying. But then the evil-doers rushed at the crowd with sticks and stones! The bandits drove away anyone who tried to stand on the walls and hear your message.

He always and consistently used the term "bandits" whenever he referred to the revolutionaries. The words "insurgent" or "freedom fighter" would never pass his lips. [40]

Agrippa nodded but continued his tale. He was clearly going to place all the responsibility for the failed expeditions on Cestius alone. He asked:

> Just then, the governor decided to set out from Gibeon. "Why?" everyone thought. Was he planning to take advantage of the confusion in Jerusalem to attack it immediately? But he only moved his camp to a site just outside the city—to Mount Scopus. [41] And again, he stood there idle for three days.

"His soldiers were busy seizing food supplies across the surrounding country," said Josephus.

The king waved his hand dismissively:

> And he didn't need to do that! After all, I was responsible for food supplies. But he missed the opportunity and did not attack the city until the fourth day!

Josephus watched this attack unfold while standing on the high temple wall. He remembered the picture of the Romans marching from Mount Scopus to the city as if it had happened yesterday:

> They marched in tight ranks right up to the third wall, the one your father had built. They breached it easily because it had never been completed. They took the district between this wall and the second wall. [42] The people of the district sought refuge behind the second wall and, whoever could, in the Temple. But the bandits called on them to remain in place and defend every house. No one listened to them, especially once fires broke out. Within hours, Cestius stood before the first wall, right next to Herod's palace. And all he needed to do was—to storm! No one defended the walls! He could have taken the city practically without a fight. The war would have been over without much loss of life. The Temple would still stand,

---

[40] Any Polish reader of these words would reflect that both Germans and Russians used the word "bandits" to describe the Polish resistance movement during World War II.

[41] Site of Hebrew University today.

[42] The New City.

Jerusalem would still stand. But that's when he ordered a halt. Why?

Agrippa pretended that he knew the answer:

> I was with Cestius. I took part in the council. [Were he to go by his own inclination], the governor may well have decided to storm the city, but some of his officers objected. Most insistent among them was the prefect of the camp, Tyranius Priscus. Honestly, I suspect that he and the others had taken money from Florus. And the latter, of course, wanted to prolong the war at all costs if only to be able to justify his own failure: "It is only natural that I didn't pacify Jerusalem—the viceroy himself and his gigantic army were unable to do it!" So, these bribed people argued endlessly that the walls were mighty, that the machines had not yet arrived, that the troops had to be regrouped and given a moment's respite.

Prudently, the king did not spell out what position he himself had taken during the council. Neither did the tactful Josephus ask. Instead, he asked something else: why had Cestius spurned the secret offer of a group of inhabitants of Jerusalem who were prepared to open the gates of the city to him? Agrippa did not know the details of the case:

> The governor seemed to think it was a trick. Anyway, even if he agreed, it wouldn't have mattered. The bandits have, by then, regained control of the city. They had already manned the walls and were hunting throughout the city for those who were prepared to negotiate.

Josephus confirmed this:

> Some were even thrown off the walls. The bandits now manned the battlements, and it must be admitted that for five days, they repulsed the Romans bravely. But on the sixth day, the legionaries approached in what they call a "tortoise formation."

Agrippa perked up, jumped up from his chair. He seemed to have the scene before his eyes. He spoke, gesticulating wildly:

> I remember this well! I saw it all from Mount Scopus! They took a formation that really looked like a monstrous turtle. They walked slowly

in tight, deep ranks. They held their shields above their heads. Only those in the outer ranks had their shields in front of them or at their sides. The defenders threw at them everything they got, but even the heaviest projectiles, even those thrown with great force, just bounced off the armor of this gigantic turtle like a fine hailstone off a mighty rock.

Josephus nodded:

> That's right! What a sight that was! The tortoise marched on like a battering ram. They came right up to the wall. Then the first ranks, protected by their comrades, began pounding the foundation of the wall with a battering ram. A dozen more hard blows would have been enough, and they would have made a wide breach. Nobody would have been able to stop them. You, king, could not see what went on in the city, but I was there: even the bravest men—men who had recently fought like lions— now ran about in panic. The people, too, came out into the streets and ran to and fro in dismay. I heard people calling for immediate surrender and the opening of the gates. And just then, just then, when Cestius was practically victorious, the tooting of Roman war trumpets and horns sounded the signal of retreat! We couldn't believe our eyes and ears. It was a miracle, I guess. Or total folly. Or maybe betrayal? But whose? After all, only the commander could have given such an order!

And here, the king, who was fond of philosophical reflections, may have said—perhaps because he did not want to dwell on the question of who had ordered the assault to be stopped—

"Imagine that in some two thousand years, someone will wonder and write, for example, how our fate and the fate of the empire—and even the world—would have turned out had the Romans not held back at that moment, at the moment when they were already entering the city; if the war had ended on that day, with little loss of life on both sides, rather than three years later with all the consequences it had! And if Jerusalem, and the Temple, and the people of Judea had been spared!"[43]

---

[43] A Polish reader of those lines would have been familiar with the endless debates current then (and now) among Poles—whether Poland should have refused Hitler's ultimatum in August 1939; or whether the Polish resistance should have gone ahead with the Warsaw Uprising in 1944.

THE BETH-HORON GORGE

Hearing the drawn-out signal of trumpets and horns, the ranks of legionaries immediately moved away from the walls and returned to the camp. The insurgents—Josephus would have said: *the bandits*—felt like lions and followed them through the rubble. They killed many of the Roman rearguard. And then, on the morning of the following day, came a surprise: the Romans folded camp on Mount Scopus and began a full retreat. The insurgents, emboldened by the preceding day's success, now attacked the column even more boldly. They attacked the legionaries mainly, for they, bearing heavy armor, could not easily pursue the agile enemy among the rocks and crevices. Many died in these continuous skirmishes, including a few officers; among them was the prefect who had supposedly been behind the retreat: Florus.

The terrain was so difficult that the next camp was pitched not far away—on the old site near Gibeon. The Romans rested in its fortifications for two days. It seems that Cestius Gallus was still hesitating whether to remain there and try to attack Jerusalem again or whether to leave Judea altogether.

How to explain this conduct of Cestius? In recalling his cohorts from the city walls, he had made a mistake, of course, but an understandable one: the governor had not been aware of how favorable to the Romans the situation in the city was. Evidently, he thought the defenders would continue to stand as fearlessly as before, and he preferred to avoid heavy casualties. When abandoning the camp on Mount Scopus, he had probably only intended to move to an area where his army could more easily be supplied with food, fuel, and building materials since the location closest to Jerusalem had already been stripped completely bare. However, during the march, he suffered such severe losses in men and equipment that it became necessary to reconsider whether to continue the attack. It was late autumn, the season of cold and rain was afoot. One had to take into account the increasingly precarious situation of provisioning, all the more so because the insurgents, controlling the countryside of Judea, might possibly cut off the Roman camp from its main supply bases on the coastal plain.

After weighing all his options, Cestius determined to pass through the dangerous gorge of Beth-Horon as quickly as possible and take up positions closer to the sea; from there, a new operation against Jerusalem could be launched the following spring. However, remembering how many casualties in men and material his recent march through this ravine had cost him, the governor decided that everything that would hinder and delay his retreat had to be destroyed. Most of the draft animals were slaughtered, saving only those that carried ammunition and war machines, for otherwise, that equipment might fall into the hands of the enemy.

On the third day, the Romans folded camp at Gibeon and immediately advanced in good order towards the gorge. At first, while they were still on the open plateau, the army advanced quickly and efficiently.

The catastrophe occurred only in the ravine itself, in the most difficult place to pass, where the road led up a steep slope. On one side, there was a perpendicular wall of rock, and on the other, a precipitous cliff. And now a hail of well-aimed bullets suddenly fell on the stretched-out column—both from above and from the opposite slope. It turned out that the enemy had closed the road in the front and attacked from the rear. There was terrible confusion and howling as if from the pit of the damned, multiplied by the echo. The howls of the wounded and enraged men, as they struggled helplessly, mixed with the attackers' shouts of triumph and joy.

Only the falling darkness saved the army of Cestius from total annihilation. Under cover of darkness, his decimated cohorts finally reached the village of Beth-Horon, lying at the mouth of the gorge on the side of the plain. But that same night, the viceroy left the village with his main force. He left behind only four hundred men. Hiding on the flat roofs of houses, they shouted all night to create the illusion that the whole army still stood there. The insurgents camping above the village discovered the ruse only at dawn. They struck at once, and, having the advantage of numbers and elevation, they routed the four hundred. Then, they went in pursuit of the main force. On the way, they found the heavy war machines and ammunition abandoned by the fleeing Romans. Thus, pursuing Cestius, they came as far as the town of Antipatris, but Cestius was already far away. So, they turned back, took the war machines and weapons, and stripped the corpses of the fallen soldiers. They entered Jerusalem intoxicated with victory, singing triumphant songs, and greeted enthusiastically. It is not certain that seeing their triumph, Josephus really made the prediction he later reported to King Agrippa and Berenice:

I said: "This victory will be the cause of our annihilation!"

It was the end of November AD 66, the twelfth year of Nero's reign. The emperor was visiting Greece.

THE SECOND MARRIAGE OF TITUS

Even before Nero departed for his beloved Hellas, dramatic events had taken place in Rome in the same year, AD 66. They affected many senatorial families, especially the House of the Flavians. Figuratively speaking, to say that lightning struck from the blue would not have been an exaggeration.

Shortly after Arruncia's death, Titus had married Marcia Furnilla. Her father, Marcius Barea Sura, belonged to the senatorial class. Marcia bore Titus a daughter, Julia. Despite this, the marriage did not last: it ended in divorce in AD 66. It is almost certain that political considerations were behind it. To put it simply: Titus chickened out. He was afraid that his association with the family of Marcius Barea might endanger him or bring down upon him the emperor's disfavor.
    The point was that Furnilla's uncle, Marcius Barea Soranus, had been accused and convicted of political crimes in the early months

of AD 66. This case began with the daughter of Soranus, Servilia, and was a shocking tale long remembered by the contemporaries.

Nero hated Soranus and wanted to kill him for two reasons: first, because the senator had been friends with Rubelius Plautus, convicted and executed for allegedly planning a coup; and secondly, he had offended one of the emperor's influential freedmen, for, while administering the province of Asia, he indirectly prevented the man from stripping the city of Pergamon of its valuable statues and images.

On the day on which the Senate was to judge the case of Soranus and several other co-accused dignitaries, two cohorts of Praetorians in full armor occupied the temple of Venus the Mother, located near the assembly hall. At the entrance to the hall itself, groups of plainclothesmen loitered in togas, intentionally clumsily concealing swords and daggers. Small detachments of armed men roamed the Forum. Each of the arriving senators got his share of menacing stares from the officers and men. The outcome of the trial was a foregone conclusion.

The prosecutor of the case started out by reminding everyone of the friendship between Soranus and Plautus. He also declared that as governor of Asia, Soranus had thought mainly about his personal glory and not about the good of the state, sometimes even inciting the local inhabitants against imperial power. Then, however, he made a new and serious accusation, striking not only at Soranus but also at his daughter, Servilia. Namely, he stated that Servilia had paid a huge amount of money to some practitioners of the arcane arts. Alas, it was not a trumped-up charge: Servilia, a young woman of twenty, moved by her love for her father and anxiety about his fate, did indeed turn to magicians and astrologers with the question of whether their house would survive and whether the emperor could be appeased. She was immediately summoned before the Senate. Father and daughter, separated from each other, stood on opposite sides of the tribunal, where the consuls presiding over the trial sat.

The prosecutor, Ostorius Sabinus, asked Servilia whether she dared to deny that she had sold her wedding dress (her husband, Annius Pollio, had been exiled previously) and a valuable necklace in order to finance secret rites. Servilia threw herself weeping on the ground. For a long time, she couldn't utter a word. Then, kneeling, she embraced the podium of the altar of the goddess of Victory. As if drawing courage from it, she began to assure the Senate that she had never cast black magic spells. If she had asked the gods for anything, it was only that the Emperor and the Senators might preserve her father. Yes, she had sold her jewels and her dresses—the badges of her high social standing—but she would have given her blood and life for the same cause just as easily if it had been demanded of her. If she had ever mentioned the name of the emperor in her supplication, it was always in association with the most benevolent of deities. Besides, no one had known about her actions, not even her unfortunate father. If she had committed a crime, the guilt was on her alone.

Soranus interrupted her, loudly reminding the Senate that his daughter had not accompanied him when he was governor of Asia; that Plautus did not know her at all, for she was still a child then; that she had nothing to do with her husband's plot. He added:

> I am ready to submit to any sentence, even the harshest, as long as my daughter, accused only of loving me too much, is spared.

The two were already walking towards each other, weeping, but the lictors interposed themselves between them. Witnesses were brought in. The first was Publius Egnatius Celer, a Stoic philosopher, once a client and an instructor of Soranus, a man of dignified and severe demeanor. But this exemplar of all philosophical virtues had been bribed. Testifying, he incriminated his former benefactor and his benefactor's daughter.

Against all expectations, the next witness—one of the wealthiest men in the province of Asia—defended Soranus with courage and gusto. He paid for his honesty with the confiscation of his estates and exile.

Soranus and his daughter received a more severe sentence: death. As a special grace, they were allowed to commit suicide in any way they chose.

Vespasian attended this Senate meeting, of course. He heard the accusations, he saw the tears of Servilia, he voted. He voted *for* the conviction, of course—he could not have voted otherwise. Not showing up at the deliberations alone would have had severe consequences, never mind abstaining from vote. Informers, hoping to earn their statutory rewards, eagerly watched every gesture of the Senators. [44]

And thus, Titus thought it expedient to divorce Soranus's niece, Marcia Furnilla. He may have felt compelled to do so because he held the office of quaestor that year (AD 66). Like all former republican offices, this too was a merely honorary dignity under the empire, but it was important because it opened admission to the Senate. [45] It was hard to ask an ambitious young man in such a post to maintain his links to a family in imperial disfavor: he would have ruined his career before it even started.

LITTLE GIRL, ARISE!

And thus, we see the daughter of a Roman Senator consulting magicians and astrologers. She took their skills seriously, perhaps even with some trepidation. She paid a lot of money for their services. It is understandable that a young Roman woman believed in the power of sorcery and wanted to learn what the future held. Even today, after twenty centuries, Servilia finds a multitude of imitators.

But the Senate? After all, it consisted of intelligent and

---

[44] By practice established in the days of Emperor Tiberius, informers were statutorily entitled to ¼ of the value of the assets confiscated by the state from the person they denounced. (See Jacek Bocheński, *Tiberius Caesar*).

[45] In the Roman Republic, quaestors had been elected officials who supervised the state treasury and conducted audits. When assigned to provincial governors, their duties were mainly administrative and logistical, but also could expand to encompass military leadership and command. It was the lowest ranking position in the *cursus honorum* ("course of offices"); by the first century BC, one had to have been quaestor to be eligible for any other posts.

generally well-educated men, most of them cynics and ruthless careerists, who assessed the affairs of this world only too soberly. And yet, the august assembly did not only receive but considered the accusation of magic and astrology with complete straight-faced seriousness! One might well conclude that this was done for political reasons, to pass a sentence Nero wanted: soberly and cynically exploiting a nonsensical case to please the ruler. Alas, the conviction of Servilia was not the only case of this kind. Dozens of them appear in the surviving records from this period—largely in part because people widely believed that witchcraft and astrology posed a threat to life, health, and safety. If magicians were often persecuted and repeatedly expelled from Rome, it happened precisely because public opinion attributed real power to them. Entrepreneurs like Simon the Magus were not looking for followers in Palestine alone. Strange tales were told about many others—also about Apollonius of Tyana.

And it so happened that Apollonius, having visited various lands and cities of mainland Greece, had just arrived in Rome. Here, if we are to believe his biographer, he became the object of great interest, arousing reverent fear and respect. Even the omnipotent Praetorian Prefect Tigellinus, who questioned him, did not dare to take any steps that would hinder his freedom of action, even though he felt offended by some actions of the ascetic. He said to him:

"I will grant you the freedom of the city: you may move about as you like. But you must name men who will guarantee for your good conduct."

But Apollonius replied:

"And who will vouch for a body that no one can imprison?"

At these words, the Prefect became terrified, thinking that he was dealing with a divine being, and he quickly withdrew his condition:

"Go wherever you want! You are too strong for me to rule you."

And now, says the biographer, walking about the streets and squares of the giant city thanks to the cowardice of the Prefect, Apollonius performed one of the most amazing miracles of his life.

The day was cool and rainy. A large and splendid funeral procession came marching down a main thoroughfare toward the gates of the city. Ear-splitting wailing resounded from a distance. Apollonius stopped. As the funeral procession approached, he saw that the body of a young girl lay on the bier. He heard from bystanders that she had come from one of the most prominent families of Rome and had consuls among her ancestors. She died suddenly, just before her wedding. The young man walking behind the bier was her fiancé.

Apollonius approached and studied the corpse. Suddenly, he shouted:

"Stop! Set the bier down! Soon, you will stop crying!"

He spoke so imperiously that they obeyed him at once: he was already a well-known person in the city. Meanwhile, he asked the deceased's name. People thought he would deliver a eulogy to comfort the family, but something completely different happened: Apollonius bent over the corpse, touched it with his hand, whispered some words, and... after a while, the girl opened her eyes.

Stunned, people asked each other:

"Perhaps Apollonius saw some faint sign of life that had escaped everyone's attention? Who knows, for example, whether there was not a slight mist above the girl's lips, the vapor of her breath (for the day, as we said, was cold and rainy). Or maybe she had really died, but her soul returned from the afterlife, summoned by a secret spell?"

However, soon after this event, an imperial edict was issued forbidding the teaching of philosophy in Rome because—it said—various subversive activities took place under the guise of its study. The edict was issued in connection with the case of Senator Thrasea Paetus.

He had been sentenced to death at the same time as Soranus and Servilia on charges just as trivial and just as fabricated. The real cause of his disgrace was his independence of spirit, and his outspoken nature, which attracted to him people with known dissident sympathies. Those closest to Thrasca included some of the Stoic philosophers and even the more moderate Cynics.

It was already evening when a certain friend of Thrasea,

coming straight from the Senate chamber, arrived at his house. The host was in the garden. There, surrounded by a large group of men and women from the most illustrious Roman families, he conversed with the Cynic philosopher Demetrius. Seeing the focused, serious faces of those gathered around him and hearing a few words of their conversation, the visitor now approaching along the garden path guessed that the discussion concerned the ultimate things: What was the soul? How did it part from the body? What happened to it after death? The visitor guessed that Thrasea had foreseen the verdict of the Senatorial tribunal. The friend to whom everyone now turned confirmed this in a few words. But he added:

"You may die by your own hand. And in any way you wish."

Crying broke out in the garden. Only Thrasea remained calm. He asked his guests to disperse as soon as possible since they put themselves in danger by staying even a minute longer in a convict's house. His wife, Arria, begged him to let her commit suicide as well. He replied firmly:

"You have to live in order to look after our daughter."

He walked over to the garden portico. Here, he met the quaestor sent by the Senate. Thrasea received him almost cheerfully, for in the meantime, he had learned that his son-in-law, Helvidius Priscus, had only been sentenced to exile.

Thrasea committed suicide in his bedroom. He had stretched out both his arms and asked Demetrius and Priscus to cut his veins.

Demetrius, the witness of Thrasea's last moments, was one of Apollonius' closest associates. For this reason alone—notwithstanding the imperial edict against philosophers—it was a good idea for the newcomer from Asia Minor to remove himself from Rome. However, he did not return to his homeland. Instead, he went in the opposite direction: he went west, to Spain. And with good reason: it was generally reported that the emperor would soon travel east, to Greece. Wishing to be as far away from the court and the imperial actor as possible, Apollonius decided to go in the opposite direction. But maybe there were other—secret—reasons which made him go to Spain?

The developments of the next 18 months would make many wonder.

THE EMPEROR'S JOURNEY TO GREECE AND THE BUSINESS AFFAIRS OF THE HOUSE OF FLAVIUS

The trials of Soranus and Servilia and of Thrasea Petus were soon forgotten. In fact, the ordinary men and women of Rome took little interest in either their course or their outcome because the emperor's advisors, acting with great public relations acumen, carried them through at the time of a state visit. The ruler of Armenia, Tiridates, came to the capital. The king paid public homage to Nero and, in return, received a royal diadem—a symbol of his reign. The magnificent and carefully orchestrated ceremony displayed the power of the Empire and the majesty of the emperor in extraordinary splendor. It completely overshadowed the judicial murders carried out almost simultaneously on several representatives of the senatorial class.

Besides, every ordinary inhabitant of Rome, relying only on official reports and on accidentally overheard gossip, was certainly convinced that the accused had conspired against their benevolent emperor. And to do so, they must have been madmen, for how could anyone possibly oppose Nero? He shored up the greatness of the state, preserved peace, and, above all, cared like a father for the widest masses of his simple, honest subjects. He gave the people bread and entertainment and was not ashamed to entertain them personally with performances as a charioteer, an actor, and a singer.

And soon, all talk turned to his upcoming journey to Greece. It was going to be a kind of triumphant artistic tour. Preparations began in early summer, and the huge retinue of the imperial court set off in September AD 66. Apart from servants and courtiers, the emperor was accompanied by selected senators. On the one hand, their dignity added splendor to the journey, and on the other, they served as hostages for the loyalty of those who remained in Rome.

Vespasian found himself among those invited to participate in the expedition. He must have owed this distinction to some political considerations, for it was generally established that he knew nothing about poetry or music. The honor came at a great cost. He had to pay all the travel expenses from his own pocket and appear in the kind of splendor that befitted a Senator and companion of the emperor. And it all came at a time when the financial situation of the Flavian family was not very robust.

It is true that some years ago, around the year 60, Vespasian was governor of the province of Africa, which is today's Tunisia. Opinions about how he performed his duties were mixed. Some praised his impeccable honesty and senatorial probity, while others claimed that he administered the province in a petty way, arousing the indignation of the natives. It was said that during some riots in the city of Hadrumetum, a commoner threw a turnip at him. But the important fact was that Vespasian fell into serious financial difficulties soon after his return from Africa. Harassed by creditors, he saved himself from bankruptcy (and the consequent loss of his seat in the Senate) by pledging his landed estates and even his house to his elder brother, Flavius Sabinus. He also engaged in some not-very honorable businesses, namely the trade in slaves and draft animals, of course, with the help of intermediaries. These ventures earned him the malicious nickname *mulio*—"the mule driver." Finally, he went so far as to take a bribe of two hundred thousand sesterces from a young man by promising him the privilege of framing his robe with a wide, senatorial purple stripe. However, the young man's father did not fancy the honor because—apparently—he did not foresee a brilliant political career for his lad. When his complaint brought the matter to light, Vespasian received a severe public rebuke during one of the Senate sessions.

Death did not spare the house of Flavius, either. Vespasian's wife, Flavia Domitilla, died about that time. She had given him three children: two sons—Titus and Domitian—and a daughter bearing the same names as her mother. The second Flavia Domitilla also died in AD 60s as a young wife, probably in childbirth. Her orphaned daughter was named after her mother and her grandmother. This third Flavia Domitilla, the granddaughter of Vespasian, has a special place in history and legend: she may have been a Christian, the first from such a high-ranking Roman family.

Newly widowed, Vespasian returned to his first love, Antonia Caenis. True, even now, he could not officially marry her, for she was a freedwoman and thus belonged to an estate too low to permit marriage with a senator, but the two lived together like an exemplary couple. Many years earlier, as a girl, the slave Caenis had served a great lady of the imperial family: Antonia, the mother of Claudius and grandmother of Caligula. Because Antonia died in AD 37, entering the house of Vespasian Caenis must have been at least forty, perhaps even fifty. Resourceful, thrifty, intelligent—her memory was so excellent that she could still recite by heart letters once dictated to her by Antonia—she was sincerely devoted to the whole family. She perfectly suited a man of common sense, love of money, simplicity of manners, and a sense of humor.

Leaving for Greece, Vespasian bid a tender farewell to the woman so dear to his heart because, as an official participant in the imperial journey, he could not take a concubine with him. Who could have expected then that their separation, which was supposed to last only a few months, would extend to four years? And who could have predicted that when they saw each other again, he would be an emperor?

But even when he eventually became the ruler of the Empire, Vespasian never abandoned Caenis. She remained in his house, enjoying great influence, and many important matters (of which, of course, the emperor knew nothing) were arranged through her. She specialized in obtaining high civil and military dignities and even priesthoods—of course, for a fee. Apparently, one could also buy from her a pardon for serious offenses. It was said in Rome:

"Vespasian differs from previous emperors in that he does not put anyone to death in order to seize his money, but rather he pardons the accused in exchange for money."

And the people praised such methods of government as more

reasonable and humane.

Caenis probably died in AD 74—and in any case, soon before the arrival of Berenice in Rome. And thus, these two women, the father's freedwoman concubine and the son's queen-lover, never met, though they certainly heard a lot about each other. We may imagine that perhaps the smart and practical but fundamentally simple Roman woman might not have taken to the sensual and pious oriental queen. What could they possibly have talked about, strolling in the Palatine Gardens, their alleys dark green with high cypresses? Berenice would have worn a robe of gold and, on her hand, would have glistened a ring with a magnificent diamond. And Caenis, glancing at the priceless gem with envy, would perhaps have thought like the rest of Rome:

"A king's gift for his shameless sister!"

NERO AND VESPASIAN IN GREECE

Having set foot in the sacred land of Greece, the emperor devoted himself exclusively to artistic pursuits. Various programs took place in different towns: singing competitions, chariot races, poetry recitations, and theatrical performances. And invariably, the world's best singer, its most excellent musician, and its most brilliant actor—Nero—performed in them all. He received frenetic applause, aroused universal enthusiasm, and won first prizes, wreaths, and memorial statuary. It was, therefore, hardly surprising that overwork and excess of impressions prevented him from dealing with trivial matters like politics. Nothing out of the ordinary was happening anyway.

But then, this blessed living for art alone was suddenly disturbed by news from Judea and, in particular, by the news of the defeat of Cestius Gallus. Of course, it was clearly not a major disaster by any means. The whole thing was a rebellion of a small people, and while, yes, it had inflicted some casualties on the Roman corps, none of it was cause for alarm. The forces led by Cestius were only part of the army stationed in Syria, and other legions could easily be moved to the Palestinian theater if necessary. Yet, it was unwise to underestimate the importance of the uprising. Rome had to suppress it as soon as possible lest it become a contagious example to other subjugated peoples.

The emperor and his advisers judged the situation well, stating publicly that the defeat in Judea was brought about, above all, by the incompetence of the commander. It, therefore, behooved the emperor to send a new general, an energetic and experienced man. We do not know what candidates were considered, but the final result is known. And we can guess why the choice fell on this particular senator and not any other.

The newly designated commander-in-chief was none other than Flavius Vespasian.

Of course, Vespasian had proven himself an effective general in Germany and Britain and possibly a capable administrator in Africa. However, there was no shortage of people with similar or even better qualifications in the Senate, so there had to have been other considerations. The decisive factor seems to have been that Vespasian did not belong to any of the great aristocratic families and was not aligned with any of them: he had no Senators among his ancestors. And all the conspiracies uncovered in recent years, both real and imagined, had all involved members of old and distinguished families. Nero and his advisers were understandably suspicious of people of that class. They certainly would not have entrusted a mighty army to any aristocrat—and to put down the uprising in Judea would require a large army comprised of several legions.

It is possible that Vespasian's candidacy was helped, somewhat paradoxically, by a small and amusing event, but one imbued with very special meaning in the eyes of Nero. It had recently been reported to the emperor that Vespasian showed little enthusiasm during the emperor's artistic performances; indeed, that he showed no interest in them at all. To speak the brutal truth—that they made him fall asleep. As soon as this matter was reported, the Senator found himself in disfavor. He was ordered to leave the imperial entourage and go to one of the small Greek towns for a while. It is easy to imagine the anxiety in which he lived there, deeply convinced that his career, and perhaps even his life, had already come to an end. When he sought help from one of the emperor's freedmen, he heard a formerly unimaginable answer:

"Get lost!"

Vespasian could only console himself with the fact that his fortune was rather small and that he was in debt, for in recent years, the emperor had tended to send only very rich people to the other world.

It is very likely that during the deliberations within the imperial entourage, someone recommended his candidacy half-jokingly and half-seriously, saying:

"Ah, Vespasian should be sent to war! He is a simpleton, he has no idea about art, he's only a pain and makes himself ridiculous. There, in the military camp, he will be at home. Let him go and fight and leave us here to delight in your art, Caesar!"

And someone else added:

"He's well over fifty, but he's still robust and healthy."

And yet someone else chimed in:

"He's just a simple peasant. Short, stocky, strong in arms and legs. Big square head and tiny eyes. He will do well."

And then someone else:

"And he certainly will feel lonely without his Caenis!"

And thus, the combination of many factors, both weighty and ridiculous, decided the future of both Rome and Jerusalem.

LEGIONS AND ROUTES

The newly appointed commander received the title of the imperial legate—*legatus Augusti*. Three legions were assigned to him. Luckily it was not necessary to bring them from distant provinces at the expense of some other army because all three were already in the East. They had been, until recently, part of a large corps operating in Armenia.

However, a few months ago, the corps had been dissolved, and the three legions were free to march to a new theater of operation.

Despite it being winter, a season unfavorable for travel, Vespasian left Greece at once. He took the overland route: from Greece via the Hellespont, then along the coast of Asia Minor to Syria. There, in the vicinity of Antioch, two legions were already awaiting him. At the same time, Titus—probably summoned all the way from Italy (because he probably had not accompanied the emperor on the Greek journey) boldly sailed straight across the stormy sea to Alexandria. There stood the third legion assigned to Palestinian duty, and Titus became its commander.

The legion was not part of the permanent garrison of Egypt: it had come to Alexandria only several months earlier. For dozens of years—up to AD 62—it had had its main camp in the town of Carnuntum on the Danube, a little east of today's Vienna. Its number was XV, and its nickname—*Apolinaris*. [46] In AD 62, it was sent to the eastern reaches of Asia Minor to be part of the Armenian campaign. When that campaign ended, the legion was moved to Alexandria, perhaps in connection with Nero's planned visit to Egypt, which in turn was to be but a prelude to a planned great voyage of discovery to the south, towards the legendary and still unknown sources of the Nile. The XVth Legion was supposed to form the backbone of the imperial army marching south.

Titus did his job perfectly. He reached Egypt quickly, took command, and made all preparations. Then he led the legion north along the coast in a series of forced marches. Already by the first months of the year 67, he stood at the appointed meeting point—in the coastal city of Ptolemais in Phoenicia, on the border of Palestine.

Vespasian brought his two legions there. One of them, V[th] Macedonian, had also once been part of the army of the Danube. It was stationed at the lower reaches of the great river in the province of Lower Moesia, in the city of Oescus, [47] in today's Bulgaria. It, too, like

---

[46] Or Apollo's: its symbol was an image of the god or of one of his animals.
[47] Northwest of the modern Bulgarian city of Pleven.

the XVth legion, marched to Armenia in AD 62; however, before it could return to its old quarters, it came under the command of Vespasian. Its commander, Sextus Vuttelenus Cerialis, came from Italy, from the land of the Sabines, that is, from Vespasian's homeland; it was a good reason to expect harmonious cooperation between the two men.

The third legion bore the number X in the traditional numbering and was called *Fretensis*.[48] Unlike the other two, it had served on the Euphrates since the time of Augustus and recently participated in the Armenian campaign. Its commander, Marcus Ulpius Trajanus, had been born in Spain. His ancestors, though wealthy and respectable, had not previously held any offices: he was the first to launch on the traditional path of a political career. The command of the Xth legion was an important step in that career. In later years, a consulship was to come, then the governorship of Syria, and finally, of Asia. His son, known to history as Trajan, would become emperor—the famous *optimus princeps*—the best ruler—and conquer Dacia, which is today's Romania.

When at the beginning of AD 67 in the city of Ptolemais, the four commanders held council together, who could have guessed that two future emperors—Vespasian and Titus—and the father of another were among them?

Vespasian's army included more than just the three legions. He also had twenty-three auxiliary cohorts under his command; ten of them had a thousand footmen each, and the others six hundred footmen and one hundred and twenty horsemen. Also, various allied kings and princes from the lands of the East sent considerable contingents of their own troops. King Agrippa himself sent two thousand foot archers and a thousand horse. And, what was more, the monarch personally took part in the expedition.

---

[48] "Of the Strait." Its symbols were a bull—the holy animal of the goddess Venus (mythical ancestor of the gens Julia), a ship (probably a reference to the battle of Actium), and a boar.

THE CASES OF PHILIP AND JUSTUS

Agrippa met Vespasian in Antioch. He then accompanied the Roman army on its march south to Ptolemais along the coast of Phoenicia. He displayed loyalty and eagerness to serve at every opportunity. But in the Phoenician city of Tyre—the city where *Ennoia*-Helen had once served in a brothel before Simon the Magus discovered her and saved her—an unpleasant adventure awaited him.

The Tyrians, evidently having some old scores to settle with the king, brought serious accusations against him. They tried to convince Vespasian that Agrippa was only pretending to be a friend of Rome, but in reality, as a Jew, wholeheartedly supported the rebels and secretly aided them, committing many cunning acts of betrayal. And the evidence? Yes, the Tyrians presented a fact. They claimed that the king's officer, Philip, had helped to murder the Roman soldiers in Jerusalem, for while defending Herod's palace alongside them, he secretly entered into an agreement with Menahem's men, unexpectedly capitulated and left the city, which, in consequence, led to the extermination of the Roman garrison.

The accusation rang reasonable. Thanks to information gathered from various sources, Vespasian already knew how the siege of Herod's palace had gone and under what circumstances the massacre of the Roman soldiers had taken place. He must have wondered why Philip's departure had surprised the Romans so much that they hadn't even had time to move their provisions to the three towers where they wanted to defend themselves further. In fact, everything happened so quickly that the insurgents entering the palace caught some of the Romans still in their former positions outside the towers. Had Philip not warned his comrades-in-arms that he was negotiating and was about to capitulate? That alone would amount to treason.

Vespasian, however, acted prudently and with great restraint. First of all, he sharply scolded the accusers of Agrippa. By what right did they dare to slander a man who bore the title of "A Friend of the

Roman People"? As such, the king was clearly beyond all suspicion! Vespasian made no further public mention of the case: he did not wish to compromise the reputation of a local ruler who mattered to him a lot. Privately, however, he advised Agrippa to send Philip to Rome to explain himself before the emperor and refute the accusation that he was responsible for the death of the Roman garrison.

And so, Philip left for Italy. Not at once, though: he took a long time to reach it—almost a year. He did not arrive in Rome until the spring of AD 68, and by then, Nero had more serious matters on his mind. And when soon thereafter, the emperor died by his own hand, Philip peacefully returned to Palestine. In the avalanche of momentous events, no one remembered to ask whether Philip had betrayed Romans in the palace of Herod: the matter seemed distant and immaterial. Clearly, Philip was an exceptionally lucky man. He kept getting into all sorts of scrapes, repeatedly stood at death's door, and escaped unscathed each and every time.

Bidding farewell to Tyre, Vespasian and Agrippa moved their army further south to Ptolemais. The inhabitants of this city, taught by the experience of the Tyrians, did not attempt to slander the king; but trouble awaited him here, too. Namely, a delegation of Greek cities from across the Jordan arrived and accused Justus of Tiberias, a man in Agrippa's retinue, of having raided their villages a few months earlier. Since Tiberias was part of Agrippa's kingdom, Vespasian decided that the king had jurisdiction in the matter. And the king would have put Justus to death had it not been for Berenice. Thanks to her intercession, Justus was only sentenced to prison, from which he was soon released. In advocating for Justus, Berenice showed a kind heart but also a good political sense: his guilt was not entirely obvious. The accusation was based only on the fact that a servant of Justus was killed in the raid across the Jordan. But did the servant participate in the raid on the orders of his master?

This mention of the queen's intercession in our sources indicates that Berenice accompanied her brother and the Roman army. And this

Roman lictors

means that she had been to Tyre, too—that Phoenician city where *Ennoia*-Helen had once lived in a brothel until Simon the Magus freed her.

Our old acquaintance, Clemens, son of Faustus, the hero of the Greek novel called *Homilies*, also visited Tyre at that time. He arrived there from Caesarea Maritima along with the twins, Aquila and Niketas. All three took up residence with a pious woman named Veronica—Veronica, that is: Berenice.

They learned from her that Simon the Magus, having been bested by Peter in the Caesarean dispute, had now moved to Tyre and performed miracles so wonderful there that many in the city worshipped him as divine. But when, on the following morning, they went looking for him, they learned that Simon had already departed for Sidon, leaving behind only a few of his disciples. Nevertheless, Clemens and the two brothers took advantage of Berenice's hospitality for several days, debating various doctrinal matters with the magician's disciples.

Who was this pious woman, named after a hot-tempered but pious Queen? Or maybe—maybe the two were one and the same?

In Ptolemais, Queen Berenice saw Titus for the first time. Briefly. The times were not conducive to long introductions. Time was pressing: there was war in Galilee.

JOSEPHUS: MY ADVENTURES IN GALILEE

After the defeat of Cestius, we called an assembly of the people in the Temple courtyard. We wanted to elect a group of elders who would henceforth direct all matters of war because, after what had happened, we all knew that there was no turning back. Why, many even dreamed of victory! What was significant, however, was this: during the elections, we managed to remove the current leadership of the Zealots. Even though the Zealots had gained a lot of respect on account of their recent victories, the authority of the priests and elders prevailed. Yes, having captured a lot of Roman weapons and money, the Zealots had a lot of influence, yet we managed to appoint to the highest offices in Jerusalem Joseph, son of Gorion, and the former high priest Ananus, son of Ananus, and other such men to all districts of the country. Galilee was entrusted to me—I was given two priests to assist me.

I went to Galilee immediately. By working hard, energetically, and systematically, I accomplished great things in a short time. I fortified many towns with walls and moats. I raised an army of many thousands—each city sent half its young men to me as soldiers and retained the other half to see to the harvest. We also had four-and-a-half thousand mercenaries in our pay, and I organized a bodyguard for myself of six hundred trusted men. There was no shortage of men, but we had problems with weapons and training. I gathered weapons from wherever I could find them, even old ones, and, in order to bring some discipline to my horde, I formed them into units led by officers with the titles of captains of tens, captain of hundreds, and captains of thousands. I had almost infinite infantry but only three hundred and fifty cavalry.

To give the Galileans a stake in the cause, I formed a council of seventy locals to assist me. I took them about with me as I traveled the country, sharing my responsibilities with them, especially adjudication of the more serious disputes (because petty disputes were handled in each locality by a team of seven judges, all appointed by me).

I was constantly on the move, rarely staying in the same house two nights in a row. I traveled all over Galilee. I tried to oversee everything personally, talk to everyone, exhort the slow to greater efforts, and temper the overzealous. But what difficulties and troubles I encountered—from my compatriots, subordinates, and co-workers! I was obliged to fight not the Romans nor King Agrippa but an enemy much more ruthless and deceitful—my own people! What intrigues were plotted against me, what slanders and abominations were cast upon me, what dangers I had to face! I could write whole volumes about it, and I still don't know if I could tell everything: memory, after all, is unreliable, and the situation changed by the hour. So, I will mention a few things at random just to show an example of what was happening then.

A scoundrel, cheater, and thief, John of Gischala—of course, I realized only too late what a faithless dog he was—asked me to let him collect the "quota grain" from the villages of upper Galilee—that is, grain which had originally been meant to go to the imperial warehouses, but as a result of the outbreak of the uprising, was collected but never shipped. He promised that he would sell the grain and use the money to reinforce the walls of Gischala.[49] Although I would have preferred to have the corn at my disposal, he insisted obstinately. It finally got to the point where he bribed both of my companion priests and got his way with their support.

Then he began to lament that our countrymen in the capital of King Agrippa, in Caesarea Philippi, had no Palestinian oil and had to anoint themselves with Greek, which is against the Law. I agreed to send Gischali oil there. But here, the price was four drachmas for two quarts! He made a huge pile of money on that shipment. Yes, he fortified the walls of Gischala, but above all, he hired four hundred thugs, mostly fugitives from Tyre. He sent them out into various towns and villages to raid and rob, and at the same time, complained to all and sundry that all this was my fault because I was unable to keep law and order and allowed robbery to thrive! He called for me to be relieved of office as soon as possible. Of course, he meant to take my place himself. He secretly sent denunciations against me to Jerusalem, saying that I was in league with the Romans and the King and that I was a traitor. He didn't even flinch from an assassination attempt. He stayed for some time—with my written consent!—at a cure in a hot spring near Tiberias. Taking advantage of the opportunity, he began to incite the local population. I hastened to Tiberias as soon as I realized what was going on. I called a rally of the people at the racecourse, which lay at the shore of the lake. I stood on a small hill. But no sooner had I opened my mouth to speak than some of those below drew their swords. I saved myself at the last moment, warned by

---

[49] Jish today.

a shout from one of my men. I risked a daring dash for the boats in the harbor. Miraculously, I escaped from my pursuers and sailed to Tarichaea.

And here's another thing. The inhabitants of Tiberias, led by Justus, took up arms against the Romans. But there was also a fanatical party of the poor, composed mainly of fishermen and rowers. They were led by Joshua, son of Sapphas, who soon became ruler of the whole city. His people burned the palace of King Agrippa in the city because it was decorated with images of animals, which is indeed contrary to the Law. But really, they just wanted to rob the place, for it was rich, and even the ceilings were gilded. They plundered most of the valuables, but I was able to gather a lot of them later and carefully guarded them to return them to their rightful owner in due course.

It also happened that the wife of Ptolemaios—he was a steward of the estates of Agrippa and Berenice—was traveling through the valley between Galilee and Samaria towards the coastal cities where the Roman garrisons stood. She had many beasts of burden, and only a few drivers for protection. So, a gang of young bandits came from a village at the foot of Mount Tabor and drove off these muleteers. The woman fled, and the robbers drove her mules, laden with sacks and chests, to Tarichaea, where I was then staying. We discovered the cargo—expensive outfits, silver dishes, and several hundred pieces of heavy gold coin. I rebuked the young men for committing robbery, for I did not want to mess with Agrippa and Berenice, especially since Ptolemaios was known to me personally.

However, I told them that since this had already happened, I would seize the booty and sell it, and I would send the money back to Jerusalem to contribute to the reinforcement of its walls. Thus, it turned out that the rogues had miscalculated badly: they had hoped to get at least part of the booty for their trouble and were left empty-handed! They did not dare to oppose me directly, but that same night they went about the neighboring villages, spreading the word that I favored the King and the Romans and that I hid their loot to return it to Ptolemaios! They demanded that I be punished immediately. In the morning, a huge crowd flocked to Tarichaea. They were led by Joshua, son of Sapphas. I was still sleeping peacefully in my house—there were only a few people with me—when they rushed the house, brandishing torches to burn me alive. But I slipped away and took a detour to the stadium where the people had gathered. I wore a black penitential robe, and I tore it at the breast, sprinkled ashes on my head, and tied my sword around my neck. Thus, I stood before them as a mourner and penitent, defenseless, subjecting myself to their judgment. Shouts soon arose: "Where is the loot? To whom did you give it?"

And I would have perished right there miserably if I had not immediately sworn a solemn promise that I would build a good wall around Tiberias and Tarichaea and a few other towns with my own money. This calmed the crowd. The people began to disperse slowly, and I returned to my home. But no sooner had I breathed a sigh of relief than my guard reported that a band of armed men with torches was approaching, shouting menacingly. I had only a handful of soldiers with me, so it was necessary to save myself by guile. I immediately went on the roof and shouted from there that I would give them the loot, but they must choose a few men from amongst themselves and send them in to collect it. Soon, a delegation was at the door. But as soon as they entered, we jumped on them, pushed them into the basement, flogged them with bull whips, and as for the ringleader, who put up the biggest fight, we cut off his hand.

They went out half-naked, smeared with blood, barely able to stand; the chief walked in front, and his severed hand hung at his breast, for we had tied it around his neck with a rope. Such treasure he got for his trouble! The others, seeing this mournful procession, stood in sepulchral silence. Then, they melted away.

Such and similar were my deeds and adventures in the winter and spring of AD 67. Then, the news came that the Roman general Vespasian was already marching toward us from Antioch. A blind man could guess that he would attack Galilee first.

PLACIDUS IN GALILEE

Fighting in Galilee had begun even before Titus arrived at Ptolemais. Vespasian sent in six thousand foot and a thousand horse under the command of Placidus, a tribune, because emissaries of the city of Sepphoris, the largest city in the province located in its very heart, had asked for a Roman garrison. During the preceding year's campaign of Cestius Gallus, Sepphoris had favored the Romans; after his defeat, it pursued a very ambiguous policy towards the insurgents and their leader in Galilee, Josephus. It now requested Roman military aid out of fear of revenge by its countrymen. Vespasian readily granted the request. He understood that with Sepphoris in his hand, he could easily take control of all of Galilee, a fertile, rich, and populous province. It contained two hundred and forty villages and towns.

Placidus' men arrived on the great plain before the city. The infantry entered Sepphoris while the cavalry set up camp outside and immediately began to lay waste the surrounding countryside, plundering what they could and mopping up insurgents. To put an end to this, Josephus attempted an attack on the city. He had recently contributed to the reinforcement of its defenses—how he rued it now!—but now the inhabitants did not even want to hear about joining the insurgents; they knew very well what would await them if they declared against Rome. Josephus's attack failed, and the only result was that the Romans felt more confident and became even more daring. Day and night, they ravaged settlements and fields, robbed civilians, killed men of military age, and drove the rest of the population into slavery. Peasants fled the land and took refuge in fortified places.

Placidus assumed that once he took the strongest of these forts, the others would capitulate, and the war in Galilee would soon end; and once that province fell, all the provinces affected by the uprising would also submit. Now, among these fortified places in Galilee, the most worthy target was Jotapata,[50] a city located slightly

---

[50] Today's Yodfat.

north of Sepphoris, right next to Cana of Galilee. Placidus tried to take it by a surprise attack, but the inhabitants of Jotapata had been expecting him. They sortied from the city and attacked the Roman marching column. Surprised in the field, the legionaries retreated, but in good order and in close formation, losing only seven dead. The insurgents showered them with projectiles from a distance and did not dare join in a melee, knowing full well that their swords would never penetrate Roman armor. Three men died on their side.

And thus, the whole thing ended in a minor skirmish. But the report of the setback prompted Vespasian to enter Galilee at the head of a larger force. He reasoned that though the fighting in Galilee had been going on for quite some time, Placidus had failed to pacify the country. And now, his newest setback, though it was in itself insignificant, could well serve to embolden the insurgents, especially if the accounts of it—passed from mouth to mouth—grew into a terrible defeat of the Romans. A decisive action by a large Roman contingent might prevent that. And now that Titus and his legion stood in Ptolemais, the whole Roman army was ready for major action.

The people of Galilee, and especially Josephus's spies, watched the march of the Roman column with horror and awe.

ROMANS ON THE MARCH AND IN CAMP

The advancing column was led by light infantry and archers of the local auxiliaries. Their job was to detect possible ambushes and screen the main force from minor attacks. This advance guard was followed by a detachment of heavily armed Romans, foot and horse. It was very numerous, for each of the sixty centuries[51] into which each legion was divided contributed ten men to it. They were heavily laden, for, in addition to their own armor and equipment, they carried tools

---

[51] A century (*centuria*) was a unit of a hundred men, led by a *centurion*.

necessary for the setting up of camp. This unit also included road builders; they straightened sections that were too winding, leveled steep slopes, and cleared vegetation. This brigade, which we should perhaps call "engineers," was followed by the baggage train, carrying the personal luggage of Vespasian and his officers and guarded by a cavalry escort. Then came the commander-in-chief, with selected infantry and cavalry, and right behind him, the cavalry of the three legions, in three squadrons, one hundred and twenty men each. Then came the beasts of burden laden with disassembled war machines and siege towers. Then, the commanders of the legions—tribunes and centurions of various ranks, surrounded by more soldiers, and later the standard-bearers of the legions with the imperial eagles and battle emblems, and the trumpeters. Then, the main legionary column marched in tight ranks: six men abreast. Their centurions walked beside them, keeping good order.

Josephus, who had seen Roman legions on the march many times, always felt pity for the common foot soldiers; he used to say they looked like pack mules. And indeed, each legionnaire carried a lot of gear. He wore a cuirass, a helmet, and a long shield; a long sword strapped on his right and a short sword on his left—a kind of dagger. In his hand, each legionary held a *pilum*, a kind of javelin with a long blade of soft iron. He also carried tools: a saw, a basket, a spade, an axe, thongs, a sickle, a chain, and finally, provisions for three days. The elite soldiers whose job was to guard the headquarters differed from ordinary privates in that they had round shields instead of long shields and long spears instead of the *pilae*. The riders also carried a longsword strapped on the right, a spear in their hand, and three long, flat-bladed projectiles in their quivers. They hung their shields at the horse's side.

The main legionary column was followed by servants, driving mules, and other beasts of burden laden with baggage. The rest of the auxiliary troops followed behind. The whole procession was closed by the rear guard, composed of light infantry, legionaries, and horsemen.

And what a show of efficiency, discipline, and order they made when they set up camp! First, a site was selected on open ground. Then, the engineers marked out the outline of the quadrangle and leveled the ground within it. Then, they proceeded to erect ramparts and towers and to dig a moat, leaving only four access routes for the four gates. At the same time, other groups set up tents along the marked-out streets, dividing the entire surface of the quadrangle into equal blocks. In the center, a square was left open, where they raised the command building—the *praetorium*. Each legion, each cohort, and each *centuria* set up camp in an area assigned to it. In prescribed order, individual units attended to the economic activities assigned to them on a given day, such as collecting firewood, drawing and carrying water, or preparing fodder and food.

Trumpet signals regulated the life of the camp. They marked the time for supper, for going to bed, for starting the day, for the morning roll call and meals. When leaving the camp, the first signal marked the command to fold the tents; the second, their loading onto pack animals and the setting on fire of those buildings that were not dismantled and taken along; and the third—the departure. The column, adhering to a predetermined order, lined up and moved off quickly, efficiently, and orderly. Everyone knew his place and his duty—on the march, in camp, and in battle.

JOSEPHUS: I RETREAT TO TIBERIAS

When Vespasian entered Galilee, I stood with my people in the town of Garis, a little east of Sepphoris. As soon as my brave warriors realized that the war had finally begun and that the Roman commander-in-chief himself was coming against us with all his army, they immediately scattered in all directions. They fled before they clapped an eye on a single legionary, and only a handful of the faithful remained with me. There was no way for me to block the advance of the enemy with their small number. And, in any case, the talk of capitulation was everywhere throughout Galilee; the only topic of conversation was whether the Romans may be persuaded to grant merciful terms.

Thus, remaining at my advance post made no sense. I gathered my people and moved further east to the city of Tiberias on the shores of the Sea of Galilee.

Meanwhile, Vespasian took the town of Arraba,[52] north of Sepphoris. He took it without a fight, for all its defenders had fled before him. Nevertheless, Vespasian ordered all able-bodied men to be slaughtered anyway; his soldiers carried out this order with great zeal, mercilessly murdering everyone, from little boys to old men. In this way, they took revenge for the defeat of Cestius. They burned Arraba and set all the neighboring villages on fire. The villagers had mostly fled earlier, but any who remained were now taken into slavery.

My arrival in Tiberias caused major panic. For who can hope that the war will end in victory when the district commander himself withdraws? And I must admit that the people guessed my innermost thoughts correctly. I had been convinced from the beginning that the whole war was a tragic mistake and that the only chance of salvation lay in surrendering to the enemy. I personally had some grounds to believe that the Romans might treat me leniently. But I would rather die many times over than betray my homeland and cover with disgrace the office entrusted to me.

So, I sent a letter to Jerusalem. In it, I presented the situation in Galilee as faithfully as possible. I carefully weighed every word of the report. I did not wish to give the impression that I was exaggerating the enemy's strength; for then I would be called a coward. Nor, on the other hand, did I want to minimize the horror of the situation because then I would weaken the arguments of the peace party. I ended my letter by saying:

"If you wish to negotiate, let me know as soon as possible. If, on the other hand, you are determined to continue the war, send me adequate reinforcements!"

I sent messengers with this letter to Jerusalem and immediately afterward received word that Vespasian was on his way to Jotapata. I did not wait for a response from the capital: I decided that my duty as a commander required me to be present at the battle which would

---

[52] Modern 'Arrabat al-Battuf.

150

decide the future of Galilee.

ROMANS UNDER THE WALLS OF JOTAPATA

I arrived in Jotapata on the 21st of Iyar (end of May). The Romans were not yet there, but their engineers, shielded by cavalry, had been preparing the road for four days, for the road led over the mountains and was so rough that pedestrians had difficulty crossing it, and horses could not cross it at all. My arrival encouraged the inhabitants of Joatapata—until my arrival, they had been terrified of the impending attack. It is only natural that they became emboldened with their commander at their side.

Almost immediately after my arrival, we saw the first Romans from the city walls. This was only the vanguard of the great army: a thousand cavalry under the command—as I soon learned—of the tribune Placidus and the *decurion*[53] Ebutius. It was the same Ebutius I had dealt with a few months before. At the head of one hundred horsemen and two hundred foot soldiers, he had roamed then the great plain of Esdraelon[54] between Galilee and Samaria. I engaged him at the head of about two thousand foot. (I had no cavalry at all). Ebutius lost three killed and hastily retreated to the west, to Gaba, a place near Ptolemais. I followed him. I stopped some 20 *stadii*[55] from Gaba in the town of Besara. There were granaries there with grain brought from the estate of Queen Berenice. Under cover of my outposts, I loaded the grain on camels and donkeys and carried it off to Galilee. But Ebutius followed and harried me. That was my first encounter with the man.

Now, below the walls of Jotapata, the men of the advance Roman guard immediately surrounded our stronghold so that no one could get in or out. The task was not difficult because Jotapata stands

---

[53] Commander of a squadron of cavalry.
[54] Today, Jezreel Valley, also known as the Valley of Megiddo.
[55] About 3 km.

on a rocky elevation that extends southwards from a much higher mountain massif. The hill has very steep slopes, almost vertical; you get dizzy merely looking down from the walls. Only from the north— that is where the hill connects with the main massif, is the access tolerable, and, at one point, it becomes easy because there, the road begins to slope downward towards the city wall. Of course, it was this section of the wall that I fortified particularly carefully. Mountains surround Jotapata on all sides so that the city can only be seen when you are near it.

I was convinced then—and remain so even now—that the news of my impending arrival at Jotapata prompted the Roman attack. The report was taken to their camp by a defector, and Vespasian rejoiced to hear it. He saw in it an act of providence: here was the man widely considered the brightest among the enemy now voluntarily falling into his hands.

The day after the arrival of Placidus, the whole Roman army reached the base of the Jotapata hill. The long column had taken the whole day to negotiate the mountain pass. The Romans then struck camp north of the city, on the ridge of our mountain, only seven *stadii* [56] from our walls. Their power, efficiency, and order were displayed for us like on the palm of our hand. They camped deliberately so close in order to strike fear into us. And indeed, no one wanted to go outside the walls. Some of us had to camp outside, for the city itself was incredibly crowded, but they camped very close so as to take refuge behind the city gates when the attack came.

That day, Vespasian did not begin operations, for the hour was late, and his soldiers were weary. However, he set up two rings of infantry outposts around the city and another ring of cavalry beyond them.

---

[56] About 1 km.

JOSEPHUS: THE OPENING DAYS OF THE SIEGE

In the days that followed, some fighting took place before our walls, that is, on the slope rising from our city northward towards the Roman camp. As the Romans approached, we made sorties. In each of these clashes, both sides lost a dozen or so dead. It was only after five days of such skirmishes that Vespasian, having studied the ground and surveyed our forces, understood that he must proceed with a real siege.

The Romans set about constructing a great earthworks ramp, by which they intended to reach the top of our wall. They built it from tree trunks hewn in the forest, boulders, and piled-up earth. To protect their workers from our missiles, they set up tall screens of pleated wicker stretched between wooden posts driven into the ground. At the same time, one hundred and sixty of their catapults and ballistae began to hurl missiles at us: heavy stones, flaming faggots, whole clouds of arrows. Not only was it dangerous to show up on the walls, but even in the streets where the missiles rained; all the more so that, apart from machines, their archers, lancers, and slingers kept up an uninterrupted barrage of projectiles. We tried sorties. Breaking out unexpectedly, we circumvented the wickerworks, set them on fire, attacked men employed at construction, and tried to demolish the ramp. Vespasian, however, soon came up with an idea of how to deal with us: he ordered his men to combine all the wicker screens into one unbroken line—and this, we were never able to penetrate.

Since the Roman ramp was going to reach the height of our walls soon, we had to raise our wall. To protect our masons, we had to imitate the Roman idea: we drove stakes into the wall and stretched ox hides between them. This screen deflected smaller projectiles and reduced the momentum of the larger ones, and unlike the Roman wicker, it was fireproof. In a day and a night of uninterrupted work, we raised the wall some forty feet and further reinforced it with turrets and battlements. We felt more confident now and resumed our sorties. But, the Romans soon abandoned the thought of an assault and gave up further engineering work. They decided to starve us.

Jotapata was well stocked with everything except salt and water. The city had neither well nor spring. During the winter rains, rainwater was collected in rock cisterns and then gradually used throughout the summer. Usually, that was enough until the next rain season; but now there were many outsiders inside the walls, apart from the permanent residents, and water had to be rationed. The introduction of rationing and the fear that water might run out made everyone try to take more than he needed and hide it. Worse still, the Romans had a good view of the city from their ramparts, and they began to shoot at the place where our people gathered with vessels to collect their rations of water. I had to find a way to convince the Romans that the city had enough water. Therefore, I ordered a lot of rags to be soaked in water and hung on the walls in such a way that the water would run down the walls in streams. The Romans were deceived; apparently, they concluded that we had a spring in the city. They reverted to their original plan to take Jotapata by force.

About this time, the Romans made a small but—for us— painful advance. They discovered a crevice in the western wall, which we used to send and receive scouts at night to bring food and take letters. (To be safe, I had made them put on shaggy skins and crawl on their fours to look from far away like dogs). Now here, too, the Romans placed their guards.

JOSEPHUS: I REMAIN IN JOTAPATA

There was no doubt that the city would fall, and that—soon. If I stayed in it, I would needlessly die along with everyone else. So, I began to consult with the other leaders on how to escape from Jotapata, but the locals soon found out about it. They caught up with me, surrounded me, and began to beg me that I do not leave them. They cried out that I was their only hope of salvation because, in my presence, everyone fought more bravely; and if they were to be taken captive, I would protect them. Some also said that it was shameful to run from the enemy and abandon one's friends; that I wanted to abandon a sinking ship; that my departure would hasten the ultimate catastrophe for all.

For my part, I tried to convince them that I wanted to leave the city not for my own safety but for their own good. I said:

"If I stay within the walls, there's little I can do to save you, and if the city falls, I'll die uselessly. But as soon as I manage to break out of here, I will be able to help you from the outside. I will gather men across all Galilee as quickly as possible and draw the Romans away from you, attacking them from all sides. How can I do this while I'm sitting here with you? On the contrary, my presence motivates the enemy to storm the walls all the harder. It's obvious the Romans want to lay their hands on me. As soon as they know that I have escaped, their attacks will surely diminish."

However, my words did not convince the crowd. Old people, children, women with babies in their arms fell on their knees before me. By weeping and wailing and embracing my legs, they begged me to share their misfortune with them. I think they did not actually envy me for my possible escape as much as they believed that my presence would be of some help to them.

I understood that if I gave in to them, their pleas would remain just that: pleas; but if I insisted and held my own, they would surround me with a strong guard and stop me by force. Besides, I must admit, my resolve to leave the city was really shaken by my pity for the despairing crowd. So, I shouted desperately:

"Well then, let's fight here and die, for there is no hope for us! At least we will earn glory!"

JOSEPHUS: THE RAM'S HEAD

On the same day, I made a raid on the Roman positions at the head of my men. We managed to scatter their guards and break into their camp, where we destroyed some tents closest to the rampart; we also set fire to some buildings. I repeated such forays continuously during the days and nights that followed. They succeeded because it was difficult for the heavily armed legionaries to catch us at night. Vespasian finally took them out of the fight altogether, and he countered our sorties with archers and slingers. And all this time, he kept up an endless barrage from his machines. These caused great losses among us, but as soon as we managed to cross the line of fire, we inflicted painful blows on our opponents in hand-to-hand combat.

Meanwhile, the Roman ramp was creeping closer to our wall. Vespasian, irritated with the length of the siege and our exploits, decided it was time to break down the walls with a battering ram. A "ram" is what they call this device. It is a long, thick wooden beam, tipped at one end with a block of iron in the shape of a ram's head. It swings back and forth on ropes hung from transverse beams. A group of strong men pulls the beam back with all their strength and lets it swing forward; and there is no wall so strong that it can withstand the repeat blows of that head.

The Romans pushed their machines closer, and the archers and slingers came closer, too. And now, amid the constant hail of projectiles, it was impossible to stand on the wall. Under this covering fire, the Romans pulled up the ram. To protect the men operating it, they surrounded it with a wicker fence on all sides and stretched animal hides on top. Already at the first blow, the wall, so recently built, visibly trembled, and at the same time, a cry of despair escaped our lips. It was obvious that the battering ram, hitting the same place time and time again, would soon break through. To protect the wall, I came up with this idea:

We used ropes to lower sacks filled with chaff to where the ram's head was striking. This caused a lot of trouble for the Romans at first because they had to constantly change the direction of their blows, for if they hit the sacks, their blows lost most of their momentum. Soon, however, they found a way to deal with the problem: they attached sickles to long poles and used them to cut the ropes holding up our sacks of chaff. The battering ram started pounding again, and the wall began to crumble.

Gathering what fuel we could—dry wood, asphalt, tar, and sulfur, we rushed out of the gates. We threw flaming faggots and torches at the Roman machines and started a fire in the blink of an eye. It burnt so hot that the enemy was helpless to put it out.

Three times we sortied like that.

It was then that Eleazar, son of Shamai, performed a heroic deed. He grabbed a huge boulder and hurled it against the ram's head with such force that its iron fittings broke off. At once, he jumped down from the wall into the midst of his stunned enemies, picked up the ferrule, and scampered back up the wall. He was almost naked and completely exposed. Five arrows pierced his torso before he stood on the wall, but he didn't seem to feel the pain. When he stood among us, we welcomed him with a shout of joy. But just at that moment, Eleazar fell, writhing in terrible torment. He soon gave up the ghost, but he never let his prize out of his hands.

And again, we made a sortie against the positions of the Xth Legion. We broke the first ranks of well-armed enemies thanks to the extraordinary courage of two brothers, Neteiras and Philip. We followed them in a swarm into the breach of the iron-clad lines, brandishing flaming torches. We succeeded in setting fire to the machines, screens, and grain storage of both the Xth legion and the neighboring Vth.

But all our efforts, ingenuity, blood, and heroism were in vain. The most dangerous weapon of the Romans was their command of resources; how were we to oppose it? By the evening of that day, a new battering ram was back in the old place and rhythmically pounding its head where the wall was already crumbling.

JOSEPHUS: VESPASIAN WOUNDED, AND THE NIGHT ATTACK

It was at this moment, already at dusk, that one of our archers shot a well-aimed arrow and struck Vespasian in the foot. The wound, as we later learned, was superficial, for, due to the distance, the projectile had lost most of its impetus. But even so, this accident caused incredible confusion among the Romans. Their commander-in-chief was bleeding!

As is usual in such situations, the news passed from mouth to mouth, morphed and grew, and took on the colors of horror. Crowds of soldiers began to run towards the wounded man. Titus was one of the first to reach him. Not yet knowing the situation, he rushed to his father's side with such obvious horror on his face that the mere sight of his pallor caused fear among the cohorts. Soon, however, Vespasian reassured his son and the soldiers. Although the pain in his foot was clearly bothering him, he traveled among the troops, showing up everywhere and to everyone. Order was soon restored. The troops again took their positions dutifully, and the legionaries attacked our walls with all the more ferocity to avenge the blood of their commander. The incident was minor, but to us, watching everything from above—it gave a brief moment of relief.

Night fell. The Roman machines had been constantly hammering us with all sorts of projectiles that flew through the air with a shrill whistle and fell to the ground with a tremendous thud. Their impact was enormous. I will give only two examples:

One missile tore off the head of a fighter standing on the wall and threw it deep into the city. Another fell upon a pregnant woman as she left her house at dawn, stabbed her in the belly, and tore out the fetus: it was found later a dozen steps from the mother's body.

The whole city was full of banging, screaming, crying, and wailing of women and children. The wounded and dying cried out desperately for help. And all these voices echoed loud and terrible from the mountain cliffs surrounding Jotapata.

Despite these horrors, our men bravely defended the wall. We hit the Romans with everything we could. They, however, hidden behind their screen and under their leather roof, safely and uninterruptedly pounded the battering ram against the weakening wall.

We threw flaming firebrands at their screens, but in doing so, we hurt ourselves more; for we illuminated ourselves as if in broad daylight and made ourselves excellent targets for the Roman machines shooting at us out of the dark. Very many of our people died or were seriously wounded that night. So many corpses lay under the wall, that it seemed almost as if one only had to step on the piles of the dead to reach the top of the wall and enter the city. But many more of our enemies were yet to fall before this happened.

It was already dawn when a breach opened in the wall. Our men tried to block it with their bodies and weapons while the rest built a replacement wall behind them in feverish haste. The Romans did not manage to break through. And soon afterward, at daybreak, Vespasian gave the order to retreat. He decided that his men had to rest for a while before the final assault.

THE 20th OF SIVAN[57]

And yet, the defenders managed to repel the all-day attack of the following day. It seemed like a miracle and probably surprised even Josephus himself. Of course, he, the commander of the besieged city, attributed his success to the bravery of his men and to his own ingenuity; to the man who advised him to pour buckets of hot oil on the closed ranks of the legionaries climbing the wall and to splash the platforms (which the Romans lowered from siege towers so that their men could step onto the city wall) with a decoction of an herb called "Greek hay"—which made the boards so slippery that the soldiers were unable to cross them. All this sounds very impressive, as does his praise for the bravery of those who fought desperately to save their women and children while the women and children screamed so shrilly that Josephus had to order them locked up in their houses.

And yet, the same Josephus reports that during the whole day, only six defenders were killed while more than three hundred were injured. Roman losses were certainly not much greater. This suggests

---

[57] 10th month of the Jewish calendar.

that the attack was not a general assault and was not carried out too energetically. The Romans seem to have struck with only a part of their forces and only as a test. And it couldn't have been otherwise: remember that Jotapata's location at the tip of a steep crest gave the besiegers access only from one side and only over a relatively narrow front. When they learned that the wall, though partly breached, still held up and the defenders fought on bravely, the Romans ultimately retreated. Vespasian wished to avoid unnecessary casualties and to save his men for the final battle within the coming days. But Josephus, with his usual panache, was inclined to overstate the successes of his leadership. In his description, he transformed these clashes into Homeric battles.

That assault took place on the 20th of Sivan, that is, at the end of June or the beginning of July. The following day and for the next few days, the Romans did not approach the walls. They used a different method. They built a much higher ramp and set on it three high towers, wooden but iron-clad, so that they would not catch fire. On these towers, hidden behind their crenellations, stood their best archers, slingers, javelin-throwers, and even light war machines. They hit the defenders of the city accurately and without stopping, not even allowing them to man the wall. Josephus's men were still trying to make sorties, but they were increasingly weaker and less and less effective, and for each sortie, they paid with ever more losses.

THE FIRST VICTORY OF TITUS

There was another reason why Vespasian did not renew his assault on Jotapata: he had sent two large units of his army to take control of two other towns.

The first unit was led by Trajanus. With a thousand horse and two thousand foot, he marched on the city of Japha,[58] in southern

---

[58] Yafa an-Naseriyye

Galilee, near Nazareth. It was very populous and fortified with a double wall, and there was some concern that its defenders might try to harass the Romans, encouraged by the long resistance of Jotapata. The siege of Japha would certainly not be easy; fortunately for Trajanus, however, its inhabitants, confident in their numerical superiority, came out of the city to fight him in the open field. The Romans drove them off with a single charge and, in hot pursuit, broke through the first wall. The defeated Jews tried to take refuge in the city behind the second wall but found the gates closed. All their screams and begging were in vain. Their compatriots, sitting safely inside, trembled with fear that as soon as they opened the gates, the Romans would rush in along with their defeated compatriots. So all the Jews darting between the first and second walls were massacred by the legionaries, some choosing to kill themselves by their own hand to deny the enemy the satisfaction.

It was now obvious that the capture of Japha, which had just lost so many of its bravest defenders, was inevitable. However, Trajanus chose loyalty to his commander over expediency; informing Vespasian of the situation, he asked him to send his son to Japha to share in the victory. And indeed, Titus soon arrived. He led five hundred horse and a thousand foot.

As expected, things at Japha turned out differently from Jotapata. The Romans did not have to conduct extensive siege works, bang the walls with a battering ram, erect ramps, or pelt the city with projectiles. Their soldiers approached the walls from all sides; they drew up ladders, gained the parapets, and soon broke into the city. On the other hand, they had to fight a hard, protracted battle in the city itself, a door-to-door fight in its narrow streets. The inhabitants put up a desperate resistance. Even the women took part in the fight, throwing whatever they could from the rooftops at the Roman ranks.

But then everything ended as usual. All men were exterminated, women and children were sold into slavery. It was the 25th of Sivan: the day of Titus's first military victory.

At the same time, Cerealis, commander of the Vth Legion, marched into Samaria and towards the holy Mount Gerizim.[59] He brought with him six hundred horse and three thousand foot. The reason for the expedition was the strange news that crowds of armed Samaritans had gathered there, expecting some miracle. The Samaritans camped at the mountaintop and behaved peacefully, and Cerealis contented himself with encircling the mountain with a cordon of his soldiers. The summit of Mount Gerizim was naked, and exposed, and the thousands camped upon it had not provided themselves with food or even water. Some, exposed all day to the scorching rays of the sun, died of exhaustion; others walked down and gave themselves up to the Romans. Only after the Samaritan forces had greatly diminished did the Roman commander lead his men higher. He surrounded those still at the top and called upon them to lay down their weapons. They refused. Everyone was killed.

It was the 27th of Sivan.

But those who killed them must have marveled at the madness of their victims. What mysterious force could have made all these people from different parts of Samaria assemble here? What were they looking for? What did they expect?

THE MYSTERY OF MOUNT GERIZIM

Pontius Pilate might have explained this to Cerealis—if he were still alive. Thirty-two years earlier, when he ruled Judea as its prefect (for he had the title of prefect, not of procurator), he had had to deal with a similar event in Samaria, also connected with Mount Gerizim. Pontius Pilate surely remembered it well, for it led to his dismissal from office.

It happened in AD 35, during the reign of Tiberius. A mysterious prophet appeared in Samaria. He claimed to know a certain

---

[59] Mount Gerizim is one of two mountains in the immediate vicinity of the Palestinian city of Nablus and biblical city of Shechem.

place on Mount Gerizim, where Moses, the prophet of the Jews, had hidden the most sacred utensils of the Jewish cult. The new prophet promised to reveal the site and the sacred objects to those who would follow him. According to an ancient Samaritan tradition, the discovery of these vessels was supposed to herald the coming of the age of glory and joy for the whole Jewish nation. The word spread throughout the country, and soon hundreds of credulous people began to come from all directions to the village of Tiratana; for there, at the foot of Gerizim, a meeting point had been appointed before the planned ascent of the holy mountain. Many who arrived carried weapons, perhaps to fight evil spirits that might interfere with the recovery of the sacred utensils; or to form the army of the new heavenly kingdom in which they expected to be noblemen. You see, messianic hopes were familiar to the Samaritans, also.

And who was this prophet? A madman? A charlatan? Or maybe a Roman agent-provocateur? Whatever the case, Pontius Pilate was soon told about the scheme. He sent one of his officers to Mount Gerizim, with cavalry and infantry. They attacked the faithful assembled at Tiratana. Many Samaritans fell in battle, and many were captured while trying to flee. On Pilates' orders, prominent captives were executed. They were almost certainly crucified.

This ruthless suppression of the movement—which perhaps had not been terribly dangerous—certainly not yet—caused a sharp protest of the Samaritan Sanhedrin. [60] The council wrote to the governor of Syria, Lucius Vitellius (Judea, being a small territory, was not a separate province, and its prefect was under the supervision of the Syrian viceroy). Vitellius reacted sharply: he sent Pilate to Rome to report to the emperor. Fortunately for Pilate, Tiberius died before he arrived in Italy, and the new ruler, Caligula, had more serious problems before him than unraveling the mysteries of Mount Gerizim.

---

[60] Josephus describes a *synhedrion* for the first time in connection with the decree of the Roman governor of Syria, **Aulus Gabinius** (57 BC), who abolished the then existing form of government of Palestine and divided the country into five provinces, at the head of each of which a *synhedrion* was placed; Jerusalem was the seat of one of these.

And now, more than thirty years later—a whole generation later—the tragedy repeated itself. Was a false prophet to blame in this case as well? But now, there was no higher authority to appeal to. Vespasian, in possession of war powers, was the master of life and death throughout Palestine.

THE ARCANA OF POWER

Vespasian himself was of this opinion, at any rate: he would resolutely refuse any outsider interfering with his army and his war in Palestine. But was his view shared by the then-governor of Syria? For he, too, was a very daring and ambitious man: Gaius Licinius Mucianus.

Cestius Gallus, the commander of the ill-fated expedition against Jerusalem in the fall of AD 66, died soon after his defeat in the Beth-Horon Gorge. His contemporaries were not sure whether this death coincided with his defeat by chance or was the result of a mental breakdown as its consequence. A few months later, in the spring of AD 67, soon after Vespasian had been sent to Palestine, the emperor appointed Gallus' successor. The successor was the current fellow, Mucianus, a senator and former consul.

And thus, both dignitaries—the governor of Syria and the supreme commander in Judea—were of equal social status and had previously held similar high offices. Both bore the same title—that of a legate. But did Vespasian's title mean that Judea, hitherto subordinated to Syria, had now been elevated to an equal status with it? Mucianus certainly did not think so. He believed that both by tradition and various administrative rules, Judea remained part of the province of Syria, and this would mean that he, the legate of Syria, had supreme authority over all officials and commanders operating in Palestine, regardless of their rank.

Vespasian categorically opposed these claims. In his opinion, upon receiving his military commission and the command of his three legions, he became governor of a separate province and was, therefore, not inferior in rank and authority to the governor of Syria and, as an imperial legate, was subject only to the emperor. In fact, it seems that Nero and his advisers had deliberately left the matter of Judea's administrative status unclear. Their goal was precisely that the two governors of adjacent provinces, each commanding a considerable military force, should have grounds for disagreement.

It seems almost certain that, when the two men were appointed, their mutual dislike and different character were dully noted, and this allowed the administration to feel confident that they would not come to an understanding and support each other's ambitious designs. This pretty simple mechanism, employed whenever new appointments were made, was among the widely recognized *arcana imperii*, "the secrets of power," which is to say, unspoken administrative principles of the empire. Basically, it was all about playing off ordinary human ambitions, weaknesses, and animosities.

That Vespasian and Licinius Mucianus differed in many respects is clearly attested by Tacitus. The great historian was still a young man when the two reached the peak of their fame. He doesn't seem to have known either personally, but he did see them both beyond any doubt. And he had access to an unfathomable abundance of archival documents, memoirs, and oral accounts, often from well-connected men in high positions.

Tacitus painted the portraits of the two men with evident relish. It is rare to find such extensive descriptions in his books. The master is more inclined to present his heroes with short, concise sketches, no more than asides, and even more often by simply presenting their deeds. In these two cases, however, it is hard for the reader to resist the impression that when describing their characters, Tacitus reveled in the contrast of their personalities and lifestyles. Here are some phrases from Books I and II of *The Annals*:

> Mucianus gained fame both on account of his successes and his misfortunes. When he was young, he very zealously sought the friendship of eminent people. However, he lost much of his fortune, and his position

became shaky. He also suspected that he had somehow brought upon himself the displeasure of Claudius. He then holed himself up in the distant lands of Asia, and his stay there was not much different from exile.

In his personality, the love of splendor cohabited with diligence, consideration with arrogance, bad traits with good. When time allowed it, he over-indulged in pleasures, but when it was worth it to do so, he was capable of showing great qualities. Thanks to various skillful tricks, he exerted a huge influence on his subordinates, his relatives, and his colleagues.

Vespasian was an excellent soldier. He personally led his columns. He selected the site of each day's camp. Day and night, he fought the enemy with all his skill and even with his own arms if it proved necessary. He ate whatever came to hand and was scarcely different in dress and appearance from a common legionary. Were it not for greed, he would be little different from the Roman commanders of old.

Mucianus, on the other hand, constantly sought to impress others with his wonderful generosity, wealth, and the fact that he exceeded the measure of a private man in every respect. He was more skillful of the two in conversation and more experienced in planning and directing policy."[61]

Apart from what Tacitus says, little is known about Mucianus's life before he became the governor of Syria. Even his lineage is unknown. Of course, he must have been wealthy since he achieved the highest offices of the state. It is also impossible to say what caused the young senator to incur the displeasure of emperor Claudius. But we do know that better times came for him when Nero came to power. He received the governorship of Lycia—a mountainous province in southern Asia Minor. Traveling around his province, he came across a delightful place, the image of which he retained in his memory for a long time.

There, a huge plane tree grew by a cold spring. It stood near the road like an inn, for its trunk was hollow and rotten; it was like a room in a palace, more than eighty feet in circumference. But its crown spread out—green and lush—very wide, overshadowing a great stretch of the surrounding field, and each of its branches could have been a

---

[61] Tacitus, *Annals* ,I, 10, and II, 5.

separate tree.

"I held a feast inside it," Mucianus said, "with eighteen companions. We rested on a soft bed of moss and leaves covering the stone benches someone had placed there. Not even the lightest gust of wind could reach inside. I listened to the sound of the rain falling on the canopy above us, and I felt happier than I did when I feasted among the glittering marbles and many-colored frescoes of palaces with gilded roofs."

Returning to Rome, Mucianus was appointed consul. In the year 67, he took over Syria as the imperial legate—one of the most important provinces of the Empire, strategically speaking. Residing in its main city, Antioch, he watched Vespasian's campaign with suspicion and displeasure, envying the other man's chance to gain fame. He must have been glad in to hear that the siege of Jotapata was taking so long—well over a month.

AT DAYBREAK, CLOAKED BY MIST

And then came the forty-seventh day of the siege. Memorable and decisive because it was on that day that the Roman ramp, stubbornly and constantly raised, rose above the walls of Jotapata. The three magnificent siege towers, covered with sheet metal, were no longer required: the judgment day had come.

Naturally, on that very day, one of the defenders defected, convinced that Jotapata's final hour had come. He was brought before Vespasian. To save his own life, he betrayed all. He said that the city's handful of fighting men were at their wits' end, exhausted from the constant fighting and vigil. The best course of action, he advised, would be to launch the attack right before dawn, when sleep weighed most on the eyes of the guard.

The fugitive's report was not a revelation—after all, it was easy to guess that this was how the besieged felt—but it accelerated the Roman decision-making process. The insight into the most opportune hour of attack seemed particularly valuable.

The day broke enveloped in a thick fog. It was the first of Tammuz, which is to say, sometime in early July. A detachment of selected soldiers from the XVth Legion, under the personal command of Titus and his tribune Domitius Sabinus, silently approached and climbed the walls. In near-total silence, the sleeping guards were cleared, and still in complete silence, the Romans entered the streets closest to the fortifications. Just behind the first detachment, the soldiers of the Vth Legion climbed over the walls. They were led by the tribunes Placidus and Sextus Calvarius.

And now cries of horror broke out in the city. Someone saw the gleam of legionary armor, someone else heard the clatter of weapons, the clopping of sandals, and hushed commands in a foreign tongue. A cry of terror flew from house to house, and the waking inhabitants saw death closing upon them. Teams of Roman legionaries rushed through the narrow streets, crushing feeble attempts at resistance by the few who took up arms in desperation and bewilderment. Some of Jotapata's last defenders were cut down with swords; others jumped—or were thrown—from the walls into the abyss, and still others killed themselves. A handful of men from among the guards had spotted the enemy's entrance in time and taken refuge in the north tower. There, they resisted for a while but soon gave up, seeing the utter hopelessness of further struggle. The Romans slaughtered them all on the spot.

Many inhabitants sought refuge underground—in cellars and sewers, and especially in the deep water cisterns cut in the rock. The victors, busy tracking down and killing the city's armed garrison, paid little attention to these hiding places at first. However, a detachment accidentally came across one.

They saw a man hiding inside. When he realized he had been spotted and nothing could save him anymore, he leaned out of the cistern and shouted to the centurion to help him out. The Roman instinctively bent down and offered him his hand, and at that moment, he fell to the ground, howling in pain: the man's spear pierced him through the belly. It was the only Roman fatality on the day of the capture of Jotapata, which most vividly illustrates how unexpectedly it had fallen.

Over the following days, the Romans made a thorough search of the entire city, including the underground channels, caves, and cisterns. As elsewhere during this war, they killed the men and took the women and children into slavery. They captured and sold over 1,200 people. They also began to demolish, destroy, and burn the buildings and fortifications of the city so that all traces of Jotapata—a city that had dared to resist Rome—would be wiped off the surface of the earth.

And from the very beginning, they sought diligently for the commander of the city—and all rebel forces in Galilee—Josephus.

JOSEPHUS: I REMEMBER MY DREAMS

The Romans were already in the city when I managed—at the last moment, and surely only with the help of providence, to sneak away and jump into a deep pit. In one of its walls, there was a side opening leading to a large room, which could not be seen from above. Forty of our leaders were already there, and we had enough provisions to last us a long time.

Throughout the first day, we did not look out of our hiding place once, for we could tell by the trampling of feet and shouting that Romans were about. I left only in the deep of the night, stealthily and as carefully as possible. I wanted to find out how the enemy outposts were set up to see whether we could try to escape. But a quick look was enough to convince me that the Roman guard was too numerous and that there was no hope of sneaking out of the city. So I returned to our cave. For two more days, we sat in that dark room in terrible stench and stuffiness. But on the third day, the Romans captured a woman who was hiding with us but had gone up for air. She gave away our hiding place and revealed that the most wanted man in all of Galilee was there.

Immediately, two tribunes sent by Vespasian stood at the opening. In the name of their chief, they solemnly promised me that I could safely put myself in their hands and that no harm would come to me if I gave up voluntarily. Of course, I did not believe these assurances. I suspected that the tribunes wanted to take me alive in order to torture and murder me as revenge for all those painful blows which I had dealt them during the siege. But soon, a third tribune, Nicanor, appeared. I had known him personally for many years because he had served with the Roman garrison in Palestine. Nicanor confirmed the words of his colleagues. He spoke very persuasively. He reminded me of all the well-known instances when Romans had shown mercy to their defeated enemies. He said that the Roman commander-in-chief was full of admiration for my courage and my military skills. He reasoned that if they wanted to kill me, there would be no need to pull me out of the ground—they could just smoke us out. Finally, he swore that he, Nicanor, would never have undertaken an ignominious mission like luring a man to his death by trickery.

But I remained deaf even to these arguments. Meanwhile, the Romans, irritated by the lack of progress in our negotiations, began to prepare a fire, which they planned to pour into our cave. I realized that it would have been all too easy to roast us alive in our cave. Yet Nicanor held them back. He spoke softly to me, but at the same time, we heard ominous grunts and shouts from the soldiers, eager to attack us like rabid dogs on a leash. It seemed to me that my last hour had come.

It was then, in that most terrible moment, that a sudden thought dawned on me. A revelation. I remembered the dreams that had haunted me at night for many years. And I should tell you that I am quite adept at interpreting dreams, which God sends in the form of riddles. I am a priest, after all, and a descendant of priests, so I know the prophecies contained in the holy books.

ON THE INTERPRETATION OF DREAMS

Like in all countries and in all ages, there existed in Palestine of that day different views on the essence and meaning of dreams, even among the priests and the learned in the scriptures. Some claimed that dreams had no influence on human fate because they were no more than a distorted echo of earlier thoughts and experiences. However, such opinions were relatively rare. The majority of scholars argued from the scripture, asking:

"If the Holy Writ so often cites prophetic and symbolic dreams, should dreams not be taken seriously? May they not constitute prophecies, instructions, or warnings?"

However, those who took this view had to deal with one constantly raised objection: why don't all dreams come true? To this, various explanations were given.

One school held that those dreams that came true were brought by angels, while those that were empty and signifying nothing were the work of evil spirits. Another line of scholarship tried to identify some feature of dreams that would allow us to distinguish between the reliable and the unreliable without the need to delve into their content. So it was said that those dreams that came in the morning were true; or those that related to another person; or those that were repeated many times; or, finally, those whose meaning was revealed at once—in the course of the dream. The more cautious, however, taught that no dream came true completely. They offered a simile:

"The vision given in a dream is like wheat standing in the field. Its edible kernel is hidden, while what is visible—the stalk—will become inedible straw. So the point is to find in every dream that kernel—that seed that is inconspicuous and small—and to throw away the straw, that is, those parts that are impressive but illusory, fragile, and devoid of meaning."

There was also the view that every dream came true, but not immediately, and that sometimes, one had to wait years for the dream to realize itself.

It was also a common opinion that a dreamer had the duty to discover the meaning of his dreams. A popular maxim went:

"An unexplained dream is like an unopened letter!"

Developing this thought further, some arrived at the apparently paradoxical assertion that a dream only came true when it was explained; for only an interpretation gave it sense, life, and value. They illustrated this view with an almost absurd parable:

"There were twenty-four good interpreters of dreams in a certain city. Each of them interpreted in a different way one and the same dream of one and the same person. And behold, all their interpretations, though so different from each other, came true!"

Among the common folk, explanations of ordinary and uncomplicated dreams circulated in everyday use. For example:

"It is good to dream of wells, rivers, birds, and cooked dishes—as long as there is no meat. A white horse also portends something auspicious; likewise, a chestnut horse, if standing still; for if it is galloping, it will bring misfortune. A camel brings rescue from mortal danger, and a saddled elephant foretells that you will witness an extraordinary event. Wheat means peace, barley forgiveness of sins, an apple—success in business, a goose—attainment of wisdom, a guineafowl—the birth of a boy. If eggs are dreamed, the heart's ardent desire will not be fulfilled; but broken eggs mean that it will be. Nuts, glass, and everything breakable carry a similar meaning. It is good to dream of every sort of animal—except a monkey, a hedgehog, or an unsaddled elephant. Similarly, it is good to dream of any fruit except unripe dates."

But Josephus, as befits the leader of an uprising, had unusual prophetic dreams and about far greater things.

JOSEPHUS: WE DRAW LOTS

At that moment, the spirit of God came to me, and I recalled the horror of a dream of long ago. Remembering it now, I offered a silent prayer to the Lord:

"Since it has pleased you, my Lord, you, who had created the Jewish people, to destroy your work and bless the Romans with good fortune and success, and since you have chosen my person to reveal the future, behold, I will now obey you by delivering myself up to the Romans and hoping to live. But I take you as my witness that I am leaving this hiding place not as a traitor but as a man obeying your command."

So I prayed, and, at once, I signaled to Nicanor that I was ready to follow him. However, my companions in the grotto noticed—for they had been watching me carefully—that I was giving up. They crowded around me, shouting and threatening. They wanted to embarrass me with beautiful-sounding talk about the duties of a commander, which (they said) I was violating shamefully, and about the glorious fame of a martyr, which I had won but was now ready to exchange for the fate of a wretched slave. They drew their swords, and they cried that if I was not brave enough to die by my own hand as befitted a chief, they would kill me as a despicable traitor. So, on the one hand, I was threatened with death by those closest to me, and on the other, I knew in my heart that I must fulfill the task that the Lord had entrusted to me.

I tried to reason with them and dissuade them from what they had decided. I said that I did not fear death at all—as long as it was death in battle, fighting against the enemy sword in hand. But now, I asked, what were we risking by surrendering to the Romans? Yes, it was possible, I said, that we would all be killed once we gave up, but it was not absolutely certain; while remaining in the cave, we would die for sure, either suffocated by the smoke of the Roman fire or burnt to death by it or murdered by our own hands. If a miserable fate awaited us with the Romans, it was probably not worse than that to which we condemned ourselves by remaining in our stinking dungeon. I also argued how cowardly suicide was, how contrary to the order of nature—because what animal kills itself?—and how insulting to the will of the Lord who had given us life and who alone had the right to take it away.

"And rightly," I cried, "are the souls of suicides cast down into the deepest pit of the nether world! For, behold, according to our Law, the corpses of those who have taken their own lives must lie unburied until sundown. And there are nations who cut off a suicide's hand. Yes, fate has thrown us into the bottomless pit of despair. Yet, it remains within our power to protect ourselves against one evil: the evil of going against the will of Him who has made us."

And then, I offered another argument:

"Say, the Romans deceive us; deceive us, and lie to us; and will kill us as soon as we surrender. But what else do you propose? That we die with by own hand? What is this whole argument really about?"

But all my arguments were in vain, however sound and wise they were: it was like talking to the deaf. These fanatics had long since decided their fate and passed their own death sentence. My talk only enraged them and drove them into a passion. They shouted ever louder that I was a villain, a coward, a traitor! Not bluffing anymore, they waved their swords in front of my nose, and in that sepulchral dungeon, it would have been all too easy to be mortally wounded, even by accident. But still, even at that moment, I had some remaining authority. I was able to stop them: stop one with a word, another with a gesture, some even with a glance—as long as something could be seen in the dim light shining from the exit. Ultimately, there was no choice. I had to give in to their passion and risk my life in order to save it. I said:

"All right. Fine. Let it be as you wish. Let us draw lots. We will all die here, everyone. We will draw lots. The one to win will fall by the hand of the next. And thus, one by one, we will all kill one another. Then, the last one will commit suicide. And I hope that the last one will not prove to be a coward and will not fail to follow his comrades to the grave."

They all agreed to this with great alacrity. I would even say—cheerfully. Perhaps fear constricted the throat of many, but none would ever admit it: we were all supposed to be fearless.

We set about drawing lots.

WHAT REALLY HAPPENED?

How did it happen that Josephus found himself in the last pair—one of whom was to be the victim and the other—the suicide? For, indeed, only Josephus and another companion remained alive in the sepulchral dungeon among fraternally intertwined corpses and the stench of blood. Thirty-eight men had gone to their deaths before them—bravely, even willingly. Everyone whom fate had chosen exposed his neck to the blow of the sword without fear or hesitation. A moment later, his killer dropped dead beside his victim. And all of them died believing unwaveringly that the next one would not renege on their deal. And so it happened, quickly and efficiently, until only two remained—and one of them was their leader, Josephus. And meanwhile, he, watching the procession of his friends departing into the world of shadows, thought pettily:

"They die so willingly because they think that I will die too. Evidently, they consider death by my side sweeter than life."

He later claimed that it was a happy accident—perhaps even divine providence—that placed him in the last pair. And yet it is difficult to dismiss the suspicion that, in reality, from the very beginning, things went differently from what his account says. It is hard to shake off the thought that Josephus knowingly and perfidiously misled his companions. It may have happened like this:

Perhaps Josephus told his companions that, as their commander, he had not only the right but even the duty to die last. That he had to ensure that no one would weasel out and that all would remain faithful to the decision they had made together. Who knows if his speech about the horror of the sin of suicide—if he delivered it at all—did not contain a heroic statement:

"I'll take this sin upon my soul. When all of you have died, I shall die by my own hand and thus save you from punishment in the next world."

But by saying this and placing himself in the last pair in the procession of death, Joseph was already deceiving those who went ahead and—paving his way to salvation. When he was left alone with his last companion, he announced firmly that he would not draw lots:

"I don't want to condemn myself to death. And I don't want to stain my hand with the blood of my countryman, either."

Josephus knew perfectly well that it would pay to surrender to the Romans. He had been convinced by the insistence of Vespasian's officers. His value to the Romans was obvious:

As one of the leaders of the uprising, he was going to be kept alive for the time being. He would then take part in the triumph that would take place in Rome after the victorious end of the war. Yes, he would then not only be humiliated—for he would be obliged to walk in chains before the victor's chariot—but also strangled, for the old Roman custom required that the defeated generals be strangled after the triumph as a sacrifice to Jupiter. But how many months, and perhaps years, would pass before the triumphal procession entered the Via Sacra on its way to the Capitol! Vespasian must first conquer the whole country and take Jerusalem. A lot can change during that time, and many opportunities for rescue might arise. The only important thing at the moment was to get out of the hands of these madmen who had lost their minds completely because of a religious delusion! They wanted to die, and therefore, let them die, but let us not be dragged into their scheme, too.

His companion allowed himself to be convinced.

Or perhaps he was overpowered.

JOSEPHUS: I PROPHESY IN ORDER TO SAVE MY LIFE

And now I walked a martyr's path. The tribunes led me down a narrow passage among the dense throng of enraged Roman soldiers. I was emaciated, spattered with blood, barely able to stand, and since I had just emerged from a dark cave, I squinted my eyes, blinded by the sunlight. But I saw their faces, and I heard their menacing cries! Some mocked and jeered me, others threatened me with torture, and still others, especially those standing farther away, cried out stubbornly: "Crucify him! Crucify him!"

But when I stood before Vespasian, Titus, and the higher officers, they looked at me not without some sympathy—or at least that was my impression. Especially Titus, nearly my age, seemed to take pity on my fate and condition. But the meeting was brief. I was immediately taken from them, put in shackles, and placed under guard.

To my horror, I soon learned from the guards that I would be leaving both the camp and Palestine and traveling to Rome to stand before the emperor. At first, it seemed to me that this was the end and that there was no escape. This turn of events seemed to thwart all my calculations. After all, I had expected to wait calmly, safely, and for a long time—albeit in shackles—for the triumph that would one day take place in Rome. But now, a much more immediate doom threatened me, and I had no illusions about it. I had been to Italy not too long ago. I knew the court, I had seen Nero, I had seen with my own eyes how he liked to enjoy himself, how much he loved games, especially blood games. It seemed certain that as soon as I was in Rome with other distinguished prisoners of Galilee, Nero, impatient and always anxious to please the people, would not wait for the fall of Jerusalem. The victories of the Roman army in Galilee were a sufficient pretext for organizing blood games. Nero would throw us to wild animals or burn us like living torches or make us fight for our lives against professional gladiators. Scarcely had I escaped the clutches of one group of madmen when a new deadly danger hung over me.

But my natural acumen and the grace of providence did not abandon me in a situation that may well have deprived others of all discernment or any will to act. I demanded that the guards lead me again before Vespasian, for I had news of great importance to him. And I demanded that the meeting be held face-to-face. Bear in mind that such a request always piques the interest of others and adds a lot of value to the speaker's words. Of course, the chief refused to talk to me without witnesses: I could have been a madman or an assassin. However, he sent away most bystanders, leaving only Titus and two trusted friends.

I said:

"You probably see me as an ordinary prisoner of war. You are mistaken, for I am the herald of great things. Were it not for the fact that God has entrusted me with His prophecy, I would know well what our Law commands us to do and how it is proper for a Jewish general to die.

"Now, I hear you want to send me to Nero. And I say to you—do not do such a thing. There is no point. Do you think that Nero will reign for a long time? Not at all. You will be the emperor soon! You don't believe me, I understand, but I'm in your hands. Order me held under guard, and then punish me severely if what I tell you today does not come to pass."

After all, what did I have to lose? What was I risking?

VESPASIAN AND DIVINATION

There is no doubt that soon after the fall of Jotapata, Josephus had a secret interview with Vespasian and Titus. It is also certain that in the course of the meeting, the captive said something which greatly moved the father and son and which they remembered for a long time.

What are the grounds for our certainty? The story, told to us by Josephus himself, might not be true at all. After all, the writer—gifted with a truly creative imagination as he was—could easily have invented any fantastic story to exalt himself and flatter the Roman generals. There are, however, two aspects of the tale that compel us to take his testimony seriously. First, we note that Josephus published the work containing the above account while both of his interlocutors were still alive. This significantly limited his freedom to fantasize. His testimony had to correspond to facts to some extent. Flattery too brazenly faked might well have missed its target and possibly offended those whom it sought to praise.

The second aspect is more puzzling. Approximately two years

after the fateful conversation, Vespasian and Titus began to treat Jotapata's commander with exceptional deference. This happened shortly after Vespasian had been hailed as emperor by his soldiers. Josephus was immediately freed. Later, he received Roman citizenship, a considerable fortune, and a regular pension. He enjoyed the thorough and unshakable trust of the entire imperial family. It seems reasonable to suppose that he had earned that special treatment by something truly extraordinary.

We should also note that Vespasian—otherwise a reasonable, thrifty, and prudent man—fully shared the then-widespread faith in all sorts of prophetic signs and omens. He remembered them. They were passed on in the family tradition and immortalized by chroniclers and historians. For example, the following stories were related regarding the period of his life when the future emperor probably had not even dreamed of higher offices:

On one occasion, Vespasian had been eating his lunch when a strange dog burst into the room, carrying a human hand in its mouth, which it had snatched somewhere at the crossroads. It dropped the hand under the table at Vespasian's feet. It was a gruesome thing, for sure, but notable and open to various interpretations.

On another occasion, an ox pulling a plow in the field suddenly threw off its yoke and burst into Vespasian's house, brushing aside the servants who tried to stop it. Then, unexpectedly, as if tired, it lay down at the feet of Vespasian and humbly lowered its neck before him.

But the strangest omen was this:

A great cypress tree once grew on Vespasian's family estate. One day, it toppled over, uprooted by some force—although there was no gale. The very next day, however, it stood erect again as if it had been lifted up at night by some extraordinary and invisible power. Since then, it has grown beautifully and flourished.

Vespasian also attached great importance to his dreams. While staying with Nero in Greece, he dreamed that everything would change for the better for him when the emperor lost a tooth. Upon entering the palace the following morning, he met a doctor, triumphantly displaying the emperor's tooth which he had just extracted. Soon afterward, he was assigned the command in Palestine.

That Vespasian willingly listened to all prophecies, Josephus could have learned in the Roman camp, but what did he say to him during their secret conversation? Certainly, he would not have dared to say that Nero's reign would soon end. Nor would the commander allow such words from the mouth of a prisoner. We guess that Josephus limited himself to some vague and ambiguous statements. Perhaps he referred to the messianic hopes and prophecies circulating among his people, promising vaguely that the future savior of the world would arise in the East? And when the time came, and Vespasian realized that these messianic prophecies had concerned him, he rewarded the Jew who had first told him about them?

THE RECAPTURE OF JOPPA

The height of summer came, and with it, as usual in Palestine, unbearable heat. It became difficult to conduct hostilities; it was all the more difficult as the army, exhausted by the long siege of Jotapata, required rest. Therefore, just four days after the capture of the city, the Romans marched back to the city of Ptolemais on the sea coast, where they had started their operations. After staying there for a few days, they moved to the larger and richer Caesarea Maritima. Its population, mostly Greek, greeted the legions enthusiastically. Almost immediately, however, popular cries rose up among the people, demanding that the captured leader of the Galileans be put to death. Vespasian rejected these calls—perhaps because he was going to send Josephus to Nero or perhaps because the man's prophecies made him hesitate.

The Vth Legion and the Xth remained in Caesarea, and the XVth was moved to the city of Scythopolis, about sixty kilometers inland as the crow flies, near the Jordan Valley. No major military operations took place that summer. The only serious action was the recapture of Joppa.

Joppa had been recovered by Cestius Gallus in the autumn of the preceding year. However, after his defeat at Beth-Horon and the subsequent departure of the Romans, refugees from various parts of the country flocked to the city. They were mostly men with nothing left to lose and ready to take on any risk. They built boats and small ships, went out to sea, and, like pirates, boldly attacked merchant ships off the coasts of Palestine, Phoenicia, and Syria. All shipping suffered greatly from this, and Vespasian sent a detachment of infantry and cavalry to Joppa. Hearing about their approach, the inhabitants hastily left the city—or rather its ruins—and spent the night on their ships. On the morning of the following day, they tried to make landfall elsewhere. Meanwhile, to their misfortune, a mighty north wind sprang up, a very dangerous phenomenon in those regions which lack good natural harbors. The wind pushed some of their ships onto the rocky shore, wrecking them and others out to the open sea, where they were swallowed up by the waves. According to Roman calculations, over four thousand people died in the storm. A garrison was left on the site of Joppa and diligently and systematically laid waste the entire surrounding area.

In the meantime, good news was received at the headquarters: King Agrippa and Queen Berenice invited the Roman commanders and their army to their capital, Caesarea Philippi. The invitation was eagerly accepted. Vespasian and Titus immediately proceeded to the royal residence at the head of a select detachment.

THE GROTTO OF PAN AND THE NYMPHS

Caesarea Philippi was situated at the foot of Mount Hermon, at the headwaters of the River Jordan, in a beautiful, mountainous, green region. One of the main sources of the river is a spring located at the foot of a high, reddish rock. Higher up, there is a large cave. Since time immemorial, the local population had paid homage to the god of fertility there. Following the conquest of Alexander the Great, Greeks settled in those parts and took over the cult center at the cave. They decided that it was a holy shrine of the Greek god Pan and his companions, the water nymphs. They erected their statues, carved numerous niches in the rock—their traces have been preserved to this day—and carved numerous inscriptions. It was from the name of this god—Pan—that this region acquired the name of *Panias* or *Paneion*.

Then, King Herod the Great received all the surrounding country as a gift from Emperor Augustus. To express and commemorate his gratitude, he erected near the red rock a magnificent temple of white stone dedicated to Augustus and placed inside it the image of the emperor. (He would never have dared to violate the Jewish Law so flagrantly in Judea). After Herod's death, his son Philip inherited the territory. He was a calm, quiet man, devoid of excessive ambitions and enamored of the comforts of life and the beauty of nature. This is illustrated by his choice of residence: Panias. Philip built a city here and named it Caesarea in honor of the emperor.

The prince almost never left the borders of his domains. Whenever he left the palace, his retinue followed him, carrying his judicial throne. He sat on it only when one of his subjects asked for a judgment. He tried to judge quickly, leniently, and justly. He died during the reign of Emperor Tiberius, leaving behind a fond memory among his subjects—the only son of Herod to do so.

His heir, King Agrippa II, Berenice's brother, also resided here. He beautified and expanded the city and eventually gave it a new name: Neronias, in honor of emperor Nero. Now, in the summer of AD 67, he entertained the Roman commanders here. The guests spent their visit in constant games and feasting, and the only duty they had was to offer sacrifices to the god of the grotto. They thanked him for the victories won and asked for more in the future. The holidays at the source of the Jordan lasted twenty days.

Unfortunately, that's all we know about this period, and that's all a historian has the right to say about it. He can add, however, that it was the first chance for Berenice and Titus to get to know each other. They had already met once some months before, in Ptolemais by the sea, when Titus brought his legion from Alexandria and Berenice and Agrippa arrived from the north with Vespasian. But, back then, there was barely enough time for introductions, perhaps at most an official reception—for the duties of war demanded immediate attention. So the romance, which was to lead Berenice to the Palatine years later, must really have started in Caesarea Philippi. One can only guess what words, signs, and gestures aroused mutual interest. The natural scenery was beautiful—rocks, the spring of a great river, the lush greenery. The splendor of the royal palace dazzled, and the refined luxury of the oriental court was downright stunning to the Romans, accustomed as they were to more simplicity.

Vespasian was charmed by the queen's generosity and gifts and his son by—her beauty. Again, the recurring image comes to mind: a brilliant diamond glistens on Berenice's finger as the queen walks in her golden dress along an avenue of dark green cypresses with Titus at her side. In the background, there is the reddish gleam of the rock from which the source of the Jordan springs.

But there were also memories of freshly spilled blood and the smell of fires that had consumed the towns and villages of Galilee. And above everything hung the constant awareness that, at any moment, one may be summoned to fight and risk his life again.

So, every pleasure was embraced greedily as if it were the last before saying goodbye forever. Already by the beginning of September, news came that fighting had renewed in Galilee.

TIBERIAS

After leaving Caesarea Philippi in September, Vespasian set about clearing the insurgents from the shores of the Sea of Galilee. He especially targeted two large cities on its western—Galilean—shore: Tiberias and Tarichaea. The commander led two of their legions: the XVth *Apollinaris* under the command of Titus and the Xth *Fretensis* under Marcus Ulpius Trajanus.

Tiberias was the larger of the two cities, and the reason why the Sea of Galilee was sometimes called Lake Tiberias. There were relatively few insurgents there. They were led by Joshua, son of Sapphas, with whom Josephus had had so much trouble a few months earlier. Vespasian wanted to spare the city and its people for the sake of Agrippa, to whom it belonged. The king had been zealously aiding Romans in their war and had lately received them so hospitably at Caesarea that it seemed fitting to protect his interests, and Tiberias brought him a substantial income. Vespasian sent ahead a party of fifty horse. They were to hold talks with the residents of the city and promise that all would be forgiven as long as they drove the insurgents away. The riders galloped up to the city wall. There, their commanding officer, Valerian, and a few soldiers dismounted: they wanted to show that they came in peace.

But just at that moment, a bunch of armed men rushed out of the gate and attacked them with such ferocity that they fled without even drawing their swords. Valerian and five others did not have time to mount their horses. The insurgents triumphantly brought them to the city as a valuable war prize.

Fortunately for Tiberias, none of the Romans were injured. However, the elders of the city were terrified by the incident—while there had been no fight and there were no killed or wounded, it had certainly been a hostile act—and everyone, rich and poor, had before their eyes the terrible fate of Jotapata. The council sent a hurried delegation to the Roman camp. There, before the commander, its delegates begged on their knees for mercy and forgiveness for the stupid provocation committed by a handful of madmen, strangers, hicks who had come to their city from the countryside, were penniless, and therefore had nothing to lose. Although Vespasian fumed, believing that the capture of his men had to be avenged, he nevertheless heeded the interests of Agrippa and accepted the city's humble plea for mercy. But he set a condition: the insurgents had to leave the city immediately.

And so it happened. Faced with the hostility of the inhabitants, Joshua and his men left Tiberias and moved to nearby

Tarichaea. The very next day, Roman troops entered Tiberias. The gates stood wide open, and where they were too narrow, a piece of the wall on the eastern side had to be demolished to allow the legions to march in in close formation. Apart from that, however, the city's fortifications were left intact. Agrippa's promise that Tiberias would remain completely loyal in the future was accepted. And the legionaries were denied plunder.

TITUS AT THE GATES OF TARICHAEA

Things went differently in Tarichaea. Since it was a smaller city, the insurgents had a significant numerical advantage over the regular inhabitants. The walls were weaker here than in Tiberias, but there was no shortage of fishing boats that could be useful in combat and facilitate retreat in the event of defeat. Joshua, son of Sapphas, saw this and took advantage of it immediately.

Vespasian encamped in the town of Amathus, between Tiberias and Tarichaea, where there was a warm spring said to have healing properties (not so long ago, John of Gischala took his cure there). The Romans, confident of their crushing numerical superiority, calmly set about constructing their camp without putting up proper guards. Unexpectedly, there fell upon them the people of Joshua, arriving by boats. They destroyed part of the completed fortifications and withdrew without any losses before the cohorts of heavy-armed legionaries arrived to defend the camp builders. The insurgents did not sail far; they moved away from the shore just far enough to stay out of range of missiles. They dropped their anchors in deeper water, lined up their boats in a straight line as if for battle, and waited patiently to see what the enemy would do.

Meanwhile, matters on land also advanced. Crowds of insurgents came out onto the plain in front of Tarichaea's walls. Vespasian sent his son against them at the head of six hundred horse. Titus, however, was not yet an experienced commander. It seemed to him that his force was too small and that he would not be able to cope with that enormous crowd. So he sent word back to camp asking for more cavalry. His subordinates, on the other hand, apparently more experienced in battle, were not at all afraid of the disorderly mob of the enemy; they advised an immediate attack without waiting for reinforcements. Meanwhile, Trajanus galloped in with four hundred horse, and two thousand Roman archers took positions on a nearby hill: from there, they were able to shoot at the men on the walls of Tarichaea so that they would not be able to sortie to aid those fighting outside.

The Roman cavalry launched its attack. It unfolded into a long line across the wide plain and crashed into the mass of insurgents. The knights rammed the enemy with their horses, stabbed them with their lances, then closed in with their long swords. What happened then was to repeat regularly in this war: Joshua's men, poorly armed, completely untrained, were unable to put up much of a resistance. They began to retreat towards the city gates. The Romans tried to maneuver in such a way as to cut them off from the city, but they managed to slip through and reenter the city.

As soon as the gates closed behind them, an argument broke out in the city between the inhabitants and the insurgents. The former wanted to save their families and possessions and demanded immediate surrender; the latter, however, having nothing to lose, insisted on continuing the fight. The screams of the quarreling crowd carried far away. Titus did not delay. He took his riders into the shallow water of the lake, made a detour along the shore, and entered the city at the head of his men from the side of the lake—for on the side where it touched the lake, the city had no fortifications.

There was no organized defense anymore. Only a few individuals or small groups put up a fight. Most of the insurgents—and they were led by Joshua himself—ran away. The Romans meanwhile set about murdering the population; they stopped the slaughter only on Titus' orders.

THE STADIUM IN TIBERIAS

By the time Vespasian arrived in Tarichaea, it was all over. The commander-in-chief did not hide his satisfaction with his son's bravery and success. He ordered the city to be placed under martial law and sealed off so that no one could escape. Now, there were many beams and planks stored along the shore, and on the following day, the legionaries used them to build wide rafts and sailed out onto the lake towards the flotilla of boats in the nearby waters. For, amazingly, the insurgents had not fled, though they could have done so easily in the night. Maybe they wanted to try their luck again? Or maybe they did not expect that the Romans could be so resourceful and efficient?

The people on the boats didn't even have proper weapons. As the slow Roman rafts made their way toward them, they hurled stones at the tight ranks of legionaries, solid as a wall of steel, but the stones bounced off the armor, shields, and helmets. Meanwhile, the Roman archers, kneeling behind the cover of the iron-clad men, shot continuously and accurately with their arrows. Then, the heavy rafts began to press against the frail and wobbly boats, crushing some and gradually enveloping the rest. The Romans were skilled at stabbing with long spears. They used their oars to bash the heads and necks of those who jumped into the water and tried to swim ashore to save themselves. Others, who clung desperately to the Roman rafts as they drowned, had their hands cut off. On the coast, Vespasian set up a cordon of horse and foot; they chased away or killed anyone who tried to come ashore.

The next day, the lake was full of floating, bloated corpses and of the wreckage of boats. In September heat, the bodies decomposed quickly, and a terrible stench hung over the city.

All this took place in a lovely, rich, smiling country on the shores of a lake with golden beaches and transparent and cool waters teeming with fish. The whole country was covered with gorgeous lush greenery because trees and shrubs of all kinds grew wonderfully on the fertile soil and in the mild spring-like climate: palms and walnuts, olives, figs, and vines.

Meanwhile, the Roman commander reviewed the thousands of prisoners taken in the city. The point was to separate not only the civilians and insurgents but also the inhabitants of the city and the recent immigrants from the countryside; the former, subjects of King Agrippa, were granted their life and freedom, but a question arose: what to do with the multitude of outsiders. Allegedly, Vespasian had initially intended to let them go as well—especially since the most ardent of the insurgents had either died in battle or fled with Joshua. However, objections were immediately raised that it would be very dangerous to do so:

"The pardoned will certainly take up arms against us at the earliest opportunity. And besides, it is necessary to show everyone how ruthlessly the Romans punish all resistance."

This view prevailed.

However, another difficulty arose—of a technical nature, so to speak. How do you shackle—or slaughter—so many people? And how to do it in Tarichaea, in front of its inhabitants? It could spark acts of rebellion and despair and may lead to the death of many people who had to be spared since they were the subjects of Agrippa and Berenice.

After a thorough analysis of the situation, the Romans decided to use a ruse. Vespasian did not explicitly tell the newcomers that he spared their lives, but he allowed them to leave Tarichaea. Leave, yes, but by one road only: the road to Tiberias.

The masses of fugitives rushed towards Tiberias, carrying and dragging all their miserable possessions. For, in many cases, they were whole families; women predominated, as well as the weak, sick, and old. The road ran along the shores of the lake; from the landward side, the refugees were hemmed in by an unbroken cordon of Roman soldiers. They consoled themselves, saying that the legionaries were only making sure that no one strayed or ran away. But when the long column finally approached Tiberias, the troops began to divert it and push it into a large suburban stadium. Then they locked it up,

Praetorians

surrounded it, and proceeded to sort the captives. The weak and infirm were put to the sword. The rest were sold into slavery. Great care was taken to hand over to King Agrippa the people who had come from his estates, but he later sold them into slavery, too.

A few thousand young, healthy men were set aside, shackled, and sent to Corinth as a gift to Nero. There, they were put to work on the construction of the Corinth Canal, which had been inaugurated by the emperor a few months earlier.

THE CORINTH CANAL AND PHILOSOPHY

The work on the waterway, which was to cut across the narrow isthmus and connect the Aegean Sea with the Ionian Sea, began in the autumn of AD 67. Nero himself inaugurated it. First, he sang a hymn to the gods of the sea. Then he struck a golden shovel into the ground three times. Then he loaded a basket of soil, lifted it on his own shoulders, and carried it off to a nearby spoil heap. The ceremonial work of the divine master was followed, equally symbolically, by the highest dignitaries in his entourage. Later, bodyguards and Praetorians got to shift some earth, and later still—in the usual course of events—criminal and political prisoners and the war captives from Palestine were set to work. These last were assigned the most difficult sections, where native rock had to be broken by hand.

However, the work did not continue for very long. First, it was rumored that the level of the Ionian Sea was much higher than that of the Aegean Sea and that if, after digging a channel, the two bodies of water were joined, a huge tidal wave would flow from the west and cause a terrible cataclysm, submerging the island of Aegina, and perhaps even tearing it from its foundations and floating it away—for the island lay opposite the eastern mouth of the future canal. These calculations were supposedly the work of Egyptian surveyors, considered to be the world's best experts in hydraulic engineering. Their work was not the cause of the halt of the construction work, however. This was interrupted by political events—events that were about to lead to a catastrophe.

Some later claimed that a certain Musonius Rufus had been among the political prisoners employed in the hardest section of the dig. Nero had had him removed from the capital for "spreading unhealthy, subversive views among the youth" and for "maintaining contacts with circles hostile to the blessings of the age." Thus, Musonius had fallen victim to the same persecutions that had caused Apollonius to leave Rome and go to Spain.

Musonius had led a philosophical school to which he accepted only a few hand-picked students. In his writings and lectures, he taught as follows:

When it comes to ethics and the question of moral conduct, one has to think of humans as sick. Like all sick, they need constant medical attention. The medicine of the soul is philosophy. Only it can lead our way to moral health. Thus, everyone should pursue philosophy, even women.

The goal of all philosophical activity is the attainment of moral health. For what does it mean to philosophize? To know and practice behavior consistent with the duties of morality. Therefore, it is completely indifferent whether we say: "He is a philosopher" or: "He is an honest man." However, all theoretical discussions are no more than mind games, for a true understanding of philosophy can be reached without any erudition and study because mental health is a derivative not of education but of strenuous work on self-improvement, and this can be practiced by doing little more than heavy physical labor, with shovel and plow. As for teachers of philosophy, the most important thing was that they live their lives in accordance with their teachings. The aim of all philosophizing is not to seek easy applause but to improve one's listeners and readers and to help them attain inner happiness. And how can that be achieved? The answer is simple: happiness is no more and no less than full and total freedom of the mind. One achieves it by managing wisely those things which are under his control and by submitting indifferently to everything that lies beyond it. Therefore, on the one hand, one must limit one's needs—so as not to depend for happiness on their fulfillment—and, on the other, rise above all the suffering that life itself inevitably brings. Everyone must die, so let us neither seek death nor try to escape it. In the same way, let us not regard exile as evil: a true philosopher feels at home everywhere, for he is a citizen not of one country but of the whole world. [62]

Nero must have felt a very strong temptation to sentence to hard labor a philosopher who talked so much about inner freedom, praised physical work, and kept proclaiming that he could be happy under any and all circumstances. It just made so much sense to put Musonius to work on building the Corinth Canal.

In fact, Nero wasn't that malicious. If Musonius had indeed found himself there, it was only briefly: he spent the greater part of his exile on the island of Gyaros. Crowds of admirers visited him there—people thought that in this way, they expressed civil courage and took an active part in the opposition movement against the tyrant.

WAR IN JUDEA AND THE DEATH OF NERO

The news of Nero's death put a stop to the construction of the Corinth Canal. It also stopped all further Roman operations in Palestine.

Nero had committed suicide by stabbing himself in the neck with a dagger. It happened at his freedman's villa near Rome on June 9, A.D. 68. The news did not arrive in Palestine until the end of June. This is how long a ship took from Rome to Palestine, even with good weather and favorable wind.

Vespasian had begun operations throughout Palestine in the early spring of AD 68. He was in a hurry, for alarming reports were already coming from the West. In early 68, Vindex, the governor of the province of Lugdunum (today's Lyon in France), rebelled. It is true

---

[62] Surviving fragments of Musonius were published by O. Hanse, Leipzig 1905.

that the Rhine legions soon suppressed him, but then reports came that they themselves were ready to rebel and acclaim their commander, Verginius Rufus, as emperor. Almost simultaneously, the administrators of the Spanish provinces declared against Nero. Their eyes turned to the oldest and most respected among them, Galba. They proposed to give the imperial purple to him, while he himself declared publicly that he considered himself not the legate of the emperor but the legate of the Senate and of the Roman People—which was tantamount to overthrowing the empire. Then, the governor of Africa broke with Nero.

Reports of these events reached Vespasian gradually while he was in the field conducting his operations. The reports motivated him to redouble his efforts. He felt he needed to achieve as much as possible as quickly as possible so that the outcome of the local war would be but a foregone conclusion by the time a civil war broke out in the West.

He was also afraid that the Jewish insurgents, likewise informed about the developments in the West, might begin to pin too much hope on them. He was guided by the simple principle: he had to show that, regardless of what happened elsewhere, Rome would neither slow nor suspend its war in Palestine and would eventually bring it to a victorious conclusion.

Starting south from Caesarea Maritima, Vespasian marched across a wide, fertile plain. Like Sherman in Georgia, he destroyed and burned everything in his way. He left the Vth Legion in the town of Emmaus to threaten Jerusalem while he himself continued south and entered Idumea. This arid, rugged land—the biblical Edom of Esau, the elder of the two sons of Isaac and the ancestral home of Herod the Great—stretched west of the Dead Sea and south of Judea proper.

In just two of its cities, Vespasian murdered tens of thousands of men of military age and took thousands of captives. The rest of the inhabitants, he drove away from their homes—he burnt their houses and chased them out into the desert. He left a considerable garrison in Idumea, ordering its commander to ravage the whole province systematically, district by district. He himself led the main body of his army to the north, bypassing Judea proper. He passed through

Emmaus again and then through the land of Samaria. Here he turned east and descended into the Jordan Valley near the village of Corea. [63] It was by then the third week of June. Vespasian now marched down the river valley, due south again, as far as the city of Jericho. There he joined Trajanus, commander of the Xth Legion. Trajanus had been operating on the eastern bank of the Jordan, bloodily pillaging all nearby settlements since March.

Hearing the news of the approach of the Romans, the people of the province of Jericho fled to the mountains towards Jerusalem. Those who dared to remain behind in their homes perished. There was hardly a soul left in Jericho.

A TRIP TO THE DEAD SEA

If not for the suffocating heat of its summers, Jericho may seem a paradise, full of all kinds of riches and charms. Thanks to the life-giving water of the Jericho Spring, which flows all year round, the surrounding country blooms with the lush greenery of gardens, palm trees, fragrant shrubs, and the balsam tree. Throughout the year, various species of plants please the eye with gorgeous flowers and the palate with delicious fruit. The sight is all the more striking because a sunburnt, tawny desert stretches all around: mountainous and rocky if one travels west towards Jerusalem, flat and utterly barren if one turns east—or south, down the Jordan valley, in the direction of the Dead Sea.

Vespasian arrived in Jericho in June AD 68. He had at his disposal the former palace of Herod the Great, splendid and equipped with swimming pools, but the air—since the summer had already begun—was so suffocating that it prevented any appreciation of the charms of the oasis. The reports that in winter, the valley experienced delightful spring weather were not much help. Yes, one could walk

---

[63] Probably modern *Tell el-Mazar*.

about Jericho in light linen clothes in January, while Jerusalem, located much higher but only a dozen or so hours away on foot, experienced freezing winds and, from time to time, driving snow. But what of it? In June, Jericho was hell.

Who knows whether it was not just this oppressive heat that drove Vespasian to the Dead Sea for relaxation—the shining surface of which was clearly visible from Jericho. He had heard curious reports about the amazing properties of that sea, and the journey to its shores took no more than two hours. The commander probably supposed that the air, as usually happens over large expanses of water, would be cooler there.

In this regard, he was disappointed. Yet, he did confirm the truth of other reports about the sea: its waters were indeed terribly bitter and salty and hostile to all life. Those who had been there before reported that no one could drown in it. To confirm this, Vespasian conducted a *scientific experiment*. He gave orders to put a few prisoners who did not know how to swim in a boat, go far out into the deep, and fling them overboard. To make double-sure, he saw to it that their hands were tied behind their backs. And behold, they all immediately came bobbing to the surface and floated without any difficulty as if held up by some invisible hand. Here and there, huge lumps of asphalt were seen swaying in the waves. They broke away from the seabed and reappeared again and again, and the natives fished for them for profit. They were used for calking boats, and some also claimed that small amounts of bitumen added to drugs enhanced their effectiveness. It was because of these lumps that many called the sea the Sea of Asphalt.

After witnessing all these miracles, Vespasian was probably disposed to believe other stories related to the area. The natives claimed that the whole region used to be fertile, rich, and populous, but the transgressions of its proud, presumptuous inhabitants, among whom not a single righteous man could be found, caused a column of fire to descend from heaven and consume the sinful cities and burn everything in the vicinity to ashes.

Yet, even now, the coast of the Dead Sea was not entirely

deserted. Spies reported that not far away, among the rocky wastes, tiny springs flowed, supporting sizeable settlements. It was also said that the followers of a strange sect lived there and that their main center was called Mesad Hasidim, which translates as The Fortress of the Pious.

This name alone had to disturb Vespasian.

PYTHAGOREISM AND THE ESSENES

How delighted Apollonius of Tyana would have been to learn of the teachings and ways of life of the inhabitants of Mesad Hasidim! They were called "Essenes" by the Greek-speaking Jews. [64] Apollonius would have been surprised that their views were so similar to what he himself preached and practiced. He would probably have concluded that there could only be one explanation for the similarity: the Essenes were, like he himself, heirs of the Pythagorean tradition. But by living in non-Greek surroundings, they have allowed the original doctrine to distort and incorporate barbarian beliefs. And perhaps Apollonius would not have been completely wrong, for even some modern scholars—meticulous, critical, and cautious—hold the view that Pythagoreanism influenced the dogmas and rules of the Essenes. Though, of course, not only Pythagoreanism did: the leading Iranian religion—Zoroastrianism—had a much stronger influence. However, no outsider could have known about this because the teachings of Iranian origin were among the most secret aspects of the Essene doctrine and were only recorded in sacred books intentionally kept out of the hands of the uninitiated. But those aspects of their dogma and practice, which most resembled Pythagoreanism, were readily discernible to any casual observer.

Josephus, son of Matthias, was not an Essene himself, but he

---

[64] Possibly from a Hebrew self-designation later found in some Dead Sea Scrolls, *osey haTorah*, "'doers' or 'makers' of Torah."

had personal contact with many members of the sect. Like many of his contemporaries, he gave the Essenes a most flattering witness. And since he did not know their secret doctrines and confined himself to what could be seen or inferred from cursory observation, the Pythagorean element seems all the stronger in his account. Had Apollonius come to Palestine at the time and spoken to Josephus or read any of the books of Philo of Alexandria while in Egypt, he would have formed a similar view:

There are about four thousand Essenes in Judea. The sect accepts only males. They form communities scattered in towns and villages all over the country, but their main center is in the west of the country, by the Dead Sea, near Jericho. They hold no personal property, not even clothing. When a man joins the sect, he donates all his property to it. In return, he gains the right to use the common property of the sect when he needs it. If he travels, he will receive food, shelter, and clothing from the Essene steward of the local commune—and they are found almost everywhere. Their needs are extremely modest anyway, for their doctrine emphasizes limiting one's desires, abstinence, and self-control. They wear the simplest possible clothing, white linen, generally. They receive new clothing only when the old is worn out. It is the same with their sandals.

They have no wives. Asked why, they answer:

"All pleasure is evil and should be avoided. And women should be avoided especially, for they are perfidious, selfish, envious, deceitful, and hypocritical and lure men with the promise of pleasures which weaken the character. A married man, and especially a man with children, becomes essentially a slave."

The sect, therefore, survives only by the continuous uptake of new mature male members, though sometimes they adopt boys and prepare them from an early age according to their principles. There is, however, a faction of Essenes who marry. They claim that they undertake this as a duty for the benefit of the community, which would otherwise die out. However, they do not marry until after three years of engagement, testing the character of their brides before they commit, and they copulate only in order to beget children.

At dawn, they recite a secret prayer to the sun. Then they go to work, as their superiors order. They cultivate land, graze cattle, keep bees, and practice some crafts. Around noon, they come together again, gird themselves with a white scarf, and take a cold bath. In the dining room of the common house—and only sect members are allowed there—they eat in silence. They receive bread and a bowl with just one dish. But none will touch his food before the elder has said a prayer. Likewise, they end each meal with a prayer. And everything they do is done in silence. If a word is uttered, it is only because it is absolutely necessary.

They are obedient to their superiors. They are not allowed to do anything without their consent—except for emergency acts of help or mercy.

They are always calm and composed, and their word is like an oath. They never swear oaths and say that an oath is a kind of blasphemy—a calling upon the name of the Lord in vain. They devote themselves diligently to their studies of old books and also of what is good for health. Many of them reach old age.

Whoever wants to join them must undergo a year of probation. He then receives an axe, a white scarf, and clothing. But even then, he does not yet participate in common meals but only in ablutions. He has two more years to train. Only then does he take a solemn oath in which he undertakes to worship God, fulfill his duties towards fellow men, not hurt anyone, not hate those who harm him, obey his superiors, love the truth and abhor lies, not steal, not keep secrets from his brothers nor reveal any of the secrets of the sect to outsiders—even if threatened with death.

Whoever breaks these rules is excluded from the fellowship, but such a verdict requires at least one hundred Essenes to gather to judge him.

They observe the Sabbath with the utmost diligence, but they send only bloodless sacrifices to the Temple in Jerusalem, for they do not recognize blood offerings at all.

They believe that an ethereal immortal soul lives in the body, imprisoned in it as if in a grave. Therefore, physical death is really the beginning of the true life of the soul, in which it will be rewarded or punished—depending on what it earned in its earthly existence. The soul of a just man goes far across the Ocean to the land of eternal happiness and spring; the evil soul, however, is sent to the underground, where there is darkness, cold, and suffering.

THE DESTRUCTION OF MESAD HASIDIM

The Roman commander paid attention neither to the sublimity of the Essene teachings nor the question of their Pythagorean or Iranian origins. For Vespasian and his officers, the only thing that mattered was this: that in the close vicinity of Jericho, there were settlements of some radical Jewish sect, supposedly fortified and armed. Their garrisons—it was said—were all men, living in a community of property, well organized, and subject to military discipline.

The operation was carried out quickly and efficiently. It was very brief and—indeed—such an insignificant undertaking that Josephus, the historian of the war, did not even mention it in his work. Admittedly, he was away at that time, held prisoner in Caesarea Maritima.

The Essenes do not seem to have resisted, perhaps because they had no weapons other than their axes. Most probably, some managed to escape in time and hide among the inaccessible rocks, chasms, and caverns of the wilderness and then wandered farther off. Some went into captivity, but most were killed.

They must have died bravely. Josephus, who often saw how they were tortured during the war in various localities, expresses his sincere admiration for their courage and endurance. Though their limbs were stretched and broken, and their flesh burned with living fire, no one could make them deny their superiors or take forbidden food into their mouths. They died without tears or groans, and some were even smiling.

Their monasteries were destroyed and burned. Clear traces of this remain to this day. Most of the rooms of their centers have collapsed, and among the rubble and the black dust of the conflagration, archeologists find iron tips of Roman arrows. But that the catastrophe came in AD 68 is evidenced only by coins. Archeologists found a lot of them among the ruins: even a small treasure hoard was discovered, no doubt hidden in haste, at the last moment before the enemy entered the house. The coins come from different periods and mints; however, in the layer affected by the destruction, the bronze coins minted by the insurgent authorities in Jerusalem are the most numerous. Almost all of them left the mint in the second year of the insurrection, that is, in 67 AD, and only a few in the third year, which began—according to Jewish count—in the early spring of AD 68. In the destruction layer, we find no later coins at all.

A Roman garrison subsequently occupied the ruined settlements, and two facts indicate this. First, some of the surviving buildings, especially the towers and defensive walls, were strengthened *after* the conflagration; and new living quarters were hastily erected on the site at the same time. The second fact involves coins again. Many were found in this layer, but most are not Jewish at all, insurgent or otherwise, but coins minted in Caesarea Maritima and in the city of Dora.[65] Those coins were minted to pay the wages of the Roman soldiers in Palestine.[66]

The conquering army occupied the main Essene site for several years. The location was excellent: it allowed the garrison to control a large area. From the high rock platform on which the settlement stood, there was a commanding view of the western and northern coasts of the Dead Sea. Maintaining a strong outpost in this place must have seemed necessary to the Romans, as less than 50 kilometers further south—and thus only a day's journey—rose the walls of the mighty Masada, occupied by the Zealots.

---

[65] Dor, south of Haifa.

[66] R. de Vaux, *L'Archéologie et les manuscrits de la Mer Morte*, London 1961, pp. 33–36

Eventually, the Romans left, but the former inhabitants never returned. They dispersed all over the world, many died in the war, others went abroad—as slaves or refugees. Nor did they return to their smaller settlement, a few miles distant from Mesad Hasidim, which was also destroyed in 68 AD.

And for centuries, no one bothered to visit the rock caverns in the area. For centuries, the holy books of the Essenes secreted there waited for their rightful owners. Gathered in great earthenware jugs lay scrolls of leather, papyrus, and even copper, brought here from the community library and hidden as the Romans approached the walls of Mesad Hassidim.

One day in March 1947, a young boy, Muhammad ad Dib, an Arab shepherd, searched among the rocky cliffs for a goat that had strayed from the flock. He saw the black opening of some fissure. Accidentally, or perhaps for fun, he threw a stone into it. Immediately, there was the dry crack of breaking pottery.

The site of the larger settlement bore by then the name of Qumran, the smaller one—of Ein Feshkha.

THE RETURN TO CAESAREA

The military garrison which Vespasian left in the destroyed Essenian settlement by the Dead Sea was not large. It was little more than an advance outpost of the main camp, which remained in Jericho. The Xth *Fretensis* remained there. It blocked the insurgents in Jerusalem from reaching the Jordan Valley and the Dead Sea. The Vth *Macedonian*, stationed on the opposite bank, on the high ground at Emmaus, blocked the roads leading to Jerusalem from the coastal plain. Returning from Jericho, Vespasian now strengthened that garrison by stationing some troops in the town of Adida,[67] near Emmaus.

---

[67] Now Hadid.

On his way to Caesarea Maritima, the commander sent one of his subordinates to the town of Gerasa. It lay in northern Judea, in the district of Acrabata.[68] (This Gerasa should not be confused with another city of the same name, much larger and more famous, inhabited mainly by Greeks, and lying quite far to the east of the Jordan and today called Jerash). The reason for the expedition was a report that a bold insurgent leader was active in the Acrabata district— *a bandit*, as Josephus or Agrippa might say: Simon, son of Gorias.

Gerasa was taken on the march. The usual methods were applied: men were executed, women and children sold into slavery, houses were looted, then burned. The surrounding villages were similarly "pacified." However, Simon was not caught. He was saved by a rather curious fact: even before the arrival of the Romans in this area, he fell into conflict with the high priests in Jerusalem. They thought that he acted too arbitrarily. So he left Gerasa and moved with his party far south—to Masada.

It was now the last days of June. Vespasian, going to Caesarea, looked confidently towards the future. He had Jerusalem, the heart of the uprising, in his grip. His armies held all the cities around it: Jericho and Emmaus in Judea, towns in Samaria to the north, and in Idumea in the south. The first stage of the campaign of 68 ended with a complete success. The next step, left for early autumn, was to attack Jerusalem itself.

But no sooner had the commander reached his headquarters than a ship brought news to the port of Caesarea. It had come from Alexandria in Egypt, perhaps even straight from Italy. The news— probably both official bulletins and private letters—related the extraordinary events in Rome: on June 8, the Senate solemnly proclaimed Sulpicius Galba as the new emperor, and a day later, Nero, abandoned by all, died a miserable death, taking his own life.

These were the first reports. However, they left many matters unclear and raised many questions that would only be answered in the future. Would Galba accept the dignity offered to him under such

---

[68] The area between Samaria and Shiloh.

circumstances? What position would the governors of the provinces take? Would they put forth their own candidacies? And what would happen if a war broke out between the armies of different provinces?

Vespasian, a sober and prudent man, immediately gave up all thought of attacking Jerusalem. Indeed, he found it advisable to cease all hostilities. For the moment, only one thing was important: hold fast the positions already seized and wait to see further developments.

When he communicated this decision to his officers, some surely objected that the enemy could exploit any suspension of hostilities to regroup and reinforce their positions. But the commander remained calm and optimistic. He said:

"Time is working for us. I don't need a spectacular victory. Left to their own devices, these bandits will tear each other to pieces. And then, when everything is ripe, we will go in to finish them off."

A lot of time would pass before that prediction came true. And a lot of blood would be spilled, not only in Jerusalem but also in Rome.

TITUS AND AGRIPPA TRAVEL TO ROME

Then Titus and Agrippa left for Rome.

Contrary to what some may have expected, Berenice did not join them. The official version was that no one, and especially no woman, went on a long journey at such an unfavorable time of year unless he absolutely had to. It was winter—the time of stormy seas. People connected with the court also noted privately that the war in Palestine required that someone from the royal family remain behind and watch over the developments—for the benefit of both the inhabitants and of the Roman rulers. Indeed, the obvious and urgent duty of King Agrippa was to go to Rome and pay homage to the new emperor, but since he was leaving, someone had to take charge of the estates and of the country in these perilous times. And whom could he trust more than his own beloved sister?

204

However, it was easy to guess other—and probably more important—reasons why the usually inseparable siblings decided to part for such a long period of time. This concerned Galba himself. He was an old man. He was seventy-three years old, raw, sick, with legs and arms so twisted by arthritis that every sandal pinched his feet, and his hands couldn't even unroll a papyrus scroll. This bitter and suffering man would have been very reluctant to welcome the queen, whose open cohabitation with her brother seemed shocking to many older Romans, otherwise very indulgent. Besides, Galba didn't like women at all. He had once been married, but his taste was primarily for boys and men.

Given this circumstance, it was indeed more diplomatic for Agrippa to go to Rome alone. But who knows—perhaps Berenice's decision not to go to Rome was even more influenced by her consideration for Titus?

The son of Vespasian was traveling along with Agrippa. He was to pay homage to the emperor on behalf of his father, present him the legions' declaration of loyalty, report on the situation in Palestine, and ask for further orders regarding the war. The mission would also give Titus the opportunity to apply for higher state offices. Yet, his love affair with Berenice was already gossipped about in the East. If the queen were now to accompany the two men on their journey, wagging tongues would go into overdrive in Rome itself. What a spicy subject for gossip! Here comes an unusual love triangle: the woman is the sister of one of the lovers but, because of her age, could well be the mother of the other (Titus was twenty-eight years old, and Berenice—over forty).

By now, almost six months had passed since the cessation of hostilities in mid-68. Roman armies remained in their camps. The insurgents, too busy fighting amongst themselves, did not attack either, and there were only minor, insignificant skirmishes. Senior officers had little to do other than inspections of troops and drills—and thus, that summer and autumn, there was a lot of free time. There were visits to the royal palaces in Caesarea, Tyre, and Berytos. Guests had fun at the tables and in the gardens. And during these months—

months about which the chronicles are silent—the romance of Titus and Berenice matured and blossomed.

One might well ask why Vespasian delayed sending his son until autumn. The answer was simple: Galba himself was traveling from Spain. He traveled slowly and with many stops. He did not arrive in Rome until mid-October.

But the upcoming journey of Titus became the subject of much political speculation even before it began, both in Rome and in the East. Namely, it was rumored that Titus was going to the capital because he had been summoned by Galba, who wanted to adopt him—which would effectively make him the designated successor to the throne.

These rumors were not entirely unfounded. The emperor was old and childless, so he had to give some thought to the question of who and how would succeed him if he wanted to save the state from the horror of another civil war. It is true that he did not know Titus— or knew him very little. However, he must have heard that this young man was intelligent, good-natured, courageous, and energetic.

There may have been another reason, too: it is quite possible that Galba ordered his confidants to spread the rumor about the possibility of such adoption in order to secure the loyalty of Vespasian, who not only controlled three legions in Palestine but could also hold in check the powerful Syrian army under the command of Mucianus. Galba urgently needed such support, considering the dangerous situation in some provinces and even in Rome itself, where many were waiting for the imperial throne to vacate again. So perhaps he deliberately spread rumors about Titus's possible adoption.

But "rumor" was all it was. The emperor was indeed thinking of adopting someone and even had a candidate in mind, but the candidate was not Titus.

If he had heard anything of the rumor, Titus must have calculated that it was not going to be appropriate for the potential adoptive son of the emperor to come to the capital with an oriental mistress in tow—and a daughter of a people with whom Rome was at war into the bargain. And she was a queen, too, and Romans had not forgotten the woeful role Cleopatra had played in their history.

So Titus and Agrippa sailed to Italy alone, without Berenice. They sailed on a Roman warship. They left the port of Caesarea Maritima in December of AD 68. Due to the inclement season, they took the long way around: along the coasts of Syria and Asia Minor to Greece. They reached the Isthmus of Corinth after January 20, 69.

THE HEAD OF GALBA

Having arrived at the eastern port of Corinth, Kenchreai,[69] Titus and King Agrippa had to disembark. There was no channel by which their ship could cross the narrow strip of land separating it from the Bay of Corinth. The short distance between the port of Kenchreai on the Saronic Gulf and the port of Leachaeum on the Bay of Corinth—just an hour on foot—allowed smaller ships to be portaged overland along a special track made of wooden beams. But warships were too large and too heavy for such portage. The king and the commander entered sedan chairs.

Along the way, they admired the enormity of the interrupted earthworks. They probably also discussed the cost and utility of the grand design and whether its enormous cost had indirectly contributed to Nero's downfall. However, soon after arriving in the city of Corinth, they had to change their topic of conversation. While still in the streets, they saw signs of an unusual commotion. To their astonishment and horror, they soon learned the cause of the excitement. Among the travelers arriving from Rome, there were eyewitnesses to the events of January 15.

Emperor Galba had been assassinated.

---

[69] Modern Kechries.

It happened in the Forum, right next to the Pool of Curtius,[70] in front of thousands of people. As soon as the trampling of horse hooves was heard coming along the cobbled streets from the direction of the Praetorian barracks, the crowds dispersed at once, and the porters of the imperial litter fled in such a panic that Galba, old and decrepit, was thrown onto the pavement. There, one of the soldiers cut his throat with a sword. The dead body was brutally mauled and repeatedly stabbed—except in the chest and belly because a cuirass protected them. The tortured corpse was left lying in the Forum until nightfall. Then a soldier cut off the head and took it to the new ruler in the fold of his cloak. Given to camp followers, the head was impaled on a spear and paraded around by a crowd amid cries of derision. It was finally redeemed for one hundred gold pieces—but not to save it from further dishonor.

The buyer had once been one of the servants of Patrobius, a freedman of Nero and the palace official in charge of organizing games and competitions. It was Patrobius who brought fine Nile sand from Egypt to sprinkle in the arenas and stadiums. A flotilla of transport ships brought heavy loads of sand while Rome experienced grain shortages. The indignation of the people at this affair was directed chiefly at Patrobius.

Immediately after his arrival in Rome in October of 68, Galba ordered Patrobius to be imprisoned along with some other freedmen of the dead emperor. First, they were paraded in shackles around the city, to the delight of the mob. Then, all were executed: Narcissus, Helios, Patrobius, and the poisoner Locusta. And now Galba paid for one of those executions: a freedman of Patrobius stuck his head on a stick in front of his master's tomb. The head was not discovered until the following day. Meanwhile, the emperor's corpse had already been cremated in the garden of his private house in via Aurelia. Someone

---

[70] Lacus Curtius ("Lake Curtius") was a pool in the ground in the Forum Romanum. The area where the Forum would later be built was originally likely a lake, as the area it is in is known to have been surrounded by brooks and marshes. One part of the area was never drained, but gradually became smaller until only a basin, known as Lacus Curtius, was left.

from among the household staff took care of the funeral. The same man also burned the head and added its ashes to the burial urn.

Consul Titus Vinius, who had accompanied Galba to the Forum, died a few minutes after the emperor. Soldiers caught up with him at the Temple of Julius Caesar; when he fell down, his leg cut off below the knee, they pierced his side with swords.

A little later on the same day, and also in the Forum, death came for the third eminent personage of the imperial retinue—Lucius Piso. At first, it seemed that he would be saved by the heroism of the centurion assigned to his defense by Galba. The officer stood alone, with only a dagger in his hand, facing a mob of enraged soldiers. He shouted in a loud voice, exhorting them to come to their senses before committing a crime. Thanks to a moment's hesitation on the part of the attackers, Piso, who had already been wounded, managed to run to the temple of Vesta and slip into the keeper's room. But the soldiers dragged him out and beat him to death at the entrance.

The severed heads of Vinius and Piso were stuck on spears and carried around the city along with the battle standards of the Praetorian cohorts and their legionary eagles. Then, they were ransomed off to their families.

In the evening of that day, the Senate solemnly awarded all the customary titles and dignities to a new emperor proclaimed by the Praetorians. He was Marcus Salvius Otho.

STARS AND COUPS

Had it not been for Ptolemy Seleucus, Otho's household astrologer, the coup would have taken place five days earlier—not on January 15, but on January 10. But Otho had followed the advice of his soothsayer for years. So when Ptolemy declared categorically that the stars bode ill for anything beginning on the 10th day of the new year, he subdued his impatience and delayed the coup. Admittedly, common sense also advised a delay as the plot was still immature, and not all details were yet fully prepared.

Ptolemy had provided Otho with astrological advice since his early youth when the senator belonged to the closest circle of Nero's friends and accompanied him in all his games and frolics. It was Otho who married the beautiful Poppaea Sabina only so that the emperor, still married to Octavia, could freely associate with her. However, Otho soon overstepped the bounds of the agreement and began to take an interest in the woman living with him as his official wife but in the character of someone else's deposit. His unhealthy advances had dire consequences. Resentful, the emperor sent him to the farthest western frontiers of the Empire as governor of the province of Lusitania. [71] That happened in the year 58. From then on, Otho remained in Lusitania for ten years, fulfilling his duties capably and honestly—to the astonishment of all who had hitherto known him only as a reveler and a libertine.

The astrologer remained in Rome, at the side of Poppea. He shared with her the hour of her triumph when the emperor, having murdered his wife, Octavia, married his lover. Thanks to his new mistress, Ptolemy now enjoyed enormous influence at court, overshadowing other practitioners of his esoteric discipline. However, the glorious times of splendor ended abruptly one day in the year 65 with the death of Poppaea. She was heavily pregnant when Nero, in a drunken fit, kicked her in the stomach. Although the emperor despaired following her death, mourned her, ordered her to be embalmed, and officially declared divine, he soon began to look for a new wife. In this situation, Ptolemy preferred to leave the capital. He rejoined his former employer, Otho.

In the last years of Nero's reign, no prominent Roman was safe. Senators, governors of provinces, commanders of legions trembled with fear. Otho also trembled, fearfully opening each letter from Rome and studying the faces of officers visiting from Italy—to see whether he might not read his death sentence in them. Still, the astrologer reassured him. He emphatically stated that Otho would

---

[71] Today's norther Portugal and Spanish Galicia.

outlive Nero: such was the irreversible decision of the stars.

Of some consolation was the arrival of Apollonius of Tyana. He left Rome—you will recall—in AD 66. He then traveled around Spain, visiting various cities, talking to many people, even conversing with governors. He reached as far as Gades, which is today's Cadiz on the Atlantic. He was an enemy of Nero and made no secret of it: his security was ensured by the general belief that he could perform extraordinary miracles. It was widely reported in Spain that Tigellinus, the praetorian prefect of Rome, had feared to quarrel with Apollonius. It was also reported that, while in Rome, the miracle worker had resurrected a dead girl lying on her bier.

The reports concerning the emperor's artistic tour of Greece offered Apollonius a convenient pretext for malicious attacks on Nero. For example, a messenger arrived at Gades with the news that the emperor had thrice triumphed at Olympia. To celebrate his victories, elaborate thanksgiving sacrifices to the gods were ordered in all the cities of the Empire. People in Gades had heard something about the Olympics, but they misunderstood the message and were firmly convinced that the Emperor had defeated some Eastern people—the Olympians—and celebrated this new success of the Roman arms with great patriotic gusto.

Why did Apollonius stay in the Spanish provinces for so long? Was he on some secret mission? Did he serve as an intermediary between the governors of different provinces of the peninsula? Who knows whether he did not play an important role in the preparation of the great conspiracy against Nero? In any case, it is noteworthy that he left Spain only in the spring of 68 when the plot of the rebellion was ripe. This time, the destination of his journey was Egypt. He traveled there by way of North Africa, Sicily, Greece, the coasts of Asia Minor, and the island of Rhodes.

Meanwhile, in the spring of 68, Otho was one of the first to endorse Galba, the then-governor of the neighboring province of Hispania Tarraconensis. He supported him courageously and energetically, although it was not yet quite certain that the rebellion would succeed. And when everything developed favorably, he arrived in Rome in October, along with Galba, as one of his closest collaborators.

Ptolemy, the astrologer, returned to the capital along with Otho. He was now prophesying to his master that he would soon become the ruler of the Empire. This seemed highly probable to many other people who watched not the stars but the realities of life and politics. Galba, an old man with no children, had to adopt someone. As for Otho, a man in his prime—he was nearing forty—he had already proven himself as an energetic administrator in Lusitania; he had been crucial in helping the new emperor gain power, and he enjoyed his trust. It was also generally known that Consul Titus Vinius, Galba's closest adviser, strongly supported Otho's candidacy, albeit for family reasons: he was going to give him his daughter in marriage. Of course, Otho also had influential opponents, opposed both to him personally and to the overly powerful Vinius. They recalled Otho's youthful excesses:

"Was Nero removed," they asked, "so that his criminal accomplice might now be placed on the throne?"

But here is the curious thing: precisely this old connection to Nero won Otho a lot of sympathy among the common people and among the Praetorians. They remembered fondly the spectacular games and the endless fun and entertainment of Nero's reign. They secretly hoped that Otho would bring back the carefree joy of those early days, so wonderful in comparison with the senile austerity and killjoy morality of Galba's regime.

Otho was aware of the mood in the capital. With the help of friends, he worked hard to exploit it for his purposes. He especially wooed the military. He won over tribunes and centurions and even simple privates—both with money and by making himself accessible.

On the eighth or ninth of January, news came to Rome that the Rhine legions had rebelled. This caused anxiety both in the city and on the Palatine, and Galba decided that he could not delay any longer the appointment of his adoptive son and heir. On the morning of January 10, he summoned Lucius Piso.

LUCIUS PISO

This relatively young man (he was thirty years old) was almost completely unknown in Rome. Yes, almost a quarter of a century earlier, his family had been on everyone's lips when a disaster struck it: Piso's father, one of the most outstanding and popular senators and a close collaborator of Emperor Claudius, died on the orders of the emperor's wife, Messalina, accused of plotting a coup. His wife and his eldest son shared his fate: all three probably committed suicide. Lucius Piso, then a small boy, went into exile. He stayed away from Rome for the rest of Claudius's reign and also during the reign of his successor, Nero. He returned to the capital only recently, thanks to Galba, because among the new emperor's first actions was to pardon almost all the victims of the previous regimes—including the philosopher Musonius. So many returned to Rome that the arrival of young Piso did not attract any attention.

And now, quite unexpectedly and against all calculations, this Piso became the new ruler's adopted son and successor! This caused a lot of head-scratching: why did Galba choose a man who had not yet held any office, had not served in the army, and had no influential friends in the capital? The malicious soon found an answer: they said that Galba liked the face of Piso—so serious that it was positively gloomy. The young man's grave disposition must indeed have appealed to the hard, stern, serious old man. Others recalled a malicious remark once made by Seneca about Piso's father: "He's so stupid he could even be an emperor!" and added that the son was a worthy heir of his father.

There is no doubt, however, that when making his choice, Galba was guided by a rational calculation. Most of all, he wanted a man who was not associated with any of the feuding coteries at court: a complete outsider. Piso's aristocratic origin also appealed to him: on his mother's side, he was a descendant of some famous personalities from the preceding century, the period of the decline of the republic:

the *triumvirs* Pompey and Crassus. The fact that Piso had suffered persecution under the emperors of the Julio-Claudian dynasty guaranteed that he would continue the policy of hostility towards all those formerly associated with it. But even the spiteful had a point: Piso's grave demeanor certainly pleased the old emperor.

On January 10, Galba summoned Piso to the Palatine. It was raining. Soon, the rain turned into a storm, with lightning and thunder, something not usual at that time of year and, therefore, some said, inauspicious. The Emperor didn't care: he had himself carried to the Praetorian camp. He summoned an *ad hoc* rally—it was assembled in such a hurry that the ushers forgot to put a chair on the rostrum, as was the ancient practice. And thus, standing on the tribune, Galba stated in a few words that he had made his decision regarding succession and adopted an heir. He introduced his adopted son. Only the officers and a handful of privates greeted the declaration with a friendly cheer—the overwhelming majority stood in stony silence.

And for a good reason: the emperor had not said a word about their traditional bonus on the transfer of power—called *donative*. Yet, under Nero, the Praetorians had received emoluments at every opportunity. However, Galba was determined to restore the strict discipline of the old days: he believed that the excessive generosity of the previous emperors had demoralized the army. Right at the outset of his reign, he replied to those demanding an increase in military pay:

"I don't buy soldiers. I draft them."

He remained steadfastly loyal to this motto to the end.

Immediately after the presentation, the emperor and Piso went to the Senate building, where they both made speeches, which were (obviously) most enthusiastically received.

Were it not for his astrologer Ptolemy, Otho, painfully disappointed in his hopes, would perhaps have struck that day. But warned by heavenly signs, he put off his attack for five days.

15 JANUARY

On the morning of 15 January, Galba offered sacrifices in front of the Temple of Apollo on Palatine Hill. The eminent priest and soothsayer Umbricius Melior, author of highly regarded books on Etruscan divination, examined the entrails of the sacrificial animals and announced in a trembling voice:

"The signs are inauspicious. They foretell treason, ambush, and domestic upheaval. You shouldn't leave the palace today."

It was decided to repeat the sacrifices—to appease the gods and obtain additional guidance. Otho stood right next to the emperor throughout. As was customary, he had come to the palace at dawn to greet the emperor, who received him very kindly and even kissed him. As the new ceremony at the altar was about to begin, a trusted freedman approached Otho and whispered—but loud enough for others to hear—that the architect and builders he had summoned were waiting. These words actually meant: everything is ready, the soldiers are assembled!

Otho immediately departed from the temple. On the way, someone from the imperial retinue asked where he was going in such a hurry. He replied:

"I'm buying a country house. But it seems to me that the building is quite dilapidated. I need to have it inspected."

Surrounded by his freedmen, he passed through the former palace of Tiberius, then descended the Palatine and walked along Via Sacra. He crossed the Forum and headed for the Capitol. Next to the temple of Saturn stood the golden milestone, the symbolic starting point of all the roads of the Empire. Twenty-three armed Praetorians were gathered there. Seeing this handful, Otho became alarmed and asked:

"Why so few? Where is the rest?"

He seemed to hesitate suddenly as if only now realizing the enormity of the risks involved. But they had already surrounded him. They shouted:

"Salve Imperator!"

Immediately and almost by force, they pushed him into the prepared sedan chair—it happened to be a woman's litter. They drew their swords and hurried towards the praetorian barracks. The barracks were quite far, outside the city walls, between Via Nomentana and Via Tiburtia. On the way, they were joined by about as many others—some were fellow conspirators, others—total outsiders who followed them out of simple curiosity. Now, there were about fifty, all told. They marched so quickly that the porters carrying the litter could not keep up. Otho got out and ran with the soldiers. He stopped for a moment to tie a sandal that had come undone: his companions took him immediately onto their shoulders. They did not have a moment to lose. Their life was at stake. Now, all were the captives of fate—no one could go back anymore.

Most soldiers in the camp did not care one way or another and would have remained passive if not for the determination of a handful of desperadoes. The overused metaphor of a small stone triggering a mighty avalanche would be apt here: the handful of daredevils was gradually joined by ever-larger groups of companions, friends, and colleagues. Soon, amid general enthusiasm, Otho was elevated to the tribune on the shoulders of soldiers, surrounded by battle emblems and saluted by the crowd as an emperor. He took the Imperial oath, he spoke, he extended his hands to the heaving throng of armed men to be kissed, he blew kisses, he cried out:

"I will take only such powers as you grant me!"

And now the Roman Empire had four Caesars. Three of them were in Rome: Galba and Piso on the Palatine Hill and Otho in the Praetorian barracks. The fourth Caesar—about whom only very few were as yet aware—was on the Rhine. He was Aulus Vitellius, elevated to the purple by the local legions on January 2. The powerful army of the Rhine considered it a dishonor that the piddly army of Spain should elevate the next emperor of Rome. By acclaiming Vitellius now, the Rhine legions corrected that mistake.

Meanwhile, on Palatine Hill, where animals were still being gutted at the altar, strange news began to arrive. First, it was said that

216

the Praetorians had kidnapped a senator from the Forum and taken him to their camp. Then, the news came that the kidnapped senator was Otho. As a precaution, Piso spoke from the steps of the palace to the cohort keeping guard on the Palatine. Most of the soldiers seemed to take to the words of the young emperor sympathetically; only some had dispersed, no one knew where and why. The cohort soon stood ready for battle with all their emblems upraised; they were told to defend the emperor and his son. Officers and senior officials were sent to various military formations stationed in the city. Soon, they all came back empty-handed. Some were met with complete indifference, while others were simply driven away.

The crowd gathered on the Palatine now began to demand the death of Otho and the other participants in the revolt. People shouted at the top of their voices, fearing nothing, for even if Otho were to be victorious, he could never hold accountable anyone lost in the sea of the multitude, and they treated these histrionics as a thrilling spectacle on par with gladiatorial games.

Galba held a feverish council of his supporters. Remain on the Palatine, fortify, arm the slaves? Such was the opinion of Consul Titus Vinius. Others, however, called for action: strike before the rebellion has had time to gain momentum! We must descend from the Palatine, occupy the Forum, occupy the Capitol! After some hesitation, the emperor agreed with this second view. He ordered Piso to go to the Praetorian barracks and try to negotiate with the men. The heir to the throne left without delay—and meanwhile—shortly after his departure, the false rumor spread that Otho had been killed. Crowds of commoners broke down the palace gates and flooded the courtyard, for every inhabitant of Rome wanted to show the emperor how devoted he was to him. Galba put on his body armor—it was a cuirass of iron scales sewn on a linen cloth—and climbed into a litter. The people pressed from every side so mightily that they nearly overturned it. A Praetorian waved a bloody sword at him, shouting that he had killed the rebel Otho with his own hand. But Galba only dared to ask sternly:

"On whose command?"

The retinue was already descending the Palatine Hill, entering the Forum. At that moment, Piso appeared. He had not reached the Praetorian camp but had inferred from the mighty shouts of "Otho, Otho!" what had happened there. Again, people began to wonder what to do next. Go back to the Palatine? Go to the Forum? Barricade themselves on the Capitol?

Crowds filled the Forum, all its temples and buildings. With bated breath, in deathly silence, they stared at the helpless group of people surrounding the imperial litter. It would seem that all this took place in some huge theater, whose stage was Via Sacra, and whose auditorium were the buildings of the Forum and their roofs.

Just then came the sound of horses galloping over the cobblestones. It was Otho's most trusted unit. At that point, everything depended on the attitude of the cohort guarding Galba. If it had remained faithful, the horsemen probably would not have dared to attack. But behold, the standard-bearer of the cohort tore off the medallion with the image of Galba, which he wore around his neck, and flung it to the ground.

And then the killing began.

PARTING AT CORINTH

Such were the events in Rome between January 10 and 15, and this is how they were narrated in Corinth to Titus and King Agrippa. On the other hand, the events on the Rhine were not so certain, although the fact that the German legions had proclaimed Vitellius Caesar seemed beyond any doubt.

If affairs indeed stood like the news from Rome reported—a coup had taken place, and one emperor replaced another, everything would be simple. Congratulations intended for Galba would now go to his killer. But with yet another claimant to the throne in the north, the burning question arose: what would the governors and armies of the other provinces do? Would they accept Otho, or would they punt for Vitellius? Or would they put forward their own candidates?

Thus, to go to Rome now and congratulate Otho would amount to making a premature decision. Even worse, it would amount to granting the current ruler of Rome, whoever he was, hostages for the loyalty of Vespasian and his legions. On the other hand, turning back would be a clear sign of open hostility towards Otho. If he were to consolidate his power, he would surely never forget this snub and would retaliate at the first opportunity.

At last, someone gave sensible advice:

"We were sent here by Vespasian and his three legions to give a soldier's salute to Galba. But since the intended addressee is dead, we must return to our commander. Let him decide what we should do. We are, after all, only the executors of other people's orders, like a postman delivering a letter."

And that's where it all ended—at least as far as Titus was concerned. However, King Agrippa made a different decision. His take on the recent events in Rome was this: he assumed that whoever became emperor of Rome, he and his people had to submit. To Otho? To Vitellius? To someone else? Whoever it was, he, Agrippa, had to present himself in the capital and pay homage. And since he was so close to Italy already, there was no point in turning back, wasting so much time, effort, and money in vain. The situation in Palestine would have to clear up pretty soon, so it was permissible to stay away. And since Berenice was watching over the affairs of the kingdom in Palestine, Agrippa was free to engage in Roman politics at the court of the new emperor—whoever that turned out to be. Such a division of labor would be the most profitable for the family fortunes.

I suspect that Titus accepted the king's arguments with honest and undisguised joy. His reason was easy to see: Berenice. The young man was happy to think that, once he was back in Palestine, he would be able to meet her freely. Finally, this somewhat embarrassing witness—this panderer/chaperone, brother-and-almost-husband— would be out of the picture. And who knows—because our sources allow this interpretation, too—perhaps Titus only decided to stop his journey and return to Palestine after he had realized that Agrippa intended to continue on to Rome.

The king, of course, was aware of the amorous longings of his companion. In the life of his court, nothing could have remained hidden for long: that's what all those armies of eunuchs, slaves, and henchmen were for. But the lustful glances and tender words that Titus directed at Berenice had only pleased Agrippa. For understandable reasons: in times of uncertainty, when Palestine was at war, when there were civil disturbances in Italy, and already the second emperor died a violent death in less than a year, it was good to know that the son of a Roman general in command of three legions had great affection for a person so close to the king. Could anyone imagine a better protection, a better guarantee for the future? The interest of the state urged Agrippa to make things easier for the two lovers by discreetly withdrawing—as far away as possible and for a longer period of time. And here was a very good excuse indeed.

Thus, thinking of the same woman—Berenice—both Titus and Agrippa made their decisions in Corinth: one to return to Palestine, the other to continue on to Rome. And their decisions had momentous consequences—especially the choice made by Titus. Had he continued on to Rome, many matters of great importance would have turned out differently. So Tacitus, a witness and historian of the time, is right to mention Agrippa's sister in this connection :

"There were those who believed that he turned back because he burned with desire for the queen. And indeed, his youthful heart did not shun Berenice."[72]

QUESTIONS

In accordance with the then common practice, observed especially in the winter months, Titus did not sail from Corinth across the open sea but along the coasts—first of Greece, then of Asia Minor. However,

---

[72] Tacitus, *Annals*, II 2.

once he reached the island of Rhodes, he decided to change his course and sail boldly straight for Cyprus and from there on to Syria. He decided to visit the shrine of Aphrodite, of which he had heard so much, and consult its oracle.

And thus, he came to the temple in Paphos. He viewed the stone pillar and the altar, marveled at the treasury full of precious votive gifts from kings and notables from many different countries. Then he asked the oracle how the rest of his journey would go. It would have made more sense, of course, if he had asked such a question on his way to Italy and not on his way back. However, Titus had other, more serious matters on his mind—not the journey alone. This first consultation was only a test to see whether the deity was well disposed towards him and inclined to give answers, for when he had received an auspicious answer, he immediately made an impressive sacrifice. As was the custom in Paphos, he probably offered baby goats—and then asked for a further unveiling of the future. The entrails of the animals were carefully examined by the priest Sostratus. He said briefly that the signs were auspicious. So much, according to witnesses, in public. Immediately afterward, however, he spoke to Titus one-on-one.

No one knows what they talked about. Many years later, a persistent rumor held that everything that was still to come had been prophesied to Titus in that conversation. O, how easy is the divination of things already accomplished! How clearly it asserts the authority of an oracle! But a question that interests us is whether, during their confidential meeting, Titus and Sostratus engaged in divination at all. After all, the priest might instead have given the Roman some secret information. Crowds of pilgrims from near and far came to Paphos to consult the oracle. This made the temple a kind of clearinghouse of information. The most private and most secret events, which took place in all the cities and courts of the Middle East, were likely consulted there.

At any rate, the young man returned to his father's winter quarters in Caesarea Maritima full of good hope, though not free of tormenting questions. He wondered anxiously how events in the West would unfold. Would there be a civil war between Otho and Vitellius? And if there, in Italy—or in Gaul—the Roman legions were to spill fraternal blood, how should the Roman army in Palestine react? Whom of the two combatants should the Flavians support? Or should they remain neutral? The victor of the civil war would never forgive it if they did. Equally important was the position of the neighboring Syrian army—the four legions commanded by Mucianus. He was not kindly disposed towards Vespasian and made no secret of it. So why not wait for the developments in the West but immediately attack Mucianus? Or maybe the opposite—maybe try to come to an arrangement with him and then make a common cause vis-a-vis the West?

And how to proceed in Palestine? Should they start military operations in order to quench the uprising as soon as possible or, on the contrary, delay the war and wait to see how the situation in Jerusalem unfolded? For there was one more partner in this multilateral game—the Jewish insurgents. What would they do? It was impossible to predict—they were not monolithic, and it was quite possible that they would end up fighting each other, as Vespaian had predicted. But what if an energetic leader should arise among them, take advantage of the Roman inertia, seize power among the Jews, and lead them on a spirited offensive? What if the defeat of Cestius Gallus were repeated, and an avalanche should start, the effects of which could not even be imagined?

These were the weighty questions concerning the affairs of state, war, and politics. But there were other questions, too, of a private nature—some were easy to guess. But others related to people with whom Titus had not yet met but who nevertheless have often appeared on the pages of this book:

Where will Apollonius of Tyana turn next? What shall he teach now, and what extraordinary miracles shall he perform? And does he serve only gods?

And what will be the fate of Clemens—the man who had come from Rome to Caesarea many years ago to seek the truth about life and death? From there, he moved to Tyre and lived for a while with a pious girl named Berenice. Is she not the future Veronica of the legend of the veil?

And what had happened to Clemens's family? Did they really all die—the mother, both twin brothers, the father? Since *Ennoia*, once lost, was found in Tyre, maybe they, too, would reappear in some unexpected circumstances? All the more so that the father had a name that is known to us from elsewhere.

His name was—Faustus.

THE END

A Note from the Author:

This story was built on the basis of accounts of ancient authors. They are, above all, the historians: Tacitus, Josephus Flavius, Suetonius, Cassius Dio, Plutarch. Works of a different nature were also consulted—the New Testament, *Pseudo-Clemens*, Christian apologies, Philostratus's *Life of Apollonius*—to name only the most important. In some cases, epigraphy and archaeological data were of primary importance. Footnotes appear only in those places where sources are quoted verbatim.

FROM YOUR TRANSLATOR

Translating and publishing this book has been a labor of love for me.
I grew up reading it, and I have always wanted to be able
to share it with my American friends. And so here it is.
It will not make me rich, but if you liked the book, would you please
recommend it to a friend?
And give it an Amazon review?
https://www.amazon.com/dp/2919820494

THANK YOU!

ABOUT THE AUTHOR

Aleksander Krawczuk (1922-2023) was a noted scholar of Greek and Roman antiquity, a professor at the Jagiellonian University, a former minister of culture, and an author of over 30 popular and widely translated books on the subject of the Antique.

ABOUT MONDRALA PRESS

Mondrala Press publishes English translations of great Polish books—books with a track record of international critical and commercial success but which, for political reasons, have never been published in English.
To see our newest titles or to subscribe
to our mailing list, please visit
www.mondrala.com
THE GREATEST BOOKS YOU HAVE NEVER HEARD OF

Jacek Bocheński

Tiberius Caesar

Terror is normal.
The horrifying tale of Tiberius Caesar, the second emperor of Rome:
the man who normalized political terror. A moral, intellectual,
emotional zero whose only skill in life was to grab and hang onto
power. At any cost. A dizzying look into
the great void of an empty soul.

Joe Alex

The Ships of Minos 1-5

A Bronze Age Saga.
1600 BC. A Minoan ship sails to the ends of the earth in search of the
sources of amber. Days without night, water turning to stone, monsters of
the deep, peoples who sacrifice their kings to their gods and build great
stone circles to worship the sun. And god's face upon the waters.
One of the greatest exploration sagas ever written.

Witold Makowiecki

Out of the Lion's Maw

570 B.C. They slip their jailors in Carthage and rush across the Mediterranean pursued by enemy agents and assassins: a mysterious oriental priest and his Greek apprentice. Their mission: to prevent the outbreak of a civil war in Egypt. Their opponents: the Great Phoenician Council and the entire state apparatus of Eternal Egypt. Their resources: the old man's wit and the young man's courage.

Wind from the Hospitable Sea

Greece 562 BC. For insolvent debtors, the price of bankruptcy is slavery. When his mother and siblings are seized for unpaid debts, little Diossos must run to fetch help. He must cross mountains, forests, and stormy seas, brave wild animals, slave catchers, pirates, and... the law. He has one month to achieve his quest but only days to grow up.

Arkady Fiedler

The White Jaguar 1-5

AD 1726. An uninhabited Caribbean island off the Spanish Main. A
Virginian renegade. Pirates, Runaway slaves. Cannibals.
The great saga of the mysterious White Jaguar, a white man named
John who became a war leader of the Orinoco Indians in their wars
against the Spanish.

Maria Rodziewiczówna

A Summer of the Forest Folk

The most beautiful book you will read this year.
Turn of the nineteenth century. Three women spend their summers in a remote
cottage deep in the last virgin forest in Europe. This summer, their teenage big-city
nephew joins them. A heart-warming, feel-good tale of love and friendship, of
coming of age, and of the healing power of nature. This is a book like nothing you
have ever read, a phenomenon, a genre of its own.

Made in United States
Orlando, FL
02 September 2025

64580752R00138